nОts

RELIGION AND POSTMODERNISM

A series edited by MARK C. TAYLOR

Mark C. Taylor

o

o

o

nO nOt

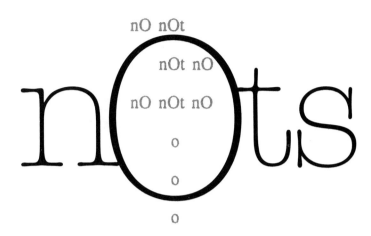

nOt nO

nO nOt nO

o

o

o

[k]nO[w] nOt

nOt [k]nO[w]

[k]no[w] nOt [k]nO[w]

o

o

o

THE UNIVERSITY OF CHICAGO PRESS

Chicago and London

MARK C. TAYLOR, Preston S. Parish Third Century Professor of Religion at Williams College, is the author of *Erring: A Postmodern A/theology* (1984), *Altarity* (1987), and *Disfiguring: Art, Architecture, Religion* (1992), and is the editor of *Deconstruction in Context: Literature* (1986)—all published by the University of Chicago Press.

The University of Chicago Press, Chicago 60637
The University of Chicago Press, Ltd., London
© 1993 by The University of Chicago
All rights reserved. Published 1993
Printed in the United States of America
02 01 00 99 98 97 96 95 94 93 1 2 3 4 5
ISBN: 0-226-79130-0 (cloth)
        0-226-79131-9 (paper)

Earlier versions of chapters 1 and 8 appeared in *Archivio de Filosofia* 58 (1990) and 60 (1992) respectively; an earlier version of chapter 2 appeared in *Derrida and Negative Theology,* edited by Harold Coward and Tony Myrthen (Albany: State University of New York Press, 1991).

Library of Congress Cataloging-in-Publication Data

Taylor, Mark C., 1945-
    Nots / Mark C. Taylor.
    p.   cm. — (Religion and postmodernism)
    Includes bibliographical references and index.
    1. Religion—Philosophy. 2. Aesthetics. 3. Postmodernism.
    I. Title. II. Series.
    BL51.T395   1993
    200'.1—dc20   92-38702
                                                       CIP

For KIRSTEN JENNIE TAYLOR

I *prefer* not.

— BARTLEBY

CONTENTS

ILLUSTRATIONS

ABBREVIATIONS

AD   *Architectural Design* 58, no. 1–2 (1989).

AT   Jacques Derrida, "Of an Apocalyptic Tone Recently Adopted in Philosophy," *Semeia* (1983): 63–97.

BL   Daniel Libeskind, "Between the Lines," *Architectural Design* 60, no. 3–4 (1990).

CD   Daniel Libeskind, *Counterdesigns* (London: Academy Editions, 1991).

EL   Edmond Jabès, *El, or the Last Book,* trans. Rosmarie Waldrop (Middletown, Conn: Wesleyan University Press, 1984).

FL   Jacques Derrida, "Force of Law: 'The Mystical Foundation of Authority'," *Deconstruction and the Possibility of Justice, Cardozo Law Review* 11, nos. 5–6 (July-August 1990): 919–1045.

FT   Søren Kierkegaard, *Fear and Trembling,* trans. Howard and Edna Hong (Princeton, N.J.: Princeton University Press, 1983).

HAS   Jacques Derrida, "How to Avoid Speaking: Denials," *Languages of the Unsayable: The Play of Negativity in Literature and Literary Theory,* ed. Sanford Budick and Wolfgang Iser (New York: Columbia University Press, 1989), pp. 3–70.

IE   Georges Bataille, *Inner Experience,* trans. Leslie Boldt (Albany: State University of New York Press, 1988).

L   G.W.F. Hegel, *The Logic of Hegel,* trans. William Wallace (New York: Oxford University Press, 1968).

MM   Arakawa and Madeline Gins, *The Mechanism of Meaning* (1971; New York: Abbeville Press, 1988).

ND   Arakawa and Madeline Gins, *To Not to Die* (Paris: Éditions de la Différence, n.d.).

NI	Daniel Libeskind, *Notes for a Lecture: Nouvelles Impressions d'Architecture* (Milan: Electa Spa, 1988).
P	Anselm, *Prosologion, a Scholastic Miscellany,* ed. E. R. Fairweather (Philadelphia: The Westminster Press, 1966).
PA	Maurice Blanchot, *Le Pas au-delà* (Paris: Gallimard, 1973).
PF	Søren Kierkegaard, *Philosophical Fragments,* trans. Howard and Edna Hong (Princeton, N.J.: Princeton University Press, 1985).
PLT	Martin Heidegger, *Poetry, Language, Thought,* trans. Albert Hofstader (New York: Harper and Row, 1971).
PN	G.W.F. Hegel, *Philosophy of Nature,* trans. Michael Petry (New York: Humanities Press, 1970).
PR	G.W.F. Hegel, *Lectures on the Philosophy of Religion,* trans. E. Speirs and J.B. Sanderson (New York: Humanities Press, 1988) vols. 1–3.
PS	G.W.F. Hegel, *Phenomenology of Spirit,* trans. A.V. Miller (New York: Oxford University Press, 1977).
RD	Arakawa and Madeline Gins, "Reversible Destiny," unpublished manuscript.
RN	Keiji Nishitani, *Religion and Nothingness,* trans. Jan Van Bragt (Berkeley: University of California Press, 1982).
SL	G.W.F. Hegel, *Science of Logic,* trans. A.V. Miller (New York: Humanities Press, 1969).
SS	Anthony Wilden, *System and Structure: Essays in Communication and Exchange* (London: Tavistock, 1972).
TCP	Arakawa and Madeline Gins, "The Tentative Constructed Plan as Intervening Device (for a Reversible Destiny)," unpublished manuscript.
U	Sigmund Freud, "The Uncanny," vol. 17 of *The Standard Edition of the Complete Psychological Works of Sigmund Freud,* trans. and ed. James Strachey (London: Hogarth Press, 1964).
VI	Maurice Merleau-Ponty, *The Visible and the Invisible,* trans. Alphonso Lingis (Evanston, Ill.: Northwestern University Press, 1968).
WP	Friedrich Nietzsche, *The Will to Power,* trans. Walter Kaufmann (New York: Random House, 1968).

1. Edward Epping, Untitled. Photograph: Mark C. Taylor.

Why Not?

The question of the not is older—dreadfully older—than theology, philosophy, and art. It is, indeed, older than thought itself, for it is impossible to think without already having thought not. To think not is not, however, to think not *as such*. The elusive complexity of the not can only be thought when reflection bends back on itself and becomes reflexive. Through this inward turn, which is intended to bring reflection full circle, thought inadvertently betrays itself by indirectly soliciting something it cannot comprehend. In a certain sense, the not is unthinkable. And yet we are always unavoidably thinking not. The question of the not, therefore, is the question of the unthinkable that we can neither think nor not think. In thinking not, thought approaches a limit that inhabits it *as if* from within. This exteriority, which is interior, rends thought, leaving it forever incomplete.

To think not is to linger with a negative, which, though it can never be negated, is not merely negative. The not is something like a nonnegative negative that nonetheless is not positive. So understood, the not does not exist; nor does the not exist. Neither something nor nothing, the not falls *between* being and nonbeing. Though thought cannot think without thinking not, the Western ontotheological tradition has, in effect, been in an extended effort not to think not. While the strategies that have been devised for negating the not have been multiple, they consistently involve the effort to turn the not into something positive that can be managed and controlled. Within such schemes, the name of the not varies: God, Satan, the good, evil, being, nonbeing, absolute knowledge, nonknowledge, the unconscious. . . . But such naming is always inadequate, for to think not is to think the unthinkable, which is unnameable or is nameable only as unnameable. Declining all nominations and eluding or resisting every oppositional structure constructed to repress it, the not entails an altarity more radical than any binary difference or dialectical other. The impossible task I set for myself in these essays is to think (the) not otherwise than by not thinking.

I have been pursued by a certain not for many years—perhaps from the beginning, even before the beginning. My earliest work on Kierkegaard and Hegel represents, inter alia, a sustained investigation of alternative dialectics of negation. The longer I have struggled with these two precursors whose grasp I cannot escape, the more I have become convinced that neither Kierkegaard's either/or nor Hegel's both/and is adequate to convey the ever-elusive not. My search for an unthinkable third that lies between Kierkegaard and Hegel has taken many unexpected twists and turns. In the course of my erring, I have wandered from theology and philosophy into areas as diverse as literature, literary criticism, cultural studies, art, architecture, and even chemistry and biology. Though apparently unrelated, these different fields all involve contrasting inscriptions of the not. As I have followed the strange course of the not, I have discovered that the problem of the not extends beyond the realm of thought and invades all domains of experience—individual as well as social, natural as well as cultural. This realization has not been easy and has often been painful—terribly painful. Day by day, I continue to learn that it is no exaggeration to insist that the not is a matter of life and death.

The question of the not is first and foremost religious and theological. God, self, and world are bound in a not of difference: God is what self/world is not, and self/world is what God is not. Accordingly, to think God would seem to be to think not. And yet, the most sustained efforts to think God rigorously have tended to erase the not without which God cannot be thought. From Anselm's classical formulation of the ontological argument for God's existence, to Hegel's reworking of the ontological argument in his systematic philosophy, rational reflection has constituted itself by negating the negation without which one cannot think. In the first chapter, "How Not to Think God," I examine Anselm's and Hegel's versions of the ontological argument in an effort to discern the not they are trying not to think. This not points to an inescapable flaw in Anselm's argument and fault in Hegel's system. Far from a shortcoming or a failure, the flaw of theology and fault of philosophy mark an opening that creates the possibility of rethinking negative theology.

Throughout the history of Western philosophy and theology, the *via negativa* has seemed to provide a way to think not. From Plato and the Neoplatonists, through the early Christian fathers, to modern reformulations of the negative way, theologians, philosophers, and artists have sought to think what cannot be thought by negating thought itself. The goal of such reflective negation is the absence of thought, which is the fullness of being. Contrary to expectation, the via negativa traditionally turns out to be a reversal that changes nothing but merely repeats, by inverting, the ontological and epistemological principles that lie at the foundation of Western thought and culture. In recent years, the emergence of post-structuralism has sparked a revival of interest in so-called negative theology. Though Derrida repeatedly insists that deconstruction *is not* negative theology, critics and supporters have repeatedly attempted to assimilate his critical strategies to the via negativa. The second chapter is devoted to Derrida's most sustained consideration of negative theology—his extraordinary essay entitled "How to Avoid Speaking: Denegations." A careful analysis of Derrida's cryptic argument suggests that his relation to negative theology is not simply negative. While insisting that the classical via negativa remains thoroughly ontotheological, Derrida's deconstructive analysis insinuates an alternative reading of negative theology that creates the possibility of thinking God otherwise by not refusing to think not.

Insofar as the question of the not is the question of thought itself, its consideration is not, of course, limited to the *Western* theology and philosophy. Perhaps the religious tradition that has been most persistently obsessed with the not is Buddhism. Members of the Kyoto school attempt to establish a dialogue between Western philosophy and Eastern religion by exploring the complex interplay between important strands in Mahayana Buddhism and leading modern philosophers like Hegel, Nietzsche, and Heidegger. In his important work, *Religion and Nothingness* (1982), Keiji Nishitani, who is the leading figure in the Kyoto school, attempts to interpret Buddhist notions of nihility and emptiness through Western philosophical categories. Though initially "the middle way" of Buddhism seems analogous to the neither/nor of the not, Nishitani's effort to reconcile East and West exposes a metaphysics of being implicit in his doctrine of nothingness. Rather than a world-negating nihilism, Nishitani's religion of nothingness ends in an affirmation of the world that leaves no space for the critical resistance necessary for ethical action.

As I have suggested, it is a mistake to restrict the importance of the not to the domain of thought. The will is, in effect, the not in action. To will is not simply to affirm but is always also to affirm not. Willing without willing not is no more possible than thinking without thinking not. The willing of the not is an act of resistance in which the subject critically engages structures—be they cognitive, moral, religious, aesthetic, social, or political—that are both inescapable and inadequate. During the past several years, events within and beyond the university have conspired to lend urgency to the question of ethics. In reaction to the perceived threat of nihilism that seems to lurk in the critique of foundationalism, many critics have resorted to a naive reassertion of traditional pieties. The result of this approach is, in my judgment, disastrous. While I fully agree that questions of ethics call for *careful* attention, I am convinced that any response that fails to take seriously the sophisticated genealogies of forms of reflection and codes of conduct that have recently been developed cannot adequately address the complexities of our situation. In a world in which moral norms and principles have become irrevocably uncertain, the problem of ethics can be rethought in terms of strategies of resistance. To act ethically in the wake of the death of God, one must enact the not otherwise than by not acting. In an effort to describe how ethical resistance might be performed, I read Kierkegaard's *Fear and Trembling* with and against Derrida's "Force of Law," and vice versa. Though often criticized for its ethical irrelevance, deconstruction actually provides rich resources for ethical reflection. These resources cannot, however, be tapped without working through the complex interplay between ethical obligations and religious commitments. By creating a dialogue between Kierkegaard and Derrida, it becomes possible to find a middle way between a resignation that flees from the world in search of a transcendent good and a resignation that merely accepts the world as it is. To avoid the nihilism inherent in the negation of "Nay Saying" and the affirmation of "Yea Saying," I argue that the enactment of the not is not just resistance. That is to say, the not is not just, nor is it just resistance; the not is not just resistance but something other that simultaneously emerges and withdraws at the elusive point where the religious and the ethical inevitably intersect.

As Kierkegaard long ago realized, the ethical and the religious do not exhaust human experience. The aesthetic is neither reducible to nor separable from ethical and religious considerations. In the course of the modern era, the complicity between art and religion has grown ever deeper. From the nonobjective paintings of Kandinsky and Mondrian to the abstract canvases of Newman and Rothko, artists struggle to figure the unfigurable that religious language cannot adequately express. By so doing, art becomes an aesthetic education whose purpose is nothing less than redemption. In the second section of this book, I examine different artistic efforts to figure not. I begin with the innovative work of Arakawa and Madeline Gins in which East and West, painting and architecture, word and image, religion and philosophy are interwoven to form a tangled web that is quasi-textual. Reconceiving the utopian hopes of the avant-garde, Arakawa and Gins attempt to save the redemptive role of art by transferring art's salvific function from society as a whole to individuals. Working out of a philosophical tradition that is deeply indebted to Western philosophy and Eastern religion, they develop an artistic strategy for transforming perception that closely approximates meditation techniques originally developed in Buddhism. When fully elaborated, the art/architecture of Arakawa-Gins presupposes a metaphysics that is strictly parallel to Nishitani's religion of nothingness. In the absence of utopia, the only salvation that remains is the apprehension of the not, which, paradoxically, constitutes the fullness of being. The point of the not is blank and this blank is the nonsense that Arakawa and Gins call us to perceive.

In chapter 6, I shift from Arakawa and Gins's artistic appropriation of Buddhist thought and practice to Daniel Libeskind's architectural rendering of important aspects of the Jewish religious tradition. Some of the most innovative recent architecture has been implicitly and explicitly informed by themes drawn from Jewish theology. Architects like Peter Eisenman and Stanley Tigerman design structures that reflect the exile, nomadism, and errancy they believe endemic to our postmodern condition. Libeskind's project for a Jewish Museum in Berlin extends the architectural effort to build not. In Libeskind's museum, the presence of the Buddhist point gives way to the absence of the Kabbalistic point in a construction that deconstructs itself as if from within. Libeskind's structure can be read as something like a reinscription of the point of Edmond Jabès's endless *Book of Questions.* Just as Jabès's book is not a book, so Libeskind's architecture is "Not Architecture."

Though the emptiness of Arakawa and Gins's art/architecture and the absence of Libeskind's Not Architecture differ significantly, it remains uncertain whether either escapes the economy of presence that informs important strands of Eastern and Western religion and philosophy. In spite of the differences that mark the hopes and expectations inspiring their work, Arakawa and Gins and Libeskind develop their artistic programs within a horizon that approaches the apocalyptic. Whether realized or delayed, eschatology remains implicitly or explicitly committed to the dream of the realization of presence in the present.

Presence, however, assumes many and often conflicting (dis)guises. While seeming to be opposites, modern iconoclasm and postmodern iconolatry both express the *desire* for presence—even when that pres-

5

ence is the presence of absence. In post-abstract expressionism, the longing for presence issues in a superficial play of images and signs that point to nothing beyond themselves. The return of the sign *as sign,* which begins with pop art and continues in video art, reflects and extends what Guy Debord describes as "the society of spectacle," which stages the disappearance of altarity in the appearance of signs that are always signs of signs and images that are only images of images. In this culture of the simulacrum, the abiding temptation is to "forget not." In chapter 7, "Adverteasing: Forget Not," I probe the importance of the shift from pop art, as it is represented in the paintings of David Salle, to pop culture, as it appears in the videos of Madonna. Salle and Madonna are preoccupied with an eroticism that harbors an undeniable violence. When approached from the perspective of Georges Bataille's heterology and Jean Baudrillard's ecstasy, this transgressive eroticism turns out to be a refiguration of the sacred that appears when God dies. With the transition from high to low culture, the incarnation of God is consummated on an altar where body and blood become sign and image. Postmodern art and electronic media involve an iconolatry in and through which the not withdraws.

To be drawn toward the withdrawal of the not is to realize that the not cannot be avoided. Though we struggle to repress it, the not inevitably returns to disrupt everything we think we are. Neither being nor nonbeing, the not resists the incarnation that manifests itself as bodily presence. The presence sacralized by the Book cannot appear either as the presence or absence of the Word made flesh. Though apparently totally present, the body is never simply itself but always betrays the not without which it cannot be. I conclude my questioning of the not—or the not concludes its questioning of me—with a chapter entitled "The Betrayal of the Body: Live Not," in which I attempt to follow traces of the not in the discourse of disease. Disease is the impossible embodiment of the not. Since the not can never be undone or overcome, disease is not accidental, episodic, or occasional. To the contrary, disease is our chronic condition. To live is to live not, and to live not is to live disease endlessly. The task of living not is not hopeless but is the only hope that remains in a world from which hope has all but vanished.

Not is never one but always many—many different Nots that resist unification and totalization. Thus, I have deliberately not attempted to force these nots into the systematic structure of a book. To have done so would not really have been to have struggled to think not(s). The more books I write, the less certain I am that it is possible to write a book. Gradually—perhaps all too gradually—I am coming to suspect that the only book worth writing is the book I cannot write. Perhaps such a book would not be a book or would be a book that is nothing but nots.

Religion

1

How Not to Think God

This Name of God conceives God only in that sphere in which he can be conceived, not *in altitudine sua,* but with great hesitation and reserve—by conceiving the manner in which he is not to be conceived.—KARL BARTH

The name of God signifies not only that what is named by it would not belong to the language in which this name occurs, but that this name, in a way that is difficult to determine, would no longer be a part of it, even apart from it. The idolatry of the name or only the reverence that makes it unpronounceable (sacred) is related to this disappearance of the *name* that the name itself makes appear and that forces us to raise the level of the language in which it occults itself to the point of giving it as forbidden. Far from raising us to lofty significations, as those that theology authorizes, it does not give place to anything that is its proper to it: pure name that does not name, but is rather always to be named, the name as name, but, in that, hardly a name, without nominative power, attached as it is by chance to language and, thus, transmitting to it the power—devastating—of nondesignation that relates it to itself.—MAURICE BLANCHOT

To think God is to think the name of God. But what is God's name? What does "God" name? How does "God" name? Does "God" name? Perhaps, as Blanchot suggests, "God" is the name that makes the *disappearance* of the name appear. "God," then, might be the name for that in language which does not properly belong to language. If it were a name that does not name, the name "God" might, in a certain sense, be a name for the unnameable . . . the unnameable that haunts language as a strange exteriority "within" discourse.

How Not to Think God./?/! A statement, a question, a command, and/or a prohibition. Is the thinking of God inevitable or impossible? Demanded or forbidden? Or (impossibly) both inevitable and impossible? Demanded and forbidden? To ask "How not to think God" is, of course, always already to have thought God. The question, then, becomes a question of thinking of the prohibition of thinking, or a thinking of the *not,* which is not precisely not thinking. To think "How not to think God" is to *think* the limit of thought. This limit, which remains unthinkable, nonetheless constitutes thought itself. Such a limit, margin, or boundary is, as Kierkegaard insists, "the passion of thought."

Fides Quaerens Intellectum

Nowhere has the name of God been thought with more rigor than in the complex history of the ontological argument. Anselm's classic proof of God's existence is, in effect, an extended meditation on the name of God. To comprehend the "proper" name of God, one must understand how *not* to think God. Though rarely noticed, Anselm's proof seems to offer no support for the necessity of *thinking* God. Thought *supplements* belief when faith seeks understanding. While Anselm believes in order to understand, there appears to be no necessary transition from belief to understanding. Anselm's efforts to the contrary notwithstanding, his so-called ontological proof seems unnecessary.

The necessity lacking in Anselm's proof appears in Hegel's reinterpretation of the ontological argument. Hegel brings to systematic

completion the insights anticipated by Plotinus and Augustine and sub-
sequently articulated by Anselm. The entire Hegelian edifice can actually be understood as a sustained argument for God's existence.
Anselm's faith seeking understanding becomes Hegel's translation of
religious *Vorstellungen* into the philosophical *Begriffe*. Inasmuch as
Hegel's system marks the closure of the ontotheological tradition, his
philosophical rendering of the ontological argument is a pivotal moment in the fulfillment of the Western philosophical quest. If the ontological argument is in any way inadequate, ontotheology inevitably fails.
Thus, philosophy's stake in the ontological argument is nothing less
than the viability of philosophy itself.

To claim that Hegel brings to systematic completion insights initially
articulated by Anselm *is not* to imply that Hegel accepts Anselm's formulation of the ontological argument. Even though he admits that the
content of Anselm's argument is true, Hegel insists that its *form* is inadequate. "But there is the following circumstance in this case," he argues, "which makes the proof unsatisfactory. That most perfect and
most real of all things is a *presupposition,* and being and the concept,
on their own account, are one-sided when measured against it."[1] Anselm, in other words, presupposes precisely what needs to be demonstrated, that is, the identity of thought (or the concept) and being. If the
ontological argument is to be convincing, its rational necessity must be
demonstrated by explicating the dialectical relation of thought and being through which each contains the other as a constitutive moment of
itself.

Before proceeding to an analysis and criticism of Hegel's reformulation of the ontological argument, it is important to recognize the precise place of the proofs in his system. Hegel's remarks on the proofs of
God's existence are scattered throughout his *Lectures on the Philosophy
of Religion.* At the time of his death, he was preparing for publication
some lectures on these proofs, which eventually were issued as an ap-
pendix to his *Lectures on the Philosophy of Religion.* Hegel begins his
account of the proofs by insisting that his comments are a *supplement*
to his lectures on *logic* rather than to his lectures on the philosophy of
religion.

12

> These lectures are devoted to the consideration of the proofs of the exis-
> tence of God. The occasion for them is this. I had at first made up my
> mind to give only one set of lectures in this summer session on philo-
> sophical knowledge as a whole, and then afterwards, I felt I would like to
> add a second set on at least one separate subject of knowledge. I have
> therefore chosen a subject that is connected with the other set of lectures

that I gave on logic, and constitutes, not in substance, but in form, a kind of supplement [*Ergänzung*] to that set, inasmuch as it is concerned with only a particular aspect of the fundamental conceptions of logic. [*PR,* 3:155]

The *Science of Logic,* however, is something like a supplement to the philosophy of religion, which, in turn, is a supplement to the *Logic.* Philosophy, as I have noted, discloses the rational truth implicit in religious images. Accordingly, the *Logic* is both a supplement to the religious imagination and the first moment, which is the structural foundation, of the system as a whole. But in a reversal that does not seem to be dialectical, Hegel also argues that the "Lectures on the Proofs of God's Existence" supplement his *Logic.* The proofs, therefore, are a supplement to the supplement to religious *Vorstellungen.* At first glance, this play of supplements appears to be an illustration of the circularity of the Hegelian dialectic. This appearance, however, is misleading, for within the Hegelian dialectic, circularity implies hierarchy. *Begriffe* surpass the *Vorstellungen,* which they both negate and preserve. In the play of supplements acted out in the relation between the *Logic* and the proofs of God's existence, the hierarchy of *Begriffe* and *Vorstellungen* gives way to an undecidable interplay of concepts and images. In ways yet to be determined, the curious "logic" of the play of supplements interrupts the dialectical logic of Hegel's system.[2]

The relation of the proofs of God's existence to Hegel's system is even more complex than this nondialectical play of supplements suggests. From a different point of view, Hegel seems unable to decide whether the proofs supplement the logic or are internal to the system as its structural foundation. Within Hegel's scheme, the three classical proofs of God's existence actually constitute three moments in a single complex proof.

We may without prejudice admit a variety of starting-points. This does not in itself in any way conflict with the demand that we considered ourselves justified in making that the true proof should be one only; insofar as this proof is known by thought to represent the inner element of thought, thought can also show that it represents one and the same path, although starting from different points. [*PR,* 3:215]

The rational, as well as the historical, order of the proofs is cosmological, teleological, ontological. Each later proof passes beyond, while at the same time assuming and preserving, its predecessor(s). Once we recognize the dialectic of these three moments of the argument for God's existence, we are in a position to grasp their relationship to Hegel's overall philosophy of religion, as well as to the logical structure of the concept and his system as a whole.

When Hegel's interpretation of religion is read in light of his analysis of the threefold proof of God's existence, it becomes apparent that each proof is the correlate of a different stage in the philosophy of religion: the cosmological proof corresponds to the religion of nature, the teleological proof to the religion of spiritual individuality, and the ontological proof to the absolute religion. Furthermore, when rationally comprehended, the dialectic of religion prefigures the conceptual progress of the logic. The logical movement from the doctrine of being, defined as determinate being (*Dasein*), to the doctrine of essence recapitulates the advance from contingency to necessity developed in the cosmological argument. Hegel characterizes necessity in the first proof alternatively as essence, cause, ground, substance, and force, which are all variations of the logical doctrine of essence. Through the concept of determination in accordance with an end, the teleological argument defines more concretely the absolute necessity of the cosmological proof. The transition from the cosmological to the teleological argument is paralleled by the logical move from the doctrine of essence to the doctrine of the concept. More specifically, the consideration of the teleological determination of the object elucidates those aspects of rational cognition defined in the teleological argument. As the ontological argument realizes the truth implicit in the cosmological and teleological arguments by disclosing the identity of being and thought, so the absolute idea reconciles being and essence, thereby revealing *veritas ipsa,* or God. Finally, in terms of Hegel's system as a whole, the movement from the philosophy of nature, through the philosophy of spirit, to the logic repeats the progression from the cosmological, through the teleological, to the ontological arguments. Since the three moments in the proof and three parts of the system are dialectically related, this movement is reversible. In other words, the progression from the ontological, through the cosmological, to the teleological proof represents the transition from the logic, through the philosophy of nature, to the philosophy of spirit.

Historically and philosophically, the first form of the proof of God's existence is *ex contingentia mundi.* Beginning with a reexamination of finitude and contingency, dialectical reason recognizes that the finite is not independent and self-identical but is inherently dependent and self-contradictory. Because the contingent or finite does not possess aseity, its being necessarily entails the being of an other (that is, its opposite or the absolutely necessary/infinite). In Hegel's form of the cosmological argument, there is no movement from independent finitude to transcendent infinity because a rational consideration of finite or contingent being discloses its dialectical, internal relation to infinity or absolute necessity. In Hegel's terms: "*The being of the finite is not only its being, but is also the being of the infinite*" (*PR,* 3:254). Finitude and contingency include within themselves their opposites as indispensable presuppositions, necessary constituents, and the essential ground of their being. The determinate identity of finitude or contingency comprehends its own difference (infinitude/necessity) in such a way that the relationship to otherness is actually a dimension of self-relation requisite for self-realization.

At this stage of reflection, there remains a specious asymmetry within the relation of the finite and infinite. The configuration of the relation is such that the determinate identity of the infinite is construed as the ground or cause of the finite, which, in turn, is identified primarily by being grounded in or caused by infinity. In different terms, God is essentially Creator and the world essentially created. The cosmological argument seeks to demonstrate that "there is only one being and this belongs to necessity; other things by their very nature form a part of it" (*PR,* 3:315). Though philosophers and theologians have used categories as different as "ideal," "essence," "ground," "whole," "substance," and "cause" to express this insight, Hegel maintains that the fundamental characteristic of the divine to emerge from the cosmological argument is more effectively captured by the terms "power or force" (*PR,* 3:328). God is the infinite power that creates and sustains all things. From Hegel's point of view, however, the conclusion of this argument is incomplete and "is not adequate to express our idea of God" (*PR,* 3:313). Although the divine is recognized as the absolute, self-determining power of the world, the infinite's self-determination is abstract, its power blind.

While the cosmological proof establishes God's power, the teleological argument reveals divine wisdom. God no longer is viewed as abstract self-determination or blind power but is known as purposive activity—the process of determination in accordance with an end. The teleological argument takes up within itself the notion of God derived from the cosmological moment of the proof and gives it a richer, more complete determination. God remains powerful, but now is known to exercise power wisely.

Hegel builds his analysis of the teleological argument on his appropriation and expansion of Kant's account of "inner teleology," which is presented in the Third Critique.[3] From the perspective of speculative

15

reason, a single end realizes itself throughout the entire cosmos. This self-realizing *telos* is not imposed from without but is the very life-force of the world. "When we grasp this life-force in its true nature," Hegel maintains, "it is seen to be one principle, one organic life of the universe, one living system. All that is, simply constitutes the organs of the one subject" (*PR,* 3:343). The activity of this "life-force" or "single subject" is governed by the principle of inner teleology. Its means are not external but are the internal, necessary condition of the possibility of the single subject's concrete actuality. Moreover, the means (that is, all particular entities in the world) possess their specific identity by virtue of their place within the self-realizing activity of the end. According to Hegel, this omnipresent and perpetually active structural ground of all determinate reality is nothing other than the sovereign *Nous* or eternal *Logos* that creates and rules the world. The speculative form of the teleological argument does not reveal the divine as an alien other who directs the world from without. To the contrary, God is the immanent structural principle that sustains and directs the universe.

When the cosmos is viewed according to the principle of inner teleology, no part of the finite world can be comprehended in isolation from the self-actualizing totality of which it is an organic member. This determinate whole is the working-out or concrete self-actualization of *Nous.* Expressed theologically, the world is the realization of God's wise purpose. The teleological argument attempts to demonstrate that "the truth of the world is the completely realized essential existence of the manifestation of a wise power" (*PR,* 2:154). Through this proof, dialectical reason renders explicit the unity of subjectivity and objectivity implicit in the notion of design. In other words, the awareness of the teleological structure of reality discloses the coincidence of intention and actualization, thought and being, subjectivity and objectivity. This coincidence is truth, and truth is God. By establishing the identity of truth, the teleological proof points to the Absolute Idea, whose exploration lies within the domain of the ontological argument.

16

Fully realizing the truth that begins to emerge in the cosmological and teleological moments, the ontological argument is the most complete form of the proof of God's existence. Hegel maintains that the overriding issue raised by the ontological argument is the problem of the relation between thought and being: "The ontological proof starts from the concept. The concept is considered to be something subjective, and is defined as something opposed to the object and to reality. Here it constitutes the starting point, and what we have to do is to show that being, too, belongs to the concept" (*PR,* 3:361). In Anselm's terms, starting from the *idea* of God, an effort must be made to establish the *being* or *existence* of God.

Hegel begins his account of the ontological argument by defining abstract or pure being as indeterminate, completely lacking concrete specification. Earlier stages of the proof have shown that determination (that is, concrete self-identity) is a function of mediation with or relation to ostensible "otherness." Indeterminate being, therefore, is immediate, unmediated, relationless being—being that is abstracted from its relation to or mediation with otherness. In short, abstract being is simple "relation-to-self." Immediacy means, in fact, being. It means this simple relation-to-self, insofar as we eliminate [the other]" (*PR*, 1:163). Hegel argues that when being (objectivity) is conceived in this way, it is one with thought (subjectivity). "Pure being . . . is, on the one hand, pure thought, and, on the other hand, pure immediacy" (*L*, par. 20).

In an effort to provide further support for his assertion of the identity of thought and being, Hegel turns from an analysis of pure being to an examination of the thinking subject. "Thought, viewed as subject," he argues, "is what is expressed by the word I [*Ich*]" (*L*, par. 20). Reflection upon the I is, of course, inevitably reflexive. In becoming objective to itself in thought, the I discloses its intrinsic bifurcation or inherent self-contradiction. Simultaneously subject and object, the self-conscious I is a self-reflexive structure in which there is an identity of subjectivity and objectivity. Although the subjective and objective moments of the I are inseparable and always exist in concrete unity with one another, they can be distinguished by reflective analysis. As subject, the I is pure thought from which all determination has been abstracted, and as object, the I is the concretization of the subject—the particular form assumed by the abstract, universal I.

Through the analysis of self-consciousness, it becomes clear that pure thought, like pure being, is utterly empty, devoid of all particularity and determination. The I, taken as subject, "is pure relation-to-itself in which we abstract from all conception and feeling, from every state of mind, and every peculiarity of nature, talent, and experience" (*L*, par. 20). In other words, Hegel defines pure thought and pure being in exactly the same way. Both are simple self-relation or mere relation-to-self. Pure thought and pure being, therefore, are essentially one. This identity can be approached from opposite directions: From the side of being: "Being [*Sein*] is not to be felt, or perceived by sense, or pictured in imagination; it is pure thought" (*L*, par. 86). From the side of thought: "the 'I,' being is simply in myself; I can abstract from everything, but I cannot abstract from thought, for the abstracting is itself thought, it is the activity of the universal, simple relation-to-self. Being is exemplified in the very act of abstraction. I can indeed destroy myself, but that is the liberty to abstract from my existence. 'I am,'—in the 'I,' the 'am' is already included" (*PR,* 1:16).

To complete his speculative interpretation of the proofs, Hegel must demonstrate the dialectical relation of the ontological argument to the cosmological and teleological arguments. As I have stressed, within the framework of the teleological argument, the cosmos is viewed as an organic process under wise and powerful divine providence. In terms more in keeping with the ontological proof, the universe is the realization of the incarnation of the divine *Logos.* "In other words, the world and finite things have issued from the fullness of divine thoughts and divine decrees" (*L,* par. 163). Thought or reason is not merely subjective but is the active essence of objectivity. Reason (*logos*) is practical and hence the world is rational (logical).

Hegel's argument grows out of his refinement of Kant's account of *Zweck* ("end," or "purpose"). In *Science of Logic,* he argues:

> But in general end is to be taken as the *rational in its concrete existence.* It manifests *rationality* because it is the concrete concept, that holds the *objective difference within its absolute unity.* . . . . It is the self-equal *universal* and this, as containing self-repellent negativity, is in the first instance universal, and therefore as yet *indeterminate, activity;* but because this is the negative relation to itself, it *determines* itself immediately, and gives itself the moment of *particularity,* which, as likewise the *totality of the form reflected into itself,* is *content* as against the *posited* differences of the form. Equally immediately this negativity, through its relation to itself, is absolute reflection of the form into itself and thus *individuality.* [*SL,* 741]

Here Hegel identifies "end" as "the rational in its concrete existence" or the "concrete concept." Elsewhere he points out that "the realized end is the posited unity of subjectivity and objectivity" (*L,* par. 210). This identity of concept and realized end, or subjectivity and objectivity is not simple or immediate but is mediated by the concept's dynamic process of self-actualization. The end is "the concept-in-action, or the active universal—the determinate and self-determining universal" (*L,* par. 57). The process through which the active concept realizes itself is tripartite. In itself (*an sich*), the concept is abstract or indeterminate. It remains a simple potentiality or is, as Hegel puts it, "the self-equal universal." But this indeterminate concept, the abstract universal, is inherently self-contradictory. As such, it is "self-repellent negativity," or "negative relation-to-self." The concept realizes its potential by deter-

18

mining itself concretely. The actualization of the concept presupposes its objective expression. In becoming itself, the active concept repels itself from itself as potentially negating its inner subjectivity and actually realizes itself in the realm of objectivity. Object and subject are not antithetical, for the object is the objective (*Zweck* as well as *objectiv*) of the subject. The self-negation of the subjective concept is really its self-realization as the objective concept. The determinate objectification of the concept (its *Fürsichsein*) is the second moment of its self-actualization. In the final phase of this process, the reunion of subjectivity and objectivity, which is implicit in the first two stages of the concept's becoming, is realized explicitly. Since objectivity is a necessary moment in the actuality of subjectivity, the subject's relation to the object is its self-relation in which the otherness (that is, the simple opposition) of subject and object is sublated. While objectivity is the first negation of subjectivity, the subject's appropriation of the object as a determinate expression (*Äusserung*) of itself is the negation of this negation by means of which the subject returns to itself through the relation to its "other." The actualization of the concept is a process of double negation in which subjectivity and objectivity are completely reconciled:

> The concept is this totality: the process, the movement of objectifying itself. . . . The concept, however, is all that is deepest and highest. The very idea of the concept implies that it has to sublate this defect of subjectivity, overcome this distinction between itself and being, and has to objectify itself. It is itself this act of producing itself as something that has being, as something objective. Whenever we think of the concept, we must give up the idea that it is something that *we* only possess and construct within ourselves. The concept is the soul, the end or goal of what is living. What we call soul is the concept, and in spirit, in consciousness, the concept as such attains to existence as a free concept existing in its subjectivity as distinct from its reality as such. [*PR,* 3:356–57]

While determinate being finds its truth in the concept, the concept becomes actual in determinate being. Apart from its appearance in objectivity, subjectivity remains unreal. Thought and being realize themselves only in and through each other. They form an inseparable dialectical unity apart from which neither is, and through which each becomes itself. This unity of subjectivity and objectivity, concept and existence, thought and being, is truth or the Absolute Idea:

> But having reached the result that the Idea is the unity of the concept and objectivity, is the true, it must not be regarded merely as a *goal* to which

19

we have to approximate but that itself always remains a kind of *beyond;* on the contrary, we must recognize that everything *is* actual only insofar as it possesses the Idea and expresses it. [*SL,* 756]

The ontological proof reveals the world as the embodiment of the divine Idea or the incarnation of the *Logos* of God. God is the "essence [*Inbegriff*] of all reality" (*L,* par. 86). Through the comprehension of God as the Creator and Sustainer of the world, and of the world as the self-realization of God, Creator and creation, God and man, infinite and finite, absolute necessity and contingency, subjectivity and objectivity are reconciled.

Within Hegel's system, God is truth and truth is the complete reconciliation of concept and reality. The ontological argument does not involve the demonstration of the necessary existence of *a* being—even if that being is the *ens realissimum.* When fully realized as the Absolute Idea, the concept is the all-encompassing totality that constitutes all existence. To think properly or truly is to think all things in God and God in all things. The thought of God is both necessary and unavoidable. For Hegel, the question "How not to think God?" is actually rhetorical. The only way not to think God is not to think and this possibility is negated as soon as the question is asked. Thought itself is impossible apart from the implicit or explicit thought of God.

The question that lingers in the wake of Hegel's speculative rendering of the ontological argument is whether the reconciliation of concept and reality upon which true thought depends can ever be realized. Between Hegel's "Lectures on the Proofs of the Existence of God" and the published text they supplement, there is another supplement of sorts. After completing his lectures on the philosophy of religion, Hegel adds a supplementary "discordant note." The reconciliation that his system is supposed to demonstrate, he admits, is not real:

> This reconciliation is merely a partial one, without outward universality. Philosophy forms in this connection a separate sanctuary, and those who serve in it constitute an isolated order of priests, who must not mix with the world, and thus guard the possession of truth. How the temporal, empirical present is to find its way out of this discord, and what form it is to take, are questions that must be left to itself to settle. [*PR,* 3:150–51]

This confession is remarkable, for it calls into question Hegel's entire philosophical enterprise. The separation of ideality and reality reintroduces precisely the unreconciled otherness that the system is constructed to overcome. In this moment, Hegelian vision becomes Kierkegaardian despair. To try to discover whether the failure that leads to Hegel's despair is unavoidable, we must return to Anselm's ontological argument.

Addressing the Exterior

Hegel, we have seen, criticizes the form but not the content of Anselm's argument. From Hegel's speculative perspective, Anselm presupposes rather than demonstrates the identity of thought and being. What Hegel's criticism of Anselm overlooks is, however, at least as interesting as what it stresses. While emphasizing the issue of form, Hegel nevertheless fails to note that in its most refined version, Anselm's ontological argument is actually an *address*. The title of the work is *Proslogion*, which is an improper Latin word created by combining *pro* (toward) and *logion* (speech). Anselm's text is an address spoken to or toward someone. But to whom is Anselm's message addressed? To whom is his letter sent? There is no simple reply to these questions because the destination of Anselm's letter is multiple.

The most obvious answer to the question of the addressee of Anselm's message is that it is directed to his "brethren." Anselm prefaces his address by recording the circumstances of its composition. He observes that *Proslogion* is a supplement to an earlier work, *Monologion*, which he had written in response to "the urgent request of some of [his] brethren" (*P*, 69). In the course of reflecting on the *Monologion*, Anselm recalls: "I began to ask myself whether *one* argument might possibly be found, resting on no other argument for its proof, but sufficient in itself to prove that God truly exists, and that he is the supreme good, needing nothing outside himself, but needful for the being and well-being of all things" (*P*, 69). *Proslogion* is the result of Anselm's further thought. Persuaded that his labors had borne fruit, Anselm reports: "I thought that the proof I was so glad to find would please some readers if it were written down" (*P*, 69).

With the transition from the spoken to the written word, at least two significant changes take place. First, the circle of addressees expands significantly. No longer are the recipients of Anselm's word merely the "closed circle" of brethren. Now anyone who is able to read can, in principle, receive the message. The second important development is closely related to the first. Anselm loses control over his work, or, more precisely, is forced to confess that he never had controlled his words. It seems that others copied Anselm's text without "proper" attribution. This practice of reinscription posed a threat to the "integrity" of the word that Anselm takes so seriously. He explains that initially he had

21

not intended to sign his works but when the written word began to circulate a bit too freely, he attempted to put a stop to its promiscuity by reasserting his paternal rights:

> Neither this essay nor the other one I have already mentioned really seemed to me to deserve to be called a book or to bear an author's name; at the same time, I felt that they could not be published without some title that might encourage anyone into whose hands they fell to read them, and so I gave each of them a title. The first I called *An Example of Meditation on the Grounds of Faith,* and the second *Faith Seeking Understanding.*
>   But when both of them had been copied under these titles by a number of people, I was urged by many people . . . to attach my name to them. In order to do this more fittingly, I have named the first *Monologion* (or *Soliloquy*), and the second *Proslogion* (or *Address*). [*P,* 70]

The inscription of the author's name and the attribution of a title to the work represent an effort to keep the written word from running wild.

When Anselm turns from the preface to the text "proper," the question of the addressee of *Proslogion* becomes even more complex:

> Now then, little man, for a short while fly from your business; hide yourself for a moment from your turbulent thoughts. Break off now your troublesome cares, and think less of your laborious occupations. Make a little time for God, and rest for a while in him. Enter into the chamber of your mind, shut out everything but God and whatever helps you to seek him, and, when you have shut the door, seek him. [*P,* 70]

This opening paragraph names at least four addressees. The "little man" of the first sentence refers to the brethren, in response to whom *Monologion* and its supplement had been written, and to the reader. After this initial address, Anselm proceeds to invoke a trope that returns repeatedly throughout the text—the apostrophe:

> Speak now, O my whole heart, speak now to God: "I seek thy face; thy face, Lord, do I desire."
>   And do thou, O Lord my God, teach my heart where and how to seek thee, where and how to find thee. Lord, if thou art not here, where shall I seek thee who art absent? But if thou art everywhere, why do I not see thee who are present? [*P,* 70]

Anselm's message is addressed not only to his brethren and readers but also to himself, as well as to God. The multiple addressees obviously are not of equal importance. Anselm sends his words first and foremost to God. The discourse directed to the brethren, reader, and himself depends upon God's receipt of, and response to Anselm's message: "The one who asks to be led by God turns himself for an instant toward another addressee, in order to lead him in turn. He does not simply

22

turn himself away from his first addressee who is *in truth* the first Cause of his prayer and already guides it. It is exactly because he does not turn away from God that he can turn toward [his brethren and readers] and *pass from one address to the other without changing direction*" (HAS, 48).

Anselm's address *to* God is an appeal to be addressed *by* God. The efficacy of Anselm's language in relation to both self and others presupposes an intervention from "beyond" that takes place through the discourse of an Other. For Anselm, the name of this Other is, of course, God. But the name "God" is a strange name. As the condition of the possibility of the efficacy of language, God, whose discourse is always the discourse of the Other, eludes the very linguistic structures, he, she, or it nonetheless makes possible. To address this Other is always already *to be addressed by* the Other. The form of address in which the Other approaches is prayer.

Proslogion is, in effect, an extended prayer. More precisely, *Proslogion* is the quotation of Anselm's prayer to an Other. Anselm, Karl Barth explains, "resumes the form of address to God, that is, he passes from the language of theological inquiry to the language of prayer. Or rather . . . he shows that the whole theological inquiry is intended to be understood as undertaken and carried through in prayer."[4] In this case, prayer is a petition addressed to an Other. To the extent that Anselm's appeal to be addressed by God is successful, the words of the text are not precisely *his* words but are the words of an Other who is never present or is present only by withdrawing. Thus, Anselm's discourse is never perfectly transparent but is forever haunted by an Other that language can neither include nor exclude.

The words of prayer point toward (without referring to) an exteriority that is "within" language itself. The event of discourse presupposes an anterior event that has always already taken place. In another sense, however, the ancient event that both binds and releases language never takes place, for it is never present but has always already occurred. This irreducible "before" renders language inescapably secondary. Never simply itself but always older than itself, language witnesses what it cannot express.

When Anselm asks "How not to think God?" he too suggests that it is impossible to avoid thinking God. For Anselm, as for Hegel, the only way not to think God is not to think and this possibility is, as I have argued, negated as soon as the question is asked. But there is a crucial difference between the unavoidable thought of God in Hegel's all-inclusive proof and Anselm's obedient prayer. Hegel's God is the

23

Logos—reason itself, which is not only the structure of subjective cognition but is also the foundation of objective reality. As such, God is completely knowable. Philosophy translates religious re-present-ations into conceptual present-ations. In the presence of philosophical knowledge, every vestige of altarity is negated. Efforts to the contrary notwithstanding, Anselm cannot erase the trace of the Other. From the opening invocation to the concluding "Amen," Anselm's text testifies to the exteriority that both makes it possible and calls into question the integrity, lucidity, and closure of the work. This exteriority, which is "within" language as its enabling condition, is not the opposite of interiority or inwardness. Such exteriority cannot, therefore, be assimilated by the Hegelian dialectic. Never present without being absent, the exteriority of discourse cannot be re-present-ed. This exteriority is, in the words of Blanchot, "the unrepresentable before" in whose debt we always remain. Derrida's comment on Pseudo-Dionysius's *Mystical Theology* and *Divine Names* underscores the significance of this terribly ancient Other:

> As for meaning and reference, here is another reminder—in truth, the recall of the other, the call of the other as recall. At the moment when the question "how to avoid speaking [*comment ne pas parler*]?" is raised and articulates itself in all its modalities—whether in rhetorical or logical forms of saying, or in the simple fact of speaking—it is already, so to speak, *too late*. There is no longer any question of not speaking. Even if one speaks and says nothing, even if an apophatic discourse deprives itself of meaning or of an object, it takes place. That which committed or rendered it possible *has taken place*. The possible absence of a referent still beckons, if not toward the thing of which one speaks (such is God, who is nothing because He takes place, without place, beyond Being), at least toward the other (other than Being) who calls or to whom this speech is addressed—even if it speaks to him only in order to speak, or to say nothing. This call of the other, having always already preceded the speech to which it has never been present a first time, announces itself in advance as a call. Such a reference to the other will always have taken place. Prior to every proposition and even before all discourse in general—whether a promise, prayer, praise, celebration. The most negative discourse, even beyond all nihilisms and negative dialectics, preserves a trace of the other. A trace of an event older than it *or* of a "taking-place" to come, both of them: here there is neither an alternative nor a contradiction. [HAS, 30–31]

To think this strange Other is to think not.

Thinking Not

How not to think God? How not to think God without not thinking? Perhaps, but in this region there is no certainty, perhaps by thinking *not.* The thinking of not is the unthinking implied in all thinking. But which not, what not remains to be thought?

To think the not that both allows and refuses thought is to think the not inherent in the name *God.* Anselm's ontological argument can be understood as a prolonged meditation on the name *God.* The name *God,* however, is, in effect, a prohibition, which (impossibly) names an unthinkable yet inescapable thought. To think God is to think the not his name names.

God, for Anselm, names that than which nothing greater can be thought. Since Anselm assumes that to exist is greater than not to exist, he maintains that God necessarily exists:

> For no one who understands what God is can think that God does not exist, even though he says these words in his heart—perhaps without any meaning, perhaps with some quite extraneous meaning. For God is that than which a greater cannot be thought, and whoever understands this rightly must understand that he exists in such a way that he cannot be non-existent even in thought. He, therefore, who understands that God thus exists cannot think of him as nonexistent. [*P,* 75]

In this text, Anselm makes it clear that the "proper" understanding of the name *God* entails a certain prohibition on thinking. This prohibition emerges when "How not to think God" is read as an imperative instead an interrogative. Some thoughts cannot, indeed *must* not be thought. Most important, one *cannot* think that God does not exist. In different terms, the nonexistence of God is unthinkable and, as such, is an impossible thought. Anselm's ontological proof of God's existence is really an *indirect* proof in which he attempts to prove that God exists by proving that it is impossible for God not to exist. To think God, then, is to think the not of his nonexistence.

If Anselm's "proof" is read in this way, the ontological argument exposes the impossibility of thought without which thinking is impossible. To think is to think not. To think the impossibility of thought is, of course, not to think. Such thinking is unthinking. If, as Hegel insists, the ontological argument is actually an exploration of the conditions of the possibility of thought, then it appears that thinking is impossible apart from the unthinking that struggles vainly to think the impossibility of thought. The coincidence of thinking and unthinking in (the) think-ing (of the) not constitutes a paradox that is utterly Kierkegaardian:

> The paradoxical passion of the understanding is, then, continually collid-ing with this unknown, which certainly does exist but is also unknown and to that extent does not exist. The understanding does not go beyond this; yet in its paradoxicality the understanding cannot stop reaching it and be-

ing engaged with it, because wanting to express its relation to it by saying that this unknown does not exist will not do, since just saying that involves a relation. But what, then, is this unknown, for does not its being the god merely signify to us that it is the unknown? To declare that it is the unknown because we cannot know it, and that even if we could know it we could not express it, does not satisfy the passion, although it has correctly perceived it as boundary [*Grœndse*]. But a boundary is expressly the passion's torment, even though it is also its incentive. And yet it can go no further, whether it risks a result through *via negationis* or *via eminentiae*. [*PF,* 44]

At this limit, along this border or margin, thought can go no further. We are always on a threshold that both solicits and resists thought. Thought needs what it cannot bear. This is the passion of thinking . . . the crucifixion of understanding.

Divine Names

To think God is unavoidably to think the name of God. But what *is* God's name? What does *God* name? How does *God* name? Does *God* name? Perhaps, as Blanchot suggests, *God* is the name that makes the disappearance of the name—every name—appear. If this is so, *God* is *in a certain sense* a name for the unnameable . . . the unnameable that haunts language as a strange exteriority "within" discourse.

"How Not to Think God." The title that frames the inquiry remains duplicitous. A statement, a question, a command, and/or a prohibition. Is the thinking of God inevitable or impossible? Demanded or forbidden? Or (impossibly) both inevitable and impossible? Both demanded and forbidden? To ask "How not to think God" is always already to have thought God. The question, then, becomes a question of the thinking of the prohibition of thinking . . . a thinking of the "not," which is not precisely the same as not thinking. To think "How not to think God" is to *think* the limit of thought. This limit, which remains unthinkable, nonetheless constitutes thought itself. Thought struggles to repress the limit that marks the exteriority inscribed within all thinking. Anselm's prayer indirectly pays homage to the Other that Hegel's system is constructed *not* to think. One of the names of this Other—there are, of course, always others—might be *God.* "The name God," Blanchot insists, "signifies not only that what is named by it would not belong to the language in which this name occurs, but that this name, in a way that is difficult to determine, would no longer be a part of it, even apart from it."[5] Though not precisely a part of language, the name *God* is never apart from language, nor is language ever apart from the impossible name of the unnameable. To learn to think God is to learn how

26

not to think God. The paradox of thinking is to learn how to think not without not thinking or ceasing to think.

When the ontological argument is read otherwise, the vicious circle of philosophy is broken and yet returns . . . eternally returns. Thinking is forever interrupted by the not it can never think. If, as Hegel confesses in his moment of despair, philosophers finally become "an isolated order of priests," their words unwittingly bear witness to the Other in whose wake they forever write. Foucault's reading of Blanchot's *récits* indirectly re-marks the failure of Hegel's system that is implied in Anselm's prayerful message:

> From the moment discourse ceases to follow the slope of self-interiorizing thought and, addressing the very being of language, returns thought to the outside; from that moment, in a single stroke, it becomes a meticulous narration of experiences, encounters, and improbable signs—language about the outside of all language, speech about the invisible side of words. And it becomes attentiveness to what in language already exists, has already been said, imprinted, manifested—a listening less to what is articulated in language than to the void circulating between its words, to the murmur that is forever taking it apart; a discourse on the non-discourse of language; the fiction of the invisible space in which it appears.[6]

A discourse on the nondiscourse of all language returns thought to the outside. The "name" of this (eternal) return is *God*. Devastating power of nondesignation, "God" is (but, of course God is not) the void circulating between words.

The name God
The "name" God
The name *God*

"Name," in-significant name that is forever taking apart. Impossible thought without which thinking is impossible. How not to think God? Perhaps by (the) unthinking (of) thinking (of the) not.

2

nO nOt nO

V iens . . . Come!" "In the name of what?" In the
name of what do we meet, linger, disperse? What calls? Calls us to
gather here and now . . . in this time? At this place? What time? What
place? What is the time and place of gathering? "What is the place, what
takes place or gives place to thought?" In the name of what or of whom
do we promise to speak and to write? Now and in the future? In the
"name" of nothing? In the "name" of not? Perhaps. Perhaps not. Perhaps
we are called by nothing, in the "name" of a certain not, in order (if it
is an order) not to speak and write "about" nothing. *Comment ne pas
parler* . . . about nothing? How to avoid speaking . . . not? How to avoid
speaking not without

> [. . . the strange syntax of the *without* that would patiently interrogate
> us . . . . This I (without I) of the *without* in (Blanchot's) texts, you come to
> see that it disarticulates the entire logic of identity or of contradiction . . .
> *without* any dialectical reappropriation . . .
>   without without without [1]]

not speaking? When all is said and done (but when is [the] all said and
done?), will all our speaking and writing have been for not/naught?
Who can no or not no? To no and/or not to no? Either too much or too
little. Questions of excess . . . Excessive questions.

o

o

o

nO nOt

nOt nO

nO nOt nO

o

o

o

[k]nO[w] nOt

nOt [k]nO[w]

[k]nO[w] nOt [k]nO[w]

o

o

o

But, then, *comment ne pas parler?*

[L]êt[t]re[s]

In the name

nOm

nO[m]

[n]Om

mOn

[m]On

of what . . . in the name of whom do we gather, linger, disperse? It is a certain negativity that draws us together while holding us apart and holds us apart while drawing us together. A certain negativity that is inscribed by (and, perhaps, *au nom de*) Jacques Derrida. Which negativity? What negativity? Whose negativity? Jacques's, of course. Jacques's negativity that is neither precisely negative nor positive, neither exactly present nor absent.

> To leave this immense place empty . . . . (HAS, 53)

There is an empty place at our table. The place is set but the most important guest has not arrived. Jacques has not come.[2] He was invited to our gathering but (politely) refused to come. In a letter dated 11 October 1989, he writes:

> *Votre projet me paraît passionnant et je vous suis très reconnaissant de songer ainsi à m'y associer. Croyez bien que j'aurai à coeur de tout fair pour vous suivre. Malheureusement, il me sera impossible, pour des raisons quasiment physiques, de participer directement au séminaire d'Octobre 1990 . . . .*

How is this *quasiment* to be read? Is it, perhaps, the *quasiment* with which Derrida "ends" "How to Avoid Speaking: Denials"?

> *Not, without, quasi* are three adverbs. *Quasiment.* Fable or fiction, everything happens as if I had wanted to ask, on the threshold of this lecture, what these three adverbs mean and whence they come. [HAS, 60]

This "quasi" is unavoidable and, thus, will return.

30

"Unfortunately, it will be impossible . . . for me to participate directly . . ." The qualification is important. While direct participation is impossible, indirect participation is possible. Derrida will participate *indirectly* . . . through texts. Though absent, Derrida is "present" in the texts he sends in his stead. Derrida's writings, in other words, re-mark the "presence" of his "absence."

Two texts: "How to Avoid Speaking: Denials" and "Of an Apocalyptic Tone Recently Adopted in Philosophy." Though both essays have been previously published at least twice, Derrida grants permission to reissue them yet again. No trace of original works here (or elsewhere). In addition to the refusal and the permission, Derrida makes a promise in his letter: "*Bien entendu, je ferai aussi tout mon possible pour écrire le post-scriptum auquel vous faites allusion.*" Will Derrida keep his promise? There is a note of qualification in his pledge: "*tout mon possible.*" Will the postman deliver his message? Will promise lead to fulfillment? It remains uncertain.

Once . . . at least once . . . Jacques failed to fulfill a promise. "Of an Apocalyptic Tone Recently Adopted in Philosophy" is prefaced by a letter dated 2 January 1981. It is a "Dear John" letter in which Derrida confesses that he cannot fulfill a promise. The "solution" is again a repetition—the republication of a text that has already been delivered.

> Dear John,
>
> Despite the delays generously granted me, I could not write the text requested, whether it be a question of an essay or a response to the studies that are to appear in *Semeia* . . . .
>
> I am simultaneously sending you the text of the lecture I gave this summer at Cerisy-la-Salle. If you yourself and the editors of *Semeia* judge that it can, in whole or in the form of fragments, figure in the collection in preparation, you naturally have my agreement . . . . [AT, 61–62]

The question of the address returns. To whom is the letter sent? Who is the addressee? What is its destination? Who is John? The answer seems obvious: John is John Leavey, Jr., one of Derrida's most accomplished translators. But who or what is a translator? This question is too complex to be treated adequately in this context. Suffice it to say that the translator is one who transmits a message received from an other he might or might not know to others he can never know. The translator, in other words, does not exist in and for himself but is always for an other. He is a site of passage, something like a "sieve [*crible*]" that is forever straining or a relay in a network of exchange whose currency is not fixed. Never speaking in her or his own voice, the translator echoes the discourse of an other. Which other? What other? For the moment, I delay responding.

But is the identity of the translator so obvious? After all, Derrida has taught us the impropriety of the proper. Since a name can never be proper *sensu strictissimo,* naming always raises an improper question about an improper noun: Who is John? What is (a) john? John is, of course, the "author" of The Apocalypse . . . The Revelation of John. But John is not really the "author" of the Apocalypse, for the author is (always) an other, perhaps even the Other. Is "The Revelation of John" the revelation of John or of someone or something else? Rather than an author, John is actually a translator who transmits a message from elsewhere:

> Disclosure of Yeshoua the messiah
> Elohim gives it to him
> to show to his servants
> what will come soon.
> He indicates it by sending it through his messenger
> to his servant Yohanan.

Derrida comments:

> So John is the one who already receives some letters [*courrier*] through the medium yet of a bearer who is an angel, a pure messenger. And John translates a message already transmitted, testifies to a testimony that will be yet that of another testimony, that of Jesus; so many sendings, *envois,* so many voices, and this puts so many people on the telephone line. [AT, 86]

Is this a party line? Which party? Whose party?

A third John (the question of the third will also return): A well-kept secret, though, like the purloined letter, publicly available for all to read—I believe the year was 1952—a little-noted entry in the student directory for École Normale Supérieure:

> Derrida, (Jackie)

Jackie! Jacques is Jackie? (*Aparté:* What *is* in a name? Would there ever have been deconstruction in America or elsewhere if Jacques had remained Jackie?) Jacques—*Maître Jacques,* Jack-of-all-trades . . . master of none? (But what does it mean to be master of none?) "Jack," of course, is the diminutive of John. Jacques, then, is Jack, and Jack is John.

The puzzle of the letter (to say nothing of the spirit) becomes more baffling. To whom is the letter sent? Who is its addressee? What is its destination? Who is John? The answer again seems obvious: John is Jacques. Is Jacques writing to himself? For himself? Does the letter return to its sender? Address unknown? Or is the address always already known before the letter is posted? Can the [l]êt[t]re return without the message arriving?

Let us return to the "Dear John" letter. John, we have discovered, is a translator: John Leavey, Jr., and John, "author" of *The Apocalypse*. Is Derrida also a translator? It would seem so. In his letter addressed to John, he writes:

> Modestly and in my own way, I try to translate (or let myself be involved, carried along, perhaps elsewhere, by and perhaps without) a thought of Heidegger that says: "If I were still writing a theology—I am sometimes tempted to do that—the expression 'Being' should not figure in it . . . . There is nothing to be done here with Being. I believe Being can never be thought as the essence and the bottoming of god . . . ." On this point the most diverse consequences and adventures can await us—from completely other routes, completely other writings. [AT, 61]

[Again problems of translation. In "How to Avoid Speaking," Derrida (or his translator) cites a different translation of this passage: "If I *were* yet to *write* a theology, as I am sometimes tempted to do, the word 'being' *ought* not to appear there (take place there, occur, figure, or happen there) (Wenn ich noch eine Theologie *schreiben würde,* wozu es mich manchmal reizt, dann *dürfte* in ihr das Wort 'Sein' nicht vorkommen)." The most puzzling enigma created by these alternative translations concerns the time of writing or, more specifically, the time of writing theology. "If I were still writing a theology . . . ." "If I *were* yet to *write* a theology . . . ." Is the time of writing theology past or future? Or is it a past that returns as future?

A further problem of translation. It is not clear whether this published letter is "original" or a translation. It appears to be a translation, for Derrida (though it might be his translator) cites the French translation of this Heidegger text. Thus, it seems that the critical passage is an English translation of a French translation of Heidegger's German.]

What does it mean to translate Heidegger? Those who have tried frequently are forced to admit that Heidegger is untranslatable. The problem of translating Heidegger is, therefore, the problem of translating the untranslatable. By struggling to translate the untranslatable, Derrida approaches, albeit indirectly, the question of negative theology. Explaining the reasons for his failure to fulfill his promise, Derrida writes to John, who, we now know, might also be Jacques:

> I have nothing to say in addition or afresh. I found these texts lucid and rigorous; and in any case, I believe I have no objection to make to them,

33

not even against some reservations or other regarding what I could say very insufficiently in the direction of negative theology. I am aware of this insufficiency and am quite convinced of the need for a rigorous and differentiated reading of everything advanced under this title (negative theology). My fascination at least testifies to this, right through my incompetence: in effect I believe that what is called "negative theology" (a rich and very diverse corpus) does not let itself be easily assembled under the general category "onto-theology-to-be-deconstructed." [AT, 61]

Derrida does not fulfill his promise because he has "nothing to say." Is he, in effect, saying: "I have nothing left to say. Always nothing left to say. But how to say it? To say it again? And again, and again?"[3] To say nothing is to speak *not* by avoiding speech. But to avoid speaking by saying that one has nothing to say is to speak—to speak in order not to speak, to speak in order to say nothing. "In addition or afresh, I have nothing to say." Strange [l]êt[t]re . . . strange message from this strange John. *Nothing arrives!*

An apocalypse without apocalypse, an apocalypse without vision, without truth, without revelation, of *dispatches* [*des envois*] (for the "come" is plural in itself, in oneself), of addresses without message and without destination, without sender or decidable addressee, without last judgment, without any other eschatology than the tone of the "Come" itself, its very difference, an apocalypse beyond good and evil. [AT, 94]

Nothing *arrives! Without* arriving. Again, "the strange syntax of the without." How to avoid speaking not without not speaking? In the name of what or of whom do we promise (not) to speak and write? Now and in the future? In the "name" of nothing? In the "name" of not? Perhaps we are called by nothing, in the "name" of a certain not in order not to speak and write "about" nothing.

In not writing or almost not writing, Derrida makes or almost makes a promise: "the most diverse consequences and adventures *can* await us—from completely other routes, completely other writings . . ." [emphasis added]. Will Derrida follow these routes? Will he complete these writings? Where might these other routes and other writings lead? Perhaps to something like negative theology. To begin to answer these and other questions, we will have to wait at least five years. In June 1986, Derrida delivered a paper at a conference in Jerusalem. On this occasion, he was present—"in person" as it were—to discuss "Absence and Negativity." Whether absence and negativity are better approached in absence or presence remains to be seen.

In the interval of the five years separating "Of an Apocalyptic Tone

Recently Adopted in Philosophy" and "How to Avoid Speaking: Denials," as well as the four or five additional years separating and joining their republication along with the supplemental texts it now is generating, two further delays "appear": "Titles" and "Recuperation."

Titles

"We are still on the threshold" (HAS, 27). A title is a threshold—a border, margin, or limit that brings together and holds apart the unwritten and the written. Neither inside nor outside the text, the title is, in a certain sense, untranslatable. The untranslatability of the title is not precisely the same as the untranslatability of the *pre*text. Rather, the pretext is inscribed "within" the text through the repeated displacement of the title. In other words, the pretext, the before-text, always comes "after" . . . always follows the title and "its" text. Hence, the pretext of the text is a before that is (always) yet to come.

It (What?) always begins with a question . . . a question of translation. How to translate . . . how to translate a title: *Comment ne pas parler?* First, the question of the question (which is, of course, a or perhaps *the* Heideggerian question). Is *Comment ne pas parler* a question or an assertion, an interrogation or a declaration? While bearing no question mark, the text is nothing if not a sustained interrogation that raises questions without offering answers. In asking/asserting *Comment ne pas parler,* what is Derrida asking/asserting? Is he asking how not to speak, how to avoid speaking, or is he asserting how to speak not, how to speak the avoidance of speaking? Is he asking/asserting the impossibility of speaking or the unavoidability of speaking? Is he asking/asserting the impossibility of speaking not or the unavoidability of speaking not? No not . . . Not no . . . No not no?/. Derrida realizes the difficulty. I quote at length, for the point (if it is a point) must not be missed (unless the point is always already missing . . . missing in translation):

> "Comment ne pas dire . . . ?" [A translation has already occurred "within" the text: *dire-parler-dire.*] The use of the French word *dire* permits a certain suspension. "Comment ne pas dire?" can mean, in a manner that is both transitive and intransitive, how to be silent, how not to speak in general, how to avoid speaking? But it can also mean: how, in speaking, not to say this or that, in this or that manner? In other words: how, in saying and speaking, to avoid this or that discursive, logical, rhetorical mode? How to avoid an inexact, erroneous, aberrant, improper form? How to avoid such a predicate, and even predication itself? For example: how to avoid a negative form, or how not to be negative? Finally, how to say something? Which

comes back to the apparently inverse question: How to say, how to speak? Between these two interpretations of "Comment ne pas dire . . . ?" the meaning of the uneasiness thus seems to turn again: from the "how to be silent?" (how to avoid speaking at all?) one passes—in a completely necessary and as if intrinsic fashion—to the question, which can always become the heading for an injunction: how not to speak, and which speech to avoid in order to speak *well?* "How to avoid speaking" thus means, at once or successively: How one must not speak? How it is necessary to speak? (This is) how it is necessary not to speak. [HAS, 15]

The duplicity of the title is repeated in the single word that serves as the subtitle of the essay: *Dénégations.* At this point, translation becomes impossible. *Dénégation* is the word the French translators of Freud use for the German *Verneinung.* There is already a certain duplicity in *Verneinung.* The prefix *ver-* can mean: removal, loss, stoppage, reversal, opposite, using up, expenditure, continuation to the end, alteration.[4] *Ver-nein-ung,* then, suggests both the presence and absence of negation, both the continuation and end of the not.[5] The complexity of *Verneinung* is not captured in the standard English translation of Freud's term as "negation." Difficulties are compounded by the choice of "Denials," for the English translation of Derrida's *Dénégations.* "Denial" is one of the English words (the other is "disavowal") used to translate Freud's *Verleugnung.* Though closely associated, *Verneinung* and *Verleugnung* are not equivalent.[6] To translate *dénégations* by *denials* is, therefore, a mistranslation. However, to translate *dénégations* "properly" (by way of *Verneinung*) by *negations* would also be a mistranslation. Moreover, the "proper" translation would be more misleading than the "mistranslation." Here, as elsewhere, mistranslation, it seems, is unavoidable.

Dénégation captures the irresolvable duplicity of *Verneinung* in which affirmation and negation are conjoined without being united or synthesized. *Verneinung* is an affirmation that is a negation and a negation that is an affirmation. To de-negate is to un-negate; but un-negation is itself a form of negation. More precisely, denegation is an un-negation that affirms rather than negates negation. The affirmation of negation by way of denegation subverts the dialectical affirmation of negation by way of the negation of negation. To think or rethink negative theology with Derrida, it is necessary to think the negative undialectically by thinking a negative that is *neither* both negation and affirmation *nor* either negation or affirmation. This strange thought or unthought is the neither/nor implied in *dénégation.* All things considered, it seems better to leave the untranslatable untranslated. It is, after

36

all, impossible to be sure whether "denegation" is or is not a translation. Thus a proposal for the retranslation of the title:

Comment ne pas parler:
Dénégations

How to Avoid Speaking:
Denegations

Moving beyond the periphery, away from the peripheral . . . from margin toward . . . what? Certainly not the center. From title to text . . . a text that is no longer (or perhaps is still) a pretext, though it is often called the body proper . . . the body of the text that is, perhaps, the word made "flesh" (But what word, which *Wort?* What is the *Ort* of the *W-Ort* . . . the place of the flesh of the word . . . of the text?) . . . in the body of the text, Derrida disavows a Freudian reading or merely a Freudian reading of *dénégation.* Pondering *"How not to divulge a secret? How to avoid saying or speaking?"* Derrida writes:

> Contradictory and unstable meanings give such a question its endless oscillation: what to do in order that the secret remain secret? How to make it known, in order that the secret of the secret—as such—not remain secret? How to avoid this divulgence itself? These light disturbances underlie the same sentence. At one and the same time stable and unstable, this sentence allows itself to be carried by the movements that here I call *denial* (*dénégation*), a word that I would like to understand prior even to its elaboration in the Freudian context. [HAS, 25]

Derrida is struggling to denegate Freud's denegation. But Freud, like Hegel (though in a different way), is inescapable. As we have discovered, according to the strange logic of denegation, un-negation repeats what it attempts to avoid, affirms what it tries to negate, owns what it seeks to disown. Thus Derrida's effort to escape Freud denegates itself.

What secret is Derrida not telling? What secret is Jacques (or is it John?) telling by not telling? Before crossing the threshold (as if the threshold could ever be crossed), a (perhaps) final deferral.

37

Recuperation

Negative theology is once again timely. But why does negative theology return today—here and now, *ici et maintenant?* Has it ever gone away? If not, how can it return? What is the time of the timely? The time of the re-turn of, or to, negative theology? What is the place of the return of, or to, negative theology? Is the time of the return the present . . . the here and now? Or is it another time? Another place?

The return of, or to, negative theology is, in most cases, a gesture of recuperation. After so many recuperative moves, I hesitate to sound an apocalyptic tone by calling such efforts final. Nonetheless, there is something desperate about these gestures of recuperation. All too often, the return of, or to, negative theology involves a dialectical move that is supposed to negate negation. If apparent opposites are really one, then the negative is at the same time positive and thus it becomes possible to discover resources for defense in criticism itself. Within this framework, deconstruction's interrogation of so-called ontotheology can be enlisted in defense of a tradition that extends beyond the early church fathers to Neoplatonists and even Plato himself. It is precisely such gestures of recuperation that lead Derrida to deny that deconstruction is, in effect, a latter-day form of negative theology: "No, what I write is not 'negative theology.'" Classical negative theology, he insists, remains committed to the "ontological wager" that characterizes Western philosophy and theology.

"No . . . not . . . ." And yet, for Derrida, negation is always denegation; disavowal is, in some sense, avowal. Negative theology does not go away by simply negating or denying it; the repressed always re-turns. This inevitability is the source of its continuing fascination. Derrida does not merely reject negative theology, for it exercises a certain "fascination" for him. Is this the "fascination" of Blanchot's *"Viens"* with which "Of an Apocalyptic Tone Recently Adopted in Philosophy" ends and "How to Avoid Speaking" begins? For Blanchot, fascination is always "the fascination of the absence of time":

> The time of the absence of time is not dialectical. What appears in it is the fact that nothing appears, the being that lies deep within the absence of being, the being that is when there is nothing, that is no longer when there is something—as though there were beings only through the loss of being, when being is lacking. The reversal that constantly refers us back, in the absence of time, to the presence of absence but to this presence as absence, to absence as affirmation of itself, affirmation in which nothing is affirmed, in which nothing ceases to be affirmed, in the aggravation of the indefinite—this movement is not dialectical. . . . In the absence of time, what is new does not renew anything; what is present is not contemporary; what is present presents nothing, represents itself, belongs now and henceforth and at all times to recurrence. This is not, but comes back, comes as already and always past, so that I do not know it, but I recognize it, and this recognition destroys the power in me to know, the right to grasp, makes what cannot be grasped into something that cannot be relinquished, the inaccessible that I cannot cease attaining, what I cannot take but can only take back and never give up.[7]

The inaccessible . . . the unavoidable . . . the ungraspable. To recuperate is to recover, but to recover is to re-cover the irrecuperable. The irrecuperable is, of course, ungraspable. "Recuperate" derives from the stem *kap,* which means grasp, take, hold. The Germanic translation of *kap* is *haf* (Old English *helfeld*), which was a thread used for weaving. A heddle, by extension, is a device that grasps the thread. The threads of *recuperate* lead back to the problem of the text by way of *textere* (to weave). If the thread is ungraspable, the text unravels. This unraveling is the failure of recuperation. The impossibility of recuperation implies the inescapability of the irrecuperable. In the absence of recuperation, disease grows, wounds fester, tears linger. Might the tear of this disease be the place or nonplace where "what is present presents nothing?" Might this "nothing" be the nothing that Derrida struggles to say or not to say? And might saying or not saying this nothing imply an opening in which it becomes possible to read negative theology otherwise—otherwise than ontotheologically?

Avoidances

Derrida avoids negative theology as long as possible. That is to say, he avoids it until it becomes unavoidable. This avoidance, however, is never complete, for he remains fascinated by an unavoidable that remains ungraspable:

> As I have always been fascinated by the supposed movements of negative theology (which, no doubt, are themselves never foreign to the experience of fascination in general), I objected in vain to the assimilation of the thinking of the trace or of difference to some negative theology, and my response amounted to a promise: one day I would have to stop deferring, one day I would have to try to explain myself directly on this subject, and at last to speak of "negative theology" itself, assuming that some such thing exists.
>   Has that day come? [HAS, 12]

In other words, is "How to Avoid Speaking: Denegations" the fulfillment of a promise or yet another promissory note? In this text, does Derrida "explain himself directly" on negative theology? Or is his language still something like what Kierkegaard describes as "indirect discourse"? Either promise or fulfillment . . . both promise and fulfillment . . . neither promise nor fulfillment? And what if "fulfilling" a promise means not fulfilling it? What if to talk or write "directly" is to talk or write indirectly? What if Derrida in this text writes more directly, which means more indirectly, about what he is always not talking and writing about?

What is a promise? A promise is, in Austin's terms, a "performative utterance." In contrast to constative utterances, which assert or describe facts or an antecedent condition, performative utterances are speech acts that realize a state of affairs that did not exist prior to the language event. In another context, Derrida defines one of the necessary conditions of performative utterances in speech act theory:

> One of these essential elements—and not one among others—classically remains consciousness, the conscious presence of the intention of the speaking subject for the totality of his locutory act. Thereby, performative communication once more becomes the communication of an intentional meaning, even if this meaning has no referent in the form of a prior or exterior thing or state of things. This conscious presence of the speakers or receivers who participate in the effecting of a performative, their conscious and intentional presence in the totality of the operation, implies teleologically that no *remainder* escapes the present totalization.[8]

In other words, an effective speech act presupposes that the participants are fully conscious of their deeds and clearly understand not only their own intentions but the intentions of each other. For Austin and his followers, a promise must always be made in the present with full self-presence.

If a promise presupposes the full presence of the present, then is a promise possible? From Derrida's perspective, there is *always* a remainder that escapes totalization and hence the present can never be totally present. Inasmuch as it requires the presence of self-consciousness and the self-consciousness of presence, the promise would seem to be impossible. And yet, Derrida insists, promising is at the same time unavoidable. Commenting on the writings of Paul de Man, Derrida argues that "the promise is impossible but inevitable. . . . Even if a promise could be kept, this would matter little. What is essential here is that a pure promise cannot properly take place, in a proper place, even though promising is inevitable as soon as we open our mouths—or rather as soon as there is a text."[9] Language, in other words, is unavoidably promissory. Derrida notes the added twist of Freud's polyvalent prefix *ver-* that de Man uses to transform Heidegger's famous "*Die Sprache spricht*" into "*Die Sprache verspricht*." "Language promises" . . . always promises . . . unavoidably promises . . . more and/or less than it delivers. But why *must* language promise? How can language promise if a promise *cannot* take place? How can language be unavoidably promissory if promising is impossible? It is a matter of time and space, or of a certain absence of time and space.

The promise, which cannot properly take place, has always already occurred. Language, like Lacan's symbolic order, precedes those who speak it or those through whom it speaks. Inscription within the symbolic order or linguistic system entails a "primal" lack that leaves an irrecuperable remainder. Language, therefore, is always lacking, which does not mean that we simply fall silent. To the contrary, lack releases the event of language. In this linguistic event, to speak is to say the impossibility of saying by promising what cannot be delivered:

> Discourse on the promise is already a promise: *in* the promise. I will thus not speak of this or that promise, but of that which, as necessary as it is impossible, inscribes us by its trace in language—before language. From the moment I open my mouth, I have already promised; or rather, and sooner, the promise has seized the *I* that promises to speak to the other. . . . This promise is older than I am. Here is something that appears impossible, the theoreticians of speech acts would say: like every genuine performative, a promise must be made in the present, in the first person (in the singular or plural). It must be made by one who is capable of saying *I* or *we*. [HAS, 14]

Though inseparable from language, the trace "in language—before language" is nonetheless "older" than language. Language is constituted by *not saying* the trace. Since such not saying is necessary rather than contingent, the unspeakable trace is unavoidable. To speak, it is necessary to avoid speaking the trace. The avoidance of language, however, is not merely negative but is at the same time the *saying* of not-saying or the saying of not. This saying not or saying *without* saying is an unsaying that is, in effect, the denegation of language.

The promise is unavoidable and impossible. To speak is to promise and yet the promise is never present; it never takes place but has always already occurred or is always about to occur. The place of the promise is not here and its time is not now. Never here and now, the time and place of the promise are past or future. The issue is tense:

> I will speak of a promise, then, but also within the promise. . . . The promise of which I shall speak will have always escaped this demand of presence. It is older than I am or than we are. In fact, it renders possible every present discourse on presence. [HAS, 14–15]

The tense of the promise is past or future, or, through a metalepsis, a past that returns as future in something like an eternally deferred future perfect. The past that haunts language is a strange, even uncanny past. As that which is always already lacking, this past was never present and thus cannot be re-presented. Though never experienced, the trace of the past is unforgettable:

Thus, at the moment when the question "How to avoid speaking?" arises, it is already too late. There was no longer any question of not speaking. Language has started without us, in us and before us. This is what theology calls God, and it is necessary, it will have been necessary to speak. This "it is necessary" (*il faut*) is *both* the trace of undeniable necessity—which is another way of saying that one cannot avoid denying it, one can only deny it—*and* of a past injunction. Always already past, hence without a past present. Indeed, it must have been possible to speak in order to allow the question "How to avoid speaking?" to arise. Having come from the past, language before language, a past that was never present and yet remains unforgettable—this "it is necessary" thus seems to beckon toward the event of an order or of a promise that does not belong to what one currently calls history, the discourse of history or the history of discourse. [HAS, 29–30]

In this case, that which does not belong to history is not eternal, though it is immemorial. Rather, the not-historical is, in Blanchot's terms, *le pas au-delà*:

Time, time: *le pas au-delà*, which is not accomplished in time, would lead outside of time, without this outside being timeless, but there where time would fall, fragile fall, according to this 'outside of time in time' toward which writing would draw us, if it were permitted of us, vanished from us, writing the secret of the ancient fear. [*PA*, 8]

Blanchot names this unnameable time the "terrifyingly ancient." In Levinas's terms, the irrecuperable past is the "unrepresentable before." This past that was never present is undeniably *provocative;* it provokes by calling (*vocare*) forth (*pro*). From whom does this call come? To whom is it directed? Even though the call is both undeniable and unavoidable, its origin and destination remain uncertain. This provocation, which approaches from elsewhere, disrupts and displaces by sending us on our way—a way from which there is no return. Such sending creates a debt (*Schuld*) that is our guilt (*Schuld*), and this guilt becomes our responsibility (*Schuld*). Like the translator named John (or is it Jacques?), we are always already in debt:

42

The translator is indebted, he appears to himself as translator in a situation of debt; and his task is to *render,* to render that which must have been given.[10]

The words and (speech) acts with which the translator attempts to discharge this debt are promissory notes (*Schuldschein*). As the term *Schuldschein* suggests, the promissory note is the appearance (*Schein*) of debt and/or guilt (*Schuld*). If, as Derrida following de Man or de

Man following Derrida insists, *Die Sprache verspricht,* then language implies a debt that entails an impossible responsibility.

To speak is to be indebted or subjected to an other for whom and to whom every subject is unavoidably responsible. As Levinas explains, responsibility is antecedent to freedom:

> The unlimited responsibility in which I find myself comes from the hither side of my freedom, from a "prior to every memory," an "ulterior to every accomplishment," from the non-present par excellence, the non-original, the anarchical, prior to or beyond essence. The responsibility for the other is the locus in which is situated the null-site of subjectivity, where the privilege of the question "Where?" no longer holds. The time of the *said* and of *essence* there lets the pre-original saying be heard, answers to transcendence, to a dia-chrony, or to the irreducible divergence that opens here between the non-present and every representable divergence, which, in its own way, . . . makes a sign to the responsible one.[11]

The subject's responsibility is actualized in its response-ability, that is, in its ability ro respond to the provocation of the other. "*Viens* . . . Come!*" We forever live in the *Wake* of this call:

> Stay awake!
>   Strengthen what is left, so near death.
> If you do not stay awake,
> I shall come like a thief:

> You will not know at what hour I shall come to you. I shall come: the coming is always to come . . . *I come* means: I am going to come, I am to-come in the imminence of an "I am going to come," "I am in the process of coming," "I am on the point of going to come." [HAS, 85]

Who calls: "Come"? "I shall come . . ."? God, perhaps? No, not God . . . not precisely God.

And yet . . . . The re-cited words are, of course, those of John, the translator, who is forever in a situation of debt to an Other. Without the gift, which is also *ein/eine Gift,* from beyond, there would be no translation. The debt of the translator is always secondary not only to a certain creditor but also to a more "original" debtor:

> Nothing is more serious than translation. . . . For if the structure of the original is marked by the requirement to be translated, it is that in laying down the law the original begins by indebting itself *as well* with regard to the translator. The original is the first debtor, the first petitioner; it begins by lacking and by pleading for translation. . . . In giving his name, God also appealed to translation, not only between the tongues that had suddenly become multiple and and confused, but first *of his name,* of the name he

had proclaimed, given, and which should be translated as confusion to be understood, hence to let it be understood that it is difficult to translate and to understand.[12]

Why is *nothing* more serious than translation? Is translation (and what is not translation?) for nothing? What gives itself to be translated? What does not give itself to be translated? What allows, indeed forces us to translate? What am *I* trying to translate—here and now—in this text? Derrida, of course. But Derrida is himself a translator whose writings, like those of Heidegger, whom he translates, we all know are untranslatable. To translate Derrida is to try (and unavoidably to fail) to translate his untranslatable translations of the untranslatable.

That which is untranslatable must remain secret. Perhaps the untranslatable secret is "the secret of the ancient fear" . . . the terrible secret that might be *provoked* by "*l'effroyablement ancien.*" Who can tell? Who could tell such a secret? Any secret? Can a secret be told—told in such a way that it remains—remains (a) secret? In telling, does a secret remain? Or must a secret be told in order to be (a) secret? Would a secret that no one knows be a secret? Is the secret that remains in telling the remains that always remain, the remainder that is always to be told, whose telling is always yet to come?

Perhaps Derrida is struggling to tell us a secret. Perhaps it is precisely the telling or nontelling of the secret that secretes the texts written in his name or in the name of an other. Derrida's fascination with the secret is no secret; it is *there,* as clear as day in his texts for anyone with eyes to see:

> Under this title, "How to avoid speaking," it is necessary to speak of the secret. . . . *How not to divulge a secret?* How to avoid speaking or saying? . . . How to make it known in order that the secret of the secret— as such not remain secret? . . . There is a secret of denial and a denial of the secret. The secret as such, *as secret,* separates and already institutes a negativity; it is a negation that denies itself. It de-negates itself. This denegation does not happen to it by accident; it is essential and originary. And in the *as such* of the secret that denies itself because it appears to itself in order to be what it is, this de-negation gives no chance to dialectic. . . . I refer first of all to the secret shared *within itself,* its partition "proper," which divides the essence of a secret that cannot even appear to one alone except in starting to be lost, to divulge itself, hence to dissimulate itself, as secret, in showing itself: dissimulating its dissimulation. [HAS, 25–26]

Promise and secret intersect in the activity of denegation. The terrifyingly ancient seems to be the secret that renders all speech and writing promissory. In the wake of the "ancient of ancients," words promise but do not fulfill. Language always implies a "profound formerly" or "unprepresentable before" that never was, is, or will be present. Since "the genesis of secrecy" is always missing, there is nothing to tell. I repeat: There is *nothing* to tell. The secret is that there is no secret:

> There is no secret *as such;* I deny it. And this is what I confide in secret to whomever allies himself to me. This is the secret of the alliance. If the theo-logical necessarily insinuates itself there, this does not mean that the secret itself is theo-logical. But does something like the secret *itself,* properly speaking, ever exist? The name of God (I do not say God, but how to avoid saying God here, from the moment when I say the name of God?) can only be *said* in the modality of this secret denial: above all, I did not want to say that. [HAS, 26]

Denials of denials; negations of negations. No not no. How not to speak? How to speak not?

It is, of course, possible that the title is *both* interrogation *and* assertion, question *and* answer: How to Avoid Speaking? Denegations. Denegation, however, is an answer that is no answer, for it *neither* asserts *nor* denies. Denegation *performs* in a way other than the performative utterance of speech act theory. When understood in terms of denegation, promising and telling (a secret) accomplish nothing. Such "accomplishment" is a failure to accomplish. The text in which this unaccomplishment is accomplished becomes a performative utterance that "says" the "unsayable" by unsaying all saying and every said. While neither autonomous nor reflexive, such a text does not refer to things or narrate events beyond itself but inscribes a more radical "beyond" that is nevertheless inscribed "within" the text itself. This is the "beyond" that Blanchot (improperly) names *le pas au-delà.* The step (*pas*) toward the not (*pas*) that is forever beyond (*au-delà*) can be taken (if at all) only in a textual "event" that performs an impossible "event." In a text entitled simply "Not [*Pas*]," Derrida offers an analysis of Blanchot's writing that indirectly describes (while performing) his own textual practice:

45

> This "terrifyingly ancient" time binds one to the *récit,* makes of the *récit,* thus determined, the sole text that places us in relation (without relation) to what passes with this past of the not [*pas*], which no concept, no poem would any longer even be able to cite. Thus to recite, since it can only be a question of that: to cite a "Come," which still has not called, which is called, after a "Come," an *already* more ancient than time, an absolute crypt. This *récit* destroys the *récit* (the one that pretends to relate, according to the current logic of these words, an event) but it does not do it in the name of the concept as a philosophical gesture, but rather in the name

of an other (dissimulated) *récit,* according to the other-event [*l'autre-evenement*], to the not of the concept. It "would" be the coming of this other-event called "Come" if this would not arrive from a simple step/not [*pas*]. Thus it would not suffice to say that the *récit* (of Blanchot [and of Derrida]) is not the relation of the event but the event itself. Rather, it "would have been" the labyrinthine and snared structure of the not of event. . . . It, the necessity, the chance, still marks the chance, the risk: that the other of language takes place in the not beyond of language. No not *its* other but the other without it.[13]

". . . *l'autre de la langue se passe dans le pas au-delà de la langue. Non pas* son *autre mais l'autre sans elle.*" "The Task of the Translator" is, indeed, infinite! Perhaps translation is the play of the infinite itself. "The other of language takes place [or passes away, fades, decays] in the not [or the step] beyond of language." "The not beyond of language" must be read in at least two conflicting ways at once: the not that *is* the beyond of language, and the not that *is not* beyond language, that is, the not-beyond of language. "*Pas* non" also remains questionable. Does it negate or not negate? Both negate and not negate? Or neither negate nor not negate? Furthermore, the *de* does not denote ownership but a certain dispossession. "No not *its* other but the other without it [that is, language]." The *pas* that is *au-delà* language, as an other that does not even belong to language as *its* other, *is not the not* of (classical) negative theology. No, not that no but an other no that is at the same time not no. A *quasi* no, a no *without* no—this is the *not* that obsesses Derrida in "How to Avoid Speaking: Denegations" and elsewhere. ". . . as if I had wanted to ask, on the threshold of this lecture, what these three adverbs mean and whence they come."

Does "How to Avoid Speaking: Denegations" fulfill Derrida's promise to speak directly about negative theology? It is impossible to say . . . always impossible to say. Not only for us but also for Derrida:

> Will I do it? Am I in Jerusalem? This is a question to which one will never respond in the present tense, only in the future or in the past. Why insist on this postponement? Because it appears to me neither avoidable nor insignificant. One can never decide whether deferring, as such, brings about precisely that which it defers and alters (*diffère*). It is not certain that I am keeping my promise today; nor is it certain that in further delaying I have not, nevertheless, already kept it. [HAS, 13]

Whether to fulfill or defer, Derrida develops a tightly structured argument that mimes the machinations of Hegel's dialectical logic in three stages or moments: Greek, Christian, and a third that is undecidable—perhaps both Greek and Christian, or perhaps neither Greek nor Chris-

tian. There is, however, something missing. Derrida (yet again) avoids
something. In fact, his whole argument is a complex strategy of avoidance. Like the secret, this avoidance is no secret, for he tells us directly
what he is *not* talking about:

> Three stages or three places in any case to avoid speaking of a question
> that I will be unable [Not unwilling but *unable*. Why?] to treat; to deny it in
> some way, or to speak of it without speaking of it, in a negative mode:
> what do I understand by negative theology and its phantoms in a tradition
> of thought that is neither Greek nor Christian? In other words, what of
> Jewish and Islamic thought in this regard? By example, and in everything
> that I will say, a certain void, place of an internal desert, will perhaps allow
> this question to resonate. [HAS, 30–31]

This internal desert is the space in which the withdrawal of the terrifyingly ancient destines its followers to err.

First Greek. But the beginning is already double. Derrida identifies
two strands of "negative theology" in the Greek tradition: one dominant, one repressed. On the one hand, something like what will become negative theology appears in Plato's *Republic* and reappears in a
variety of Neoplatonisms. Within this framework, the idea of the Good
"has its place beyond Being or essence. Thus the Good is not, nor is its
place. But this not-being is not a non-being" (HAS, 32). To the contrary,
the beyond-Being of the Good is a Being-beyond that is "surreal" or
"hyperreal." Since this hyperessentiality surpasses both beings and Being, it resists positive predication. One can only express the surreal in
negative terms. In this case, negation is at the same time affirmation.
The surreality that is affirmed through the process of negation does not
break with Being but is its eternal origin and goal. The Go[o]d is the
Alpha and Omega of everything that *is*. On the other hand, there is a
repressed "tropic of negativity" that insinuates itself within the Platonic
text at pivotal points. The return of the repressed implies a "third species" that "is" *neither* being *nor* nonbeing. It is crucial to distinguish
this nondialectical third from the dialectical third that also inhabits the
Platonic corpus:

> After having raised the question of nonbeing, which is in itself unthink-
> able . . . , ineffable . . . , unpronounceable . . . , foreign to discourse and
> to reason . . . , one arrives at the presentation of dialectic itself. Passing
> through the parricide of the murder of Parmenides, this dialectic receives
> the thinking of nonbeing as *other* and not as absolute nothingness or
> simple opposite of Being. . . . This confirms that there cannot be an abso-
> lutely negative discourse: a *logos* necessarily speaks about something; it is
> impossible for it to refer to nothing. [HAS, 34]

Though this third is "beyond" the opposites it unites, it still "concerns Being." It "gathers" or "interweaves" the terms of every relationship. This gathering is the labor of the *logos.*

Beyond the gathering of the *logos,* Plato glimpses a different third that is resolutely nondialectical. He associates this third alternative with the strange space or spacing of the *khora.* In the *Timaeus,* the *khora* "appears" as the place or nonplace into which the Demiurge introduces images of the paradigms that are essential to the process of creation. As such, the *khora* "must have been *there,* as the 'there' itself, beyond time or in any case beyond becoming, in a beyond time without common measure with the eternity of the ideas and the becoming of sensible things" (HAS, 35). The *khora* marks the margin of the neither/nor: *neither* either/or *nor* both/and. "It is necessary to avoid speaking of *khora* as of 'something' that is or is not, that could be present or absent, intelligible, sensible, or both at once, active or passive, the Good . . . or the Evil, God or man, the living or the nonliving" (HAS, 37). Neither being nor nonbeing, the *khora* involves a negativity that escapes both the positive and negative theological register. As such, the *khora* is *atheological:*

> Radically nonhuman and atheological, one cannot even say that it *gives* place or that *there is* the *khora.* The *es gibt,* thus translated, too vividly announces or recalls the dispensation of God, of man, or even that of the Being of which certain texts by Heidegger speak (*es gibt Sein*). *Khora* is not even *that* (*ça*), the *es* or *id* of giving, before all subjectivity. It does not give place as one would give something, whatever it may be; it neither creates nor produces anything, not even an event insofar as it takes place. It gives no order and makes no promise. It is radically ahistorical, because nothing happens through it and nothing happens to it. [HAS, 37]

Within the Platonic text and the traditions to which it gives rise, the thought of the *khora* remains oblique and unstable. Neither/nor tends to slip into both/and in a move intended to reappropriate the *khora* for ontology. But the *khora* resists every effort to domesticate it.

Then Christian. Though Derrida's account of Christian negative theology is extensive, his point is simple: "My first paradigm was Greek and the second Christian without ceasing to be Greek" (HAS, 53). Among the Christian writers he considers are Pseudo-Dionysius, Meister Eckhart, Bernard of Clairvaux, and Augustine. In each case, Derrida maintains, the via negativa turns out to be implicitly affirmative. Christians have, for the most part, extended and elaborated the dominant strand in the Platonic tradition. In Christian theology, God, who is beyond Being, is not discontinuous with it. The apophatic God, like the

Platonic Good, is surreal, hyperreal, hyperessential, or "supereminent Being." When carried to completion (and completion *is* possible for the *theologian*), the negative becomes positive. This form of negation, according to Derrida, is a "negativity without negativity" (HAS, 44). As Eckhart stresses, the goal of the via negativa is the uninhibited enjoyment of the "pure, clear, limpid One, separated from all duality." Eckhart speaks of this One as "Nothing" or "hyperessential nothingness." "We must," Eckhart insists, "eternally sink ourselves in this One, from the Something to the Nothing" (HAS, 52). This Nothing, however, is a nonbeing that is actually identical with the fullness of Being. As Eckhart's successor, Hegel, argues in his *Science of Logic,* Being and Nothing are One. When *dialectically* understood, nothing and nonbeing turn out to be every bit as ontological as beings and Being. Within the dialectics of christo-logic, negation implies affirmation, death leads to life, and crucifixion harbors resurrection:

> Contrary to what seemed to happen in the "experience" of the place called *khora,* the apophasis is brought into motion—it is *initiated,* in the sense of initiative and initiation—by the event of a revelation that is also a promise. This apophasis belongs to a history; or rather, it opens up a history and an anthropo-theological dimension. [HAS, 48–49]

The history that the event of revelation opens is the history of salvation whose goal is the re-covery of the "absolute crypt" of the *khora.*

The empty tomb, however, can be understood in at least two ways: as a sign of the reality of resurrection or as a sign of the impossibility of resurrection. Even in the midst of the Christian effort to re-cover the "absolute crypt" of the *khora,* Derrida espies an irrecuperable trace.[14] What is Eckhart *not* saying? Or what is he saying by not saying? Is denegation quietly at work in Eckhart's text as well as in the text of all apophatic theology? Derrida comments on Eckhart's mystical theology:

> This is to speak in order to command not to speak, to say what God is not, that he is a non-God. How may one hear the copula of being that articulates this singular speech and this order to be silent? Where does it have its place? Where does it take place? It is the place, the place of this writing, and more precisely, a threshold. [HAS, 52]

Remember, "we are still on the threshold." Not just here and now but always. The threshold is the site (or nonsite/nonsight) of passage. But does a threshold permit translation (*trans,* across + *latus,* carried)? Can a passage—any passage—be translated? Eckhart attempts to translate the threshold by carrying the reader beyond the limit.

The place is only a place of passage, and more precisely, a threshold. But a threshold, this time, to give access to what is no longer a place. A subordination, a relativization of the place, and an extraordinary consequence; the place is Being. What finds itself reduced to the condition of a threshold is Being itself, Being as a place. Solely a threshold, but a sacred place, the outer sanctuary (*parvis*) of the temple. [HAS, 52]

Which temple? What if Eckhart's temple stands in the midst of "The Origin of the Work of Art"? Or what if Heidegger's temple, which is really Greek, stands in the midst of Eckhart's temple? It is well known that Heidegger sustained a lifelong interest in Eckhart. *If* Eckhart's temple is Heideggerian and Heidegger's temple is Greek, then which strand of the Greek tradition is woven into the text of the via negativa? As we have seen, Derrida argues that Christian negative theology extends and expands the domination of Greek ontology. Domination, however, requires repression and the repressed never goes away but always returns to disrupt, interrupt, and dislocate. The origin of the work of art, in whose cleft Heidegger's Greek temple stands (and falls), is a certain *Riss*—tear, tear, fissure, gap, flaw, crack. Perhaps this *Riss,* which rends the text of negative theology, points toward a different space and time. "Temple," after all, derives from the Latin *templum,* which, like *tempus* (time), comes from the Greek *temnos.* While *temno* means "cut," *temnos* designates that which is "cut off." Accordingly, *templum* is a section, a part cut off. What, then, is the time and place of the severed part . . . *la part madudite?* [15] Perhaps the time/place of the *templum* is the time/place of a threshold that cannot be crossed or erased. Something like an invisible sieve . . . a filter that allows the eye to see:

> The soul, which exercises its power in the eye, allows one to see what is not, what is not present; [16] it "works in nonbeing and follows God who works in nonbeing." Guided by this *psyche,* the eye thus passes the threshold of Being toward nonbeing in order to see what does not present itself. Eckhart compares the eye to a sieve [*crible*]. Things must be "passed through the sieve [*gebiutelt*]." This sieve is not one figure among others; it tells us the difference between Being and nonbeing. There is no text, above all no sermon, no possible predication, without the invention of such a filter. [HAS, 52–53]

". . . the difference between Being and nonbeing . . ." So interpreted, the sieve is a figure for Heidegger's "ontological difference."

Un crible, however, is not only a sieve; it is also a riddle. To riddle is to pierce with holes, to perforate. But to riddle can also mean to speak enigmatically. A riddle, of course, is a puzzle, conundrum, insoluble problem, mystery. In some cases, however, a riddle is actually a sieve—a coarse-meshed sieve, used for separating wheat from chaff, sand from gravel, ashes from cinders. And what of the "rid" in riddle? Of what does the riddle rid us? What of the wheat? In which book is it to be found? What of the sand? Is this the sand of a certain interior desert? Or the sand of another "book" . . . an "older," perhaps terrifyingly ancient testament? And what of the ashes? Whose ashes? Of what . . . of whom are riddled ashes the trace?

> Ash.
> Ash. Ash.
> Night.
> Night-and-Night.[17]

Riddles. Riddles that riddle the Heideggerian text. First Greek. Then Christian. Then "neither Greek nor Christian." But first, a further delay—a supplementary deferral in which Der-rid-a again tells us what he is not telling us or is telling us by not telling us:

> I thus decided *not to speak* of negativity or of apophatic movements in, for example, the Jewish or Islamic traditions. To leave this immense place empty, and above all that which cannot connect such a name of God with the name of the Place, to remain thus on the threshold—was this not the most consistent possible apophasis? [HAS, 53]

By re-citing the avoidance to which his *récit* is devoted, Derrida refigures the third in a nondialectical and nonsynthetic way. Is the *aparté* with which the third (non)moment of Derrida's argument begins really a deferral? Or is he telling us what he will be addressing when he writes about Heidegger?

Questions continue to proliferate. How is Heidegger to be read? Derrida has always insisted that Heidegger must be read with "two hands" at once. But whose hands are these? What is the place of the hand in the Heideggerian text? "Two texts, two hands, two visions, two ways of listening. Together simultaneously and separately."[18] Two texts . . . two hands: On the one hand, but on the other hand:

> My first paradigm was Greek and the second Christian, without ceasing to be Greek. The last will be neither Greek nor Christian.[19] If I were not afraid of trying your patience, I would recall that which, in Heidegger's thinking, could resemble the most questioning legacy, both the most audacious and the most liberated repetitions of the traditions I have just invoked. [HAS, 53]

Again it is a question of tense. The tense is conditional . . . always conditional: "*ce qui, dans la pensée de Heidegger, pourrait ressembler.*" Not

51

does but *could* resemble. Heidegger repeats the traditions that Derrida has just invoked: Greek and Christian. It can be argued, indeed some have already argued, that Heidegger brings together—perhaps even synthesizes—the Greek and Christian traditions so as to create new possibilities for theology. When read in this way, Heidegger perpetuates the very ontotheological tradition he attempts to dismantle. The arguments are too well known to be repeated here.

But there are gaps in Heidegger's arguments. And these gaps suggest other traditions. As we have discovered, the Greek and Christian traditions of apophatic thought are themselves riddled. Philosophers and theologians from Plato on repeatedly have said something other than what they intended or thought they were saying. From time to time, Heidegger glimpses this *other* that inhabits the theologico-philosophical text. At one point, he goes so far as to write: "If Plato takes the *khorismos* into consideration, the difference of place [*die verschiedene Ortung*] between Being and beings, he thus poses the question of the wholly other place [*nach dem ganz anderen Ort*] of Being, by comparison with that of beings" [HAS, 54]. Derrida explains: "I merely underscore this movement toward a *wholly other* place [*un lieu* tout autre], as place of Being or *place of the wholly other:* in and beyond a Platonic or Neoplatonic tradition. But also in and beyond a Christian tradition of which Heidegger—while submerged in it, as in the Greek tradition—never ceased claiming, whether by denial or not, that it could in no case entertain a philosophy" (HAS, 54–55). The question that remains is whether the place of the wholly other is a place of Being or is a wholly other "place."

In probing this question, Derrida returns to the task of the translator defined in his letter to John: "Modestly and in my own way, I try to translate . . . a thought of Heidegger." Near the end of "How to Avoid Speaking: Denegations," Derrida repeats Heidegger's thought: "If I *were* yet to *write* a theology, as I am sometimes tempted to do, the word 'being' *ought* not to appear there" (HAS, 58). The question that Derrida poses is whether Heidegger has not, in fact, done what he said he had not done, done what he said he ought to avoid doing:

> Hasn't Heidegger written what he says he would have liked to write, a theology *without* the word *being?* But didn't he also write what he says should not be written, what he should not have written, namely a theology that is opened, dominated, and invaded by the word *being?*
>
> With and without the word *being,* he wrote a theology with and without God. He did what he said it would be necessary to avoid doing. He said, wrote, and allowed to be written exactly what he said he wanted to

avoid. He was not there without leaving a trace of all these folds. He was not there without allowing a trace to appear, a trace that is, perhaps, no longer his own, but that remains as if (*quasiment*) his own. [HAS, 60]

The trace that is neither Heidegger's nor not Heidegger's is the trace that Derrida follows. If Derrida's writings are translations of the Heideggerian text, then Derrida's questions of Heidegger can be turned back on the Derridean text. "Hasn't [Derrida] written what he says he would have liked to write? . . . Didn't he also write what he says should not be written?" In the midst of his text on Heidegger's text, Derrida offers another important parenthetical re-mark: "(*To say nothing,* once again, of the mysticisms or theologies in the Jewish, Islamic, or other traditions)" [HAS, 55]. *To say nothing* . . . once again. Is Derrida saying nothing once again? Saying nothing by what he is not saying? Isn't his nonsaying nonetheless a saying? A denegation? Isn't his avoidance of speaking the only way he has to speak about that which he knows he cannot speak about? Isn't the unspoken third that is *neither* Greek *nor* Christian the third of "the Jewish, Islamic, or other traditions rather than a Heideggerian third?" "I do not intend to respond to these questions nor even to conclude with them" (HAS, 59).

"Autobiography"

A final note, which, of course, is not final. On the threshold of his account of Greek, Christian, and neither Greek nor Christian, at the precise moment he tells us what he is *not* going to tell us (that is, "Jewish and Islamic thought in this regard"), Derrida adds an unexpected note—note 13:

> Despite this silence, or in fact because of it, one will perhaps permit me to interpret this lecture as the most "autobiographical" speech I have ever risked. One will attach to this word as many quotation marks as possible. It is necessary to surround with precautions the hypothesis of a self-presentation passing through a speech on the negative theology of others. But if one day I had to tell my story, nothing in this narrative would start to speak of the thing itself if I did not come up against this fact: for lack of capacity, competence, or self-authorization, I have never been able to speak of what my birth, as one says, should have made closest to me: the Jew, the Arab. [HAS, 66]

"If one day I had to tell my story." "If I *were* yet to *write* a theology." The tense remains conditional. Might Derrida's story be a retranslation of Heidegger's neither/nor? Are Derrida's denials to be believed? Is he not speaking of his birth and of what is closest to him—the Jew, the

Arab? And what could be more important than speaking of the Jew and the Arab today, here and now?

For many years—at least since *Glas* and I suspect long before, perhaps even from the beginning—Derrida has been struggling with the question of autobiography. As time passes and the texts accumulate, I begin to suspect that Derrida's deepest *desire* is to write an "autobiography." But how could he ever fulfill this desire? How could he write an autobiography without at the same time writing a theology? Derrida could (or would) no more write an autobiography than he could (or would) write a theology. If, however, he were to write (or were always already writing) an "autobiography," it would seem that he must write (or have always already been writing) an *atheology*.[20] Atheology "has nothing to do with negative theology; there is reference neither to an event nor to a giving, neither to an order nor to a promise, even if, as I have just underscored, the absence of promise or of order—the barren, radically nonhuman and atheological character of this 'place'—obliges us to speak and to refer to it in a certain and unique manner, as to the wholly other who is neither transcendent, absolutely distanced, nor immanent and close" (HAS, 39) Neither transcendent nor immanent, the wholly other is traced in an immemorial past, which, though never present, eternally returns as an outstanding future that never arrives. As we have seen, the trace of this strange altarity haunts the Western theologico-philosophical tradition—from Plato's *khora,* and Eckhart's sieve, to Heidegger's *Riss,* and beyond. It is not impossible that this wholly other is the "terrifyingly ancient" that approaches from another yet more ancient tradition. This *tout autre* might imply the denegation of Jewish and Islamic traditions that Derrida's quasi-"autobiographical," atheological text performs. Perhaps. Perhaps not.

o

o

o

3

Nothing Ventured
Nothing Gained
Nothing Ventured

Néant: né en . . . It is nothingness we are born in. . . .
—EDMOND JABÈS

But I cry out to the sky: "I know
nothing." And I repeat in a
comical voice (I cry out to the
sky, at times, in this way):
"absolutely nothing."
—GEORGES BATAILLE

What is left for you to do:
to undo yourself in this nothing
that you do.
—MAURICE BLANCHOT

Nothing is not and yet not is not precisely nothing. To think not is in a certain sense to venture nothing. But what does it mean to venture nothing? Is such a venture an absolute risk or the absolute absence of risk? What does it mean to gain nothing? Is such a gain a loss? Is the price of gaining nothing losing everything? Is such absolute loss the loss of the absolute? Must the loss of the absolute be counted a gain? And again? And again? If nothing is ventured, is nothing gained? Can nothing ever be ventured? Can nothing really be gained?

Where to begin? How to begin thinking about nothing without not thinking?

> Language can only begin with the void; no plenitude, no certainty can ever speak; something essential is lacking in anyone who expresses himself. Negation is tied to language. When I first begin, I do not speak in order to say something, rather a nothing demands to speak, nothing speaks, nothing finds its being in speech and the being of speech is nothing. This formulation explains why literature's ideal has been this: to speak and say nothing.[1]

Beginagain.

There is Nothing to fear.

Nothing to rely on.

Overcoming Nihilism

During the modern period, the question of nothing returns repeatedly as the problem of nihilism. It is, of course, Nietzsche who identifies nihilism as the symptom of modern European decadence. His richest and most problematic text, *The Will to Power,* opens with the question of nihilism. "Nihilism stands at the door: whence comes this uncanniest of guests?" (*WP,* 7). From Nietzsche's point of view, nihilism and religion are inseparable. In the Western tradition, nihilism, which is implicit in the moral codes of Christianity, becomes explicit in the will to truth that grows out of religious belief. Though rarely noted, Nietzsche does not limit his genealogy of nihilism to a consideration of *Western* religious belief. At several important points in his writings, he claims that Buddhism issues in a nihilism that is at least as problematic as that engendered by Christianity. Responding to his own question about the origin of nihilism, Nietzsche asserts that this uncanny guest arrives with religion:

> It is in one particular interpretation, the Christian-moral one, that nihilism is rooted. The end of Christianity—at the hands of its own morality (which cannot be replaced), which turns against the Christian God (the sense of truthfulness, developed highly by Christianity, is nauseated by the falseness and mendaciousness of all Christian interpretations of the world and of history; rebound from "God is truth" to the fanatical faith "All is false"; Buddhism of *action*—).
>
> Skepticism regarding morality is what is decisive. The end of the moral interpretation of the world, which no longer has any sanction after it has tried to escape into some beyond, leads to nihilism. "Everything lacks meaning." . . . Buddhistic tendency, yearning for Nothing. (Indian Buddhism is *not* the culmination of a thoroughly moralistic development; its nihilism is therefore full of morality that is not overcome: existence as punishment, existence construed as error, error thus as a punishment— a moral valuation.) Philosophical attempts to overcome the "moral God" (Hegel, pantheism). [*WP*, 7]

In this important text, Nietzsche brings together morality, religion, and nothingness in a way that creates the possibility of a comparative analysis of the interplay of the not and nothing in certain strands of Christianity and Buddhism. The questions of nihilism, negation, and nothingness intersect to form the focus of Keiji Nishitani's philosophical inquiry. As the leading figure of the Kyoto school, Nishitani is particularly interested in creating a constructive dialogue between Eastern and Western philosophy and religion. Having studied with Heidegger, Nishitani is acutely aware of the importance of nihilism for the Western tradition and clearly recognizes the significance of Hegel and Nietzsche for any adequate understanding of Western thought and society. Drawing freely on the work of Hegel, Nietzsche, and Heidegger, Nishitani addresses the problem of nihilism through a careful exploration of the religious dimensions of nothingness. Appropriating important aspects of Buddhist interpretations of nothing, Nishitani effectively extends many of the insights first advanced in Western philosophy. By reading Nietzsche (or, more precisely, Heidegger's Nietzsche) through Buddhism and vice versa, Nishitani arrives at a position that is, in many ways, strikingly similar to Hegel's speculative philosophy. The problems that plague Hegel continue to haunt Nishitani.

To insist that Nietzsche attributes the origin of nihilism to religion in general or Christianity in particular is an oversimplification, for he recognizes that both nihilism and Christianity are complex cultural phenomena with multiple and often conflicting implications. "What does nihilism mean?" Nietzsche asks. "*That the highest values devalue themselves*. The aim is lacking; 'Why?' finds no answer" (*WP*, 9). In the absence of every aim that might respond to the "why?" of existence, nihilism is *Leben ohne Warum*. Aimlessness and errancy emerge when the center of value and meaning that grounds and organizes life disappears or becomes unbelievable. Though uncertainty often begins innocently, it quickly becomes all-encompassing. Nietzsche explains that "the untenability of one interpretation of the world, upon which a tremendous amount of energy has been lavished, awakens the suspicion that *all* interpretations of the world are false" (*WP*, 7). Paradoxically, the recognition of the untruthfulness of all interpretations is really the result of the relentless quest for truth that religious belief itself engenders. If God is truth, God harbors his own death, for the "truth" of truth turns out to be its untruth. The death of God, in which, contrary to expectation, God is fully realized, is the end of truth. The end of truth, in turn, is the beginning of nihilism.

Nietzsche's analysis of the complex interplay between nihilism and religion becomes clearer when it is approached from a slightly different angle. The religious awareness that has characterized Western Christendom is, according to Nietzsche, irreducibly dualistic. Nietzsche's Christian is a paradigm of what Hegel describes as "unhappy consciousness." Convinced of the transcendence of God and hence the otherness of truth, beauty, and goodness, unhappy consciousness suffers inward dismemberment as a result of the inescapable conflict between appearance and reality, or between what is and what ought to be. When God is other, the affirmation of God seems to presuppose the negation of self and vice versa. Nietzsche maintains that the bifurcation of actuality and ideality presupposed by morality is nihilistic. The Christian moralist is inevitably a "Nay Sayer" who denies the world and the fullness of human experience. Since morality engenders rather than abolishes nihilism, to surmount nihilism, it is necessary to move beyond good and evil.

Nietzsche, who is repeatedly described by his critics as one of the most dangerous nihilists in the Western tradition, is actually obsessed with finding a way to overcome nihilism. He is persuaded that nihilism can be surpassed by neither nostalgia nor evasion. To move beyond nihilism, one must pass through it. Toward this end, the negation inherent in the nihilism that grows out of Christian belief and practice must be negated. The immoralist, in other words, says "No!" to the "not" of Christianity. In terms of Hegel's speculative logic, negation must be doubled in order to become absolute. Absolute negation is not simply negative but is at the same time positive. To negate negation is to say "Yes" by saying "No to No." The world and our lives in it can only be affirmed by *denying* religious and moral denial. While the believer/moralist affirms God or the good by negating self and world, the atheist/immoralist *affirms* self and world by *denying* God and the good. Contrary to expectation, Nietzsche finds the seeds of atheistic affirmation in the religion of Jesus. Jesus, one might say, was the first to declare "the death of God."[2] The incarnation of the divine in the human is the disappearance of transcendence in immanence:

> The Kingdom of Heaven is a condition of the heart (—it is said of children "for theirs is the Kingdom of Heaven"): Not something "above the earth." The Kingdom of God does not "come" chronologically-historically, on a certain day in the calendar, something that might be here one day but not the day before: it is an "inward change in the individual," something that comes at every moment and at every moment has not yet arrived—. . . .
>
> "Bliss" is not something promised: it is there if you live and act in such and such a way. [*WP*, 99]

But how is one to act? How must one live to enjoy the bliss that issues from overcoming nihilism? According to Nietzsche, one must live a *Leben ohne Warum* by affirming what is, rather than negating what is by affirming what is not, but ought to be. Radical affirmation is a *total* affirmation that "accepts the everlasting flow; . . . accepts honey and vinegar":

> Midnight is also mid-day—Grief is also a joy, curses are also blessings, night is also a sun—go away, or else learn: a sage is also a fool.
>
> Did you ever say "Yes" to one joy? Oh my friends, then you also said "Yes" to *all* pain. All things are entwined, enmeshed, enamoured—
>
> —did you ever want Once to be Twice, did you ever say "I love you, bliss—instant—flash" then you wanted *everything* back.
>
> —Everything anew, everything forever, everything entwined, enmeshed, enamoured—oh, thus you love the world—
>
> —you everlasting ones, thus you live it forever and for all time; even to pain you say: Refrain but—come again! *For joy accepts everlasting flow!*[3]

Thus to love the world is, in a certain sense, *radically* nihilistic. The death of God, which is the end of transcendence, is the disappearance of anything beyond, which can give meaning and purpose to life. In the uncanny absence of "why," *nothing is left, nothing remains.* There is, in other words, *nothing to rely on.* But what does it mean to rely on nothing? To rely on nothing is to venture everything by affirming what is as what ought to be. Such affirmation is at once terrifying and liberating. To say "Yes" to the everlasting flow is to live without why.

Standing at the threshold of the twentieth century, Nietzsche ventures nothing. He realizes that to venture nothing is both to lose and gain everything. Life beyond good and evil, life beyond why and wherefore, is life that discloses the nihilism at the heart of religion. This nihilism that is the union of religion and nothingness.

From Nullification to "Beification"

Modernity ended and postmodernity began in Hiroshima on 6 August 1945. Insofar as the history of modernity is the culmination of the history of the West, Hiroshima and Nagasaki mark both the closure of Western history and the opening of the East. This end is no accident but, according to Heidegger, is implicit in the beginning of the West. The history of the West is prefigured in the metaphysical tradition that dates back to ancient Greece. Western metaphysics culminates in modern philosophy, which is concretely embodied and enacted in the atomic age. From this perspective, the devastation visited upon Hiroshima and Nagasaki is the tragic consequence of the exercise of humankind's "will to power."

In his richly suggestive book, *Religion and Nothingness,* Nishitani appropriates the general thrust of Heidegger's interpretation of modern philosophy. Modern philosophy, which begins with Descartes's turn to the subject, ends with Nietzsche's will to power. Cartesian doubt collapses truth in certainty, thereby establishing the subjectivity of truth and the truth of subjectivity. The subject that is certain of itself presupposes an autonomy established and secured through the negation of the social and natural world. Echoing Heidegger's analysis of technology, Nishitani writes:

> [Descartes's] *cogito, ergo sum* expressed the mode of being of that ego as a self-centered assertion of its own realness. Along with this, on the other hand, the things in the natural world came to appear as bearing no living connection with the internal ego. They became, so to speak, the cold and lifeless world of death. . . . To the self-centered ego of man, the world came to look like so much raw material. By wielding his great power and authority in controlling the natural world, man came to surround himself with a cold, lifeless world. Inevitably, each individual ego became like a lonely but well-fortified island floating on a sea of dead matter. [*RN,* 11]

The negativity of the autonomous ego is not original but emerges from a more primordial unity. In a manner strictly parallel to Hegel, Nishitani argues that unity is ontologically and chronologically prior to division:

> The idea of life as a living bond had been central to the prescientific, pre-Cartesian view of the world. . . . It was as if each human being were born from the same life, like the individual leaves of a tree that sprout and grow and fall one by one and yet share in the same life of the tree. Even the soul (or psyche) was nothing more than life showing itself.[4]

The opposition between living bond and dead matter structures Nishitani's argument. Having lost the vitality of the prescientific, pre-Cartesian world, the modern subject closes in on itself and is unable to establish contact with either other people or the natural world, which now appears to be thoroughly mechanized. Such isolation, opposition, and fragmentation are constitutive of contemporary nihilism:

> When the unique existence of all things and multiplicity and differentiation in the world appear on the field of nihility, all things appear isolated from one another by an abyss. Each thing has its being as a one-and-only, a solitariness absolutely shut up within itself. We call such a state of absolute self-enclosure "nihilistic." [RN, 145]

Throughout *Religion and Nothingness,* Nishitani attempts to find a way to overcome nihilism.

For Nishitani, as for Nietzsche, to move beyond nihilism it is necessary to experience it. The negation inherent in the nihilism that grows out of Cartesian philosophy must be negated. This negation of negation harbors an affirmation that is supposed to restore a sense of wholeness and totality. To break open the self-enclosed ego, Cartesian doubt must be radicalized by turning it back on the doubting subject:

> The *cogito* of Descartes did not pass through the purgative fires in which the ego itself is transformed, along with all things, into a single Great Doubt. The *cogito* was conceived of simply on the field of the *cogito.* This is why the reality of the ego as such could not but become an unreality. Only after passing through those purgative fires and breaking through the nihility that makes itself present at the ground of the ego, can the reality of the *cogito* and the *sum,* together with the reality of things, truly appear as real. [RN, 19]

62

Doubt establishes the certainty of the self only if it is not carried through to its final conclusion. When doubt is radicalized, it becomes what Nishitani describes as "Great Doubt" in which the self itself is doubted:

What I am talking about is the point at which the nihility that lies hidden as a reality at the ground of the self and all things makes itself present as a reality to the self in such a way that self-existence, together with the being of all things, turns into a single doubt. When the distinction between the doubter and the doubted drops away, when the field of that very distinction is overstepped, the self becomes the Great Doubt. I term it "Great" because it does not restrict its concern to the isolated self of self-consciousness but embraces at once the existence of the self and all things. This Doubt cannot, therefore, be understood as a state of consciousness but only as a real doubt making itself present to the self out of the ground of the self and of all things. In appearing out of the depths of the one ground of self and world this Doubt presents itself as *reality*. [*RN*, 17–18]

When doubt is great, it opens the self to the "ground" of all things. This ground initially appears to be thoroughly negative. The nihility that lies hidden in the ground of the self as well as all other things opens with the "nullification" of particular entities as well as the isolated subject of self-consciousness. The nihility of this ground exposes the nothingness of the Cartesian ego. "The essence of nihility," Nishitani explains, "consists in a purely negative (antipodal) negativity" (*RN*, 137).

The notion of negation that structures Nishitani's argument is quite complex. The autonomous ego, which is characteristic of modernity, emerges through the negation of a primordial unity or totality. This negation, in turn, is negated in the nihility that issues from Great Doubt. Such nullification, however, remains "relative" and thus negative. Nishitani argues that "the nihility seen to lie at the ground of existence is still looked upon as something outside of existence; it is still being viewed from the side of existence. It is a nothingness represented from the side of being, a nothingness set in opposition to being, a *relative nothingness*" (*RN*, 123). "Relative nothingness" becomes "absolute emptiness" when the negation of nihility, which is itself the negation of a negation, is negated. With this further negation, nihility is converted into *sunyata*.

Sunyata, in contrast to nihility, is not simply negative but is absolute negation, which, as such, is total affirmation. "Sunyata represents the endpoint of an orientation to negation. It can be termed an *absolute negativity,* inasmuch as it is a standpoint that has negated and thereby transcended, nihility, which was itself the transcendence-through-negation of all being" (*RN*, 97). Transcending nihility, sunyata discloses the interplay of being and nothingness. Within the nondualism of the Mahayana tradition, being and nothingness are neither perfectly identical nor completely different. Absolute emptiness empties

63

the self of itself by overcoming its self-centeredness. This self-emptying is not, however, the mere negation of the self but is a recentering in which the self returns to its true "home-ground." "In its ultimate home-ground," Nishitani contends, "the self-being of man is not human. Human Dasein may be said to emerge as the 'conformation' of the form of the human and the 'trans-form' of being into a single whole. At the ground of our human being lies a level of *pure* being beyond any determination to the human" (*RN*, 248). Though invoking Heideggerian language, Nishitani's argument is actually reminiscent of Hegel's analysis of the dialectical relation of being and nothing in *Science of Logic*.[5] The being that is the *home-ground* of the self is not different from nothing:

> The emptiness of sunyata is not an emptiness represented as some "thing" outside of being and other than being. It is not simply an "empty nothing," but rather an *absolute emptiness*, emptied even of these representations of emptiness. And for that reason, it is at bottom one with being, even as being is one with emptiness. [*RN*, 123].

The nondifference of being and nothing ("being-*sive*-nothing"), which is established through sunyata, transforms the negative negativity of nihility into the positivity of the "Great Affirmation." Nishitani's "Affirmation" repeats, in a Mahayana register, Nietzsche's "Yes." "Emptiness," Nishitani avers, "might be called the field of 'be-ification' (*Ichtung*) in contrast to nihility which is the field of 'nullification' (*Nichtung*). To speak in Nietzschean terms, this field of beification is the field of the Great Affirmation, where we can say yes to all things" (*RN*, 124).

"Beification" simultaneously empties everything of itself and establishes everything in its "suchness." Suchness is not simple identity but involves an intricate interplay of self-identity and its negation. Implicitly evoking the memory of Heraclitus, who, it is important to remember, was central to Heidegger's rethinking of the question of being, Nishitani uses the metaphor of fire to explain his interpretation of suchness:

64

> We have to admit that even the self-identity of a fire as the fire it is, is unthinkable without its non-combustion. Self-nature is such as it is only as the self-nature of *non*-self-nature. The true self-identity of fire does not emerge from the self-identity it enjoys in combustion as a "substance" or a "self-nature," but only from the absolute negation of that self-identity, from its non-combustion. Put in more concrete terms, genuine self-identity consists in the self-identity of the self-identity of self-nature (as being) on the one hand, and its absolute negation on the other. . . . "This is not fire, therefore it is fire"—to adopt a formula from the *Diamond Sutra*—is the truth of "this is fire." [*RN*, 117–18]

Suchness recenters everything by decentering all that is centered on itself. Within the field of sunyata, everything settles in itself and yet is not self-enclosed. This self-settling that unsettles the (centered) self is called *samadhi:*

> The mode of being of things in their selfness consists of the fact that things take up a position grounded in themselves and settle themselves on that position. They center in on themselves and do not get scattered. From ancient times the word *samadhi* ("settling") has been used to designate the state of mind in which a man gathers his own mind together and focuses it on a central point, thereby taking a step beyond the sphere of ordinary conscious and self-conscious mind and, in that sense, forgetting his ego.[6]

When the ego is forgotten, fragmentation is overcome and unification is realized.

In seeking to recover lost unity, Nishitani resists reducing differences to identity. According to Nishitani, efforts to solve the problem of the one and the many in the Western tradition invariably have been characterized by the tendency to secure unity at the expense of difference.[7] This "solution" merely repeats the difficulty. Neither a monism that erases differences nor a pluralism that resists unity can overcome the impasse of nihilism. In the former case, the differences that constitute life in the world are regarded as simply illusory; in the latter, differences are reified, thereby generating conflict that fragments self and world. Nihilism can be overcome only if unity is established without negating difference.

> On the field of sunyata, however, things are brought back again to the possibility of existence. Or rather, things are made to appear in the possibility of existence that they possess at bottom. They appear from the home-ground (elemental source) of their existence, from the selfness lying at their home-ground. This means that the sensible and rational forms of a thing recuperate original meaning as apparitions of the non-objective mode of being of the thing in itself, as the *positions* of that thing. This is what was referred to earlier as the process of "beification." To return to our analogy, the field of sunyata is a void of infinite space, without limit or orientation, a void in which the circles and all the tangents that intersect them come into being. Here the mode of being of things as they are in themselves, even though it arises from the sort of center where "All are One," is not reduced to a One that has had all multiplicity and differentiation extracted from it. [*RN*, 146]

When "All are One" in such a way that multiplicity and differentiation nonetheless remain, *"the center is everywhere.* Each thing in its own selfness shows the mode of being of the center of all things. Each and every thing becomes the center of all things and, in that sense, becomes the absolute center" (*RN*, 146). The home-ground or elemental source indwells all things in their suchness so that each thing becomes an absolute center. The absolute center, in other words, is *polycentric* without being dispersed. This decentering, which is recentering, does not lead to the fragmentation characteristic of the self-centered ego. Rather, when the center is everywhere, that is, when the center is the absolute center of each thing, all things are drawn together instead of driven apart:

> To treat each thing as an absolute center is not to imply an absolute dispersion. Quite to the contrary, as a totality of absolute centers, the All is One. The analogy of the circle used up to this point is incapable of illustrating such a state of affairs in which the center of all things is everywhere, and yet all things are One. What we are speaking of here cannot be thought of as a system of "being." "All are One" can only really be conceived in terms of a gathering of things together, each of which is by itself the All, each of which is an absolute center. [*RN*, 146]

Nishitani's critique of Western metaphysics notwithstanding, it is clear that the solution to the problem of the one and the many for which he is searching is anticipated in Hegel's dialectical analysis of identity and difference.[8] When read in terms of Nishitani's synthetic philosophy, sunyata involves a kenotic process that creates an all-encompassing field where there is unity-in-multiplicity and multiplicity-in-unity. Within the polycentric totality of sunyata, each thing is gathered together in the All through what Nishitani describes as "circuminsession."[9]

The circuminsessional interpretation of being is neither monistic nor dualistic. As such, circuminsession points to something like the Mahayana "middle way" that lies between unity and plurality. When everything is emptied of itself, it becomes apparent that nothing is itself by itself. All things are "codependent" or constituted in and through an infinitely complex web of interrelations. Nishitani develops his account of circuminsession by reading Heidegger's concept of being-in-the-world through Nāgārjuna's notion of codependent origination and vice versa:

> In this existence of mine, the whole world-nexus, linked together in mutual reliance and cooperation through causal kinship, is at all times coming to light. While determining my Dasein to be the Dasein it is, this infinite nexus is bound to it in causal kinship. This makes it necessary to consider the whole of mankind, the whole of living beings, the whole world, as "destined" to form a single whole with my existence and my work. At the

home-ground of my Dasein, directly beneath my work, this whole labors to make this Dasein what it is, that is, to determine it. My own labors all become in each case one with the ebb and flow of the whole nexus since time past without beginning. They become manifest, as it were, as a focal point of the total ebb and flow. [*RN,* 241]

While not immediately obvious, Nishitani's insight can be expressed in Hegelian terms. According to Hegel, identity is necessarily a function of difference. The relation to that which is other or different is not extrinsic or accidental but is intrinsic to identity itself. The logical and ontological structure of identity-in-difference defines the Hegelian notion. One of the most suggestive instances of this speculative concept is the phenomenon of force. Force, Hegel points out, is *irreducibly* relational. Inasmuch as force presupposes resistance, there can never be simply one force. Force can be actual only as the interplay of *forces.* Hegel explains the dialectic of force in the *Phenomenology of Spirit:*

From this we can see that the Notion of force becomes *actual* through its duplication in two forces, and how it comes to be so. These two forces exist as independent essences; but their existence is a movement of each towards the other, such that their being is rather a pure *positedness* or a being that is *posited by an other,* i.e., their being has really the significance of a sheer *vanishing.* They do not exist as extremes that retain for themselves something fixed and substantial, transmitting to one another their middle term and in their contact a merely external property; on the contrary, what they are, they are, only in this middle term and in this contact. In this, there is immediately present both the repression within itself of force, or its *being-for-self,* as well as its expression: force that solicits and force that is solicited. Consequently, these moments are not divided into two independent extremes offering each other only an opposite extreme: their essence rather consists simply and solely in this, that each *is* solely through the other, and what each thus is it immediately no longer is, since it *is* the other. [*PS,* 85–86]

For Hegel, force is but one instantiation of the universal structure of *Geist.* Though rarely recognized, Nietzsche develops an account of force that strictly parallels Hegel's analysis. Force, according to Nietzsche, is the category through which the entire world can be interpreted. In the final aphorism of *The Will to Power,* he writes:

This world: a monster of energy, without beginning, without end; . . . a play of forces and waves of forces, at the same time one and many, increasing here and at the same time decreasing there; a sea of forces flowing and rushing together, eternally changing, eternally flooding back, with tremendous years of recurrence, with an ebb and a flood of its forms; . . . a becoming that knows no satiety, no disgust, no weariness: this, my *Dionysian* world of the eternally self-creating, the eternally self-destroying, this mystery world of the twofold voluptuous delight, my "beyond good and evil," without goal, unless the joy of the circle is itself a goal. . . . *This world is the will to power—and nothing more!* And you yourselves are also this will to power—and nothing more! [*WP,* 550]

The play of forces establishes the complex interrelation of everything. There is no thing-in-itself, for all things are what they are only in relation. In Nishitani's terms, things "become manifest . . . as a focal point of the total ebb and flow." I have previously noted that within Nietzsche's everlasting flow, "everything [is] entwined, enmeshed, enamoured." To accept this everlasting flow, one must say "Yes" to everything—good and evil, joy and terror. This "Great Affirmation," which Dionysus pronounces, overcomes nihilism. In the eternally self-creating, eternally self-destroying world of Dionysus, there is no transcendence and hence no goal beyond the eternally returning play of forces. To affirm this play is to say "Yes" to what is rather than to deny what is for the sake of what ought to be.

When approached from the perspective of Hegel's account of the identity-in-difference of force, as well as Nietzsche's view of the play of forces, Nishitani's interpretation of sunyata, codependence, and circuminsession becomes considerably clearer. In the field of sunyata, everything is emptied of itself as a result of the codependence established by circuminsessional interrelation. In an unusually revealing passage, Nishitani explains sunyata in terms of force:

> Now the circuminsessional system itself, whereby each thing in its being enters into the home-ground of every other thing, is not itself and yet precisely as such (namely, as located on the field of sunyata) never ceases to be itself, is nothing other than the *force* that links all things together into one. It is the very force that makes the world and lets it be a world. The field of sunyata is a *field of force.* The force of the world makes itself manifest in the force of each and every thing in the world. [*RN,* 150]

As the home-ground of everything, force is neither one nor many. Force *as such* does not exist; rather, force, as Hegel points out, becomes actual in the play of forces. This play gathers everything together by drawing all things out of self-enclosure. In this way, the force of sunyata overcomes the nihilism of the autonomous ego and sublates nullification in beification. Indirectly recalling Hegel, Nishitani claims that in "the moment of conversion to birth through death . . . absolute negation and absolute affirmation are one" (*RN,* 29).

This conclusion brings Nishitani's argument full circle. Having begun with the modern or Cartesian ego, which emerges with the loss of the unity of the prescientific world, Nishitani examines the negation of the isolated self in the nihility that issues from Great Doubt. This nihility, in turn, is negated, thereby opening the home-ground in and through which everything is established in its suchness. Suchness simultaneously centers everything in itself and draws everything out of itself by relating it to all else in an all-encompassing totality. This totality is the polycentric field of force that draws together what previously had been held apart. The emptiness of sunyata recovers lost unity without losing the differences characteristic of everyday life. To embrace sunyata is to affirm this play of forces, which is "at the same time one and many." As Nietzsche insists, this Dionysian world is "without goal." To live sunyata is to live a *Leben ohne Warum:*

> On the field of emptiness, then, all our work takes on the character of play. When our doing-being-becoming, when our existence, our behavior, and our life each emerges into its respective nature from its outermost extreme, that is, when they emerge from the point where non-ego is self into their own suchness, they have already cast off the character of having any why or wherefore. They are without aim or reason outside of themselves and become truly autotelic and without cause or reason, a veritable *Leben ohne Warum.* At bottom, at the point of their original, elemental source, our existence, behavior, and life are not a means for anything else. Instead, each and every thing exists for its sake, and each gets its meaning from its relationship to them, while they themselves are their own *telos.* To the extent that they become manifest at that point of their elemental source, existence, behavior, and life assume the character of play. [*RN,* 252]

This is the world of sunyata—and nothing more! And you yourselves are also this sunyata—and nothing more!

Decentering Polycentrism

Play . . . *Leben ohne Warum.* Nothing more. . . . More nothing! Nishitani ventures nothing. The risk he takes is less than absolute, for his gain is infinite. As "Yes" displaces "No," death gives way to life. The question that lingers is whether Nishitani thinks nothing radically enough.

In his effort to establish a dialogue with the Western philosophical tradition, Nishitani reinscribes much of the language and many of the values that Heidegger labels ontotheological. The commitment to something like ontotheology is reflected in many of Nishitani's most important categories: "ground," "home-ground," "elemental," "elemental source," "the thing itself," "things as they are in themselves," "original self," "primal fact," "gathering," "assembling," "absolute center," "All are One," and "totality." The overall argument in which

Nishitani develops these notions falls into three dialectically related stages: primal unity, the loss of unity with the emergence of difference and opposition, and the recovery of unity through an absolute negation that is an absolute affirmation. As we have seen, the notion of force provides a way for Nishitani to think the return of all things to a home-ground that does not destroy differences:

> The "force" by virtue of which each and every thing is able to exist, or perhaps better, the force by virtue of which all things make one another exist—the primal force by virtue of which things that exist appear as existing things—emanates from this circuminsessional relationship. All things "are" in the home-ground of any given thing and make it to "be" what it is. With that thing as the absolute center, all things assemble at its home-ground. This assembly is the force that makes the thing in question be, the force of the thing's own ability to be. In that sense, we also said that when a thing *is,* the world *worlds,* and that, as the field of circuminsessional interpretation, the field of sunyata is a field of force. [*RN,* 159]

When all things assemble in and through the home-ground, the absolute center is in everything and all things are in the absolute center. Though this center is empty, it nonetheless recenters everything in such a way that all is gathered together in an inclusive totality. The unifying principle of the All is nothing other than force itself:

> Every human being in its selfness contains the field of that force by virtue of which the selfness of all things is gathered into one as a world. This field contains a roothold for the possibility of all things that become manifest in the world. And yet each human being, as such, is but one illusory thing in the world among others. When we say that our self in itself is most elementally "middle," we are not thinking in terms of the "middle" that Aristotle, for instance, spoke of as the "mean" between too much and too little. Nor are we thinking of the role of go-between that Hegel attributed to reason as a "mediation" between contradictories. Whereas these are both "middles" projected on the field of reason, the "middle" seen as a mode of being on the field of emptiness cannot be projected on any other field whatsoever. It is immediately present—and immediately realized as such—at the point that we ourselves actually are. It is "at hand" for us and "underfoot." Just as no one else can see for us or hear for us, so too *none* of our actions can be performed by proxy. All actions imply, as it were, an absolute immediacy. And it is there that what we are calling the "middle appears." [*RN,* 166]

70

Absolute immediacy is completely purposeless—it points to nothing—nothing beyond itself. Sunyata is the *Leben ohne Warum* that is embodied in the perfect spontaneity of play. "At the point that our work becomes play," Nishitani argues, "it is at the same time an elemental *earnestness.* In reality, there is no more unrestricted, take-things-as-they-come sort of play than the emergence of self into its nature from non-ego; and, at the same time, there is nothing more serious and earnest. In the state of 'dharmic naturalness'—of natural and spontaneous accord with the dharma—this is how it is with all things. That is why from time immemorial the image of the child has so often been invoked to portray such an elemental mode of being. For the child is never more earnest than when engaged in mindless play" (*RN,* 255).

Force, however, is not always so gentle, and play not always so childish. It is possible to interpret the play of forces as decentering in a way that forecloses every possibility of recentering. Force, I have stressed, is never present as such but appears only as the disappearance enacted in and through the eternal return of different forces. Force, therefore, is never simply one but is always already divided *between* forces. This between *is not* a home-ground that serves as a secure base or faultless foundation. To the contrary, the turning and re-turning of the play of different forces inscribes the *absence* of every ground and the *impossibility* of all grounding. Within the endless alternation of the play of forces, everything is mediated and thus nothing is immediate. In the absence of immediacy, nothing is present to itself and hence there is no-thing in itself. The play of differences does not simply gather and assemble; it also distends and disperses. The return of force is never the return of the same but is always the return of difference(s) in which difference forever returns differently.

The between of differences staged in the play of forces opens the space of the not in which nothing appears and/or disappears. This not does not simply repeat the Hegelian-Nietzschean "No to No," which is a "Yes" to "both Yes and No." The not of the play of forces is more unsettling than the negation of negation, for it calls forth resistance, which can take place, if at all, only along a constantly shifting border that is neither simply affirmative nor negative. To heed this call is to engage in a "no play" that is not child's play. There is nothing elemental about the not, for nothing is elemental. Nor is this "no play" primal, for nothing is primal. If, however, nothing is elemental, if nothing is primal, then there is no home-ground. In the absence of a home-ground, any return to the All is impossible. Loss is not only inevitable and irrevocable but is absolute. When loss is absolute, nothing can be gained. Then and only then can nothing be ventured.

> (If) nothing (is) gained,
> Nothing (is) ventured,
> (If) nothing (is) gained.

4

Not Just Resistance

In reality, of course, it was
not he who seized the power, nor
is he a tyrant. It has just come
about over the years that the chief
tax-collector is automatically
the top official, and the colonel
accepts the tradition just as we do.
Yet while he lives among us
without laying too much stress on
his official position, he is
something quite different
from the ordinary citizen.
When a delegation comes
to him with a request, he stands
there like the wall of the world.
Behind him is nothingness,
one imagines hearing voices
whispering in the background,
but this is probably a delusion;
after all, he represents the end
of all things, at least for us.
—FRANZ KAFKA

If, hypothetically, it had a
proper place, which is precisely
what cannot be the case, such a
deconstructive "questioning" or
meta-questioning would be more
at home in law schools, perhaps
also—this sometimes
happens—in theology or architecture departments, than in
philosophy departments and
much more than in the literature
departments where it has often
been thought to belong.
—JACQUES DERRIDA

We are forgetting—indeed, might already have forgotten—when and how to resist. With the effort to domesticate altarity in the postmodern culture of the simulacrum, the space of resistance seems to be disappearing and its time eclipsed. It is no longer clear whether resistance is possible or has become impossible. Moreover, one cannot be certain whether resistance is just or not just. Perhaps resistance is not enough; perhaps something other, something that is *not just resistance* is unavoidable.

To resist is to enact the not by saying "No!" This "No" is, more or less, a question of more or less. In other words, the not that is active in "No" is a question of excess: "No, enough!" "Not enough!" "No more!" "No, more!" "No, not enough, more!" From one point of view, the "No" of resistance is a negation or an avoidance of affirmation—two gestures that are not the same. But resistance is not merely negative; nor does it simply avoid affirmation. To resist is also to affirm—even when it is not clear what is being affirmed. A certain affirmation—and, as we shall see, the qualification is important—inhabits the negation of resistance as an anteriority that can never be escaped or erased. Resistance is always performed indirectly "in the name of" an an-archic "before" that must remain unnameable. Resistance, after all, is secondary and, as such, is a response to that which it follows. Its following, however, is a following "not," which is not only negative. As the *re-* of resistance implies, resistance reinscribes what it resists. Thus, resistance involves an unavoidable duplicity: it affirms what it seems to deny, and denies what it seems to affirm. Resistance needs, and, therefore, inevitably repeats, what it nonetheless cannot sanction. Though resistance remains exterior to what it resists, there is (impossibly) nothing outside resistance.

The question of resistance is the question of ethics and, by extension, of politics. Though we live in an age of all kinds of fanatical moralisms, it is no longer obvious that ethics is possible. Nor is it clear what it might mean for ethics to be impossible. As yet another century draws to a close, we seem to be approaching that point foreseen by Nietzsche

73

at the end of the last century. Perhaps the vehemence of contemporary moralism, which, I would insist, *is not* ethical, is a symptom of the implicit awareness that we have actually passed "beyond good and evil." In pursuing the question of resistance, we are called to interrogate this "beyond," which must be described as neither good nor evil. How is "beyond" to be understood? Is this beyond, which is not ethical, the condition of the possibility of morality? Does ethics presuppose something that is not ethical? And might this not-ethical have something to do with religion?

Nowhere has the recent discussion of ethics been more heated than in the debates surrounding what has come to be known as "deconstruction." Since its emergence in the late 1960s, deconstruction has been ethically and politically suspect for opponents who lean toward the right as well as the left ends of the political spectrum. According to conservatives, deconstruction represents a nihilistic attack on the stability and decidability of meaning. For leftists, deconstruction effectively extends the aestheticization of the avant-garde that leaves artists and critics politically disengaged or paralyzed. While from the former point of view, deconstruction threatens radical change, from the latter perspective, it appears essentially conservative. Neither of these interpretations of deconstruction recognizes anything that might reasonably be described as an ethical dimension of this critical strategy.

Questions about the ethical and political status of deconstruction have become more pressing in the wake of the continuing controversies surrounding Heidegger's political allegiances and the disclosure of the troubling shadows that darken Paul de Man's past. For many of his opponents, Derrida's debt to Heidegger and association with de Man confirm long-held suspicions about deconstruction's nihilistic implications. Though the issues are urgent, the analyses and arguments of critics have been anything but rigorous. All too often, innuendo and free association replace careful and responsible consideration of Derrida's demanding texts. Furthermore, opponents of deconstruction fail to realize that questionable relations to fascism are not unique to Heidegger and de Man. The entire economy of modernism is implicated in fascism in disturbing ways that have yet to be adequately assessed. Ironically, it is Derrida who has initiated an inquiry into the complicity between modernism and fascism. Long before his critics unleashed their assaults, Derrida was arguing that modernism brings to completion the Western politico-philosophical tradition, which has been constructed to exclude, dominate, and repress that which is different and other. Totalitarianisms of the left and the right are political expressions of this governing ideology. Though the complete overcoming of repression remains a utopian dream that can never be realized, the deconstruction of exclusive structures can create an opening where it becomes possible to work through resistance. *Working through resistance* is the only ethical alternative that remains in a world where it has become obvious that the desires of modernism end in tragedy.

At the same time that deconstruction has been under attack for its alleged lack of ethical concern and political will, two other important developments have been taking place. Legal scholars have borrowed deconstructive strategies of interpretation to form what is currently described as Critical Legal Studies, and interpreters of religion have turned to deconstruction as a resource for critically reassessing the Western theological tradition. While these two appropriations of deconstruction seem to have little in common, they are both deeply concerned with questions of ethics. In spite of this shared interest, there has been no effort to create a dialogue between Critical Legal Studies and theology or religion.

This situation is puzzling, for Derrida has long insisted on the ethico-political motivation of his work and has repeatedly suggested the importance of a certain reading of theology for his deconstructive enterprise. The intersection of deconstruction, ethics, and religion is most obvious in Derrida's readings of the work of Emmanuel Levinas. Ever since the publication of *Writing and Difference,* the importance of Levinas for Derridean deconstruction has been evident. In subsequent essays devoted to Levinas, Derrida elaborates a reading of "the ethical" that remains implicit in his other writings. When Derrida's defenders attempt to respond to charges of ethical nihilism and political quietism or conservatism, they usually turn to Levinas for support. While this strategy is often effective, it can be misleading. Those who cite Levinas to defend Derrida consistently exhibit a strange aversion to the *theological* dimensions of Levinas's ethics. It is impossible to understand Levinas's account of ethics without an appreciation for his interpretation of the Jewish theological tradition. What Levinas means by "the ethical" *is not* simply a code of conduct that regulates sociopolitical life but is, more importantly, the designation of the relationship of the individual to altarity, which, in one of its guises, appears to be God. So understood, "the ethical" is neither reducible to nor irrelevant for morality and ethics in the commonly accepted use of these terms. Critics as well as supporters of deconstruction have not addressed the question concerning the relationship between "the ethical" and ethics. A critical evaluation of the ethico-political implications of deconstruction presupposes an account of the interplay between religion and ethics. In the following pages, I will develop such an analysis by reading Derrida's major contribution to Critical Legal Studies, "Force of Law: The 'Mystical Foundation of Authority,'" through Kierkegaard's *Fear and Trembling,* and reading Kierkegaard's text through Derrida's writings.

Derrida mentions Kierkegaard only once in "Force of Law": "The instant of decision is a madness, says Kierkegaard" (FL, 967). The lack of any further consideration of Kierkegaard's writings in no way negates the significance of his work for the issues Derrida explores in this essay and elsewhere. To the contrary, Kierkegaard's absence becomes such an overwhelming presence that the reader begins to suspect that it is not insignificant. Though Derrida occasionally refers to Kierkegaard, he has long resisted developing a sustained reading of his texts. While this exclusion is not necessarily deliberate, it is hardly accidental. Shared suspicions of Hegel's systematic philosophy bring Kierkegaard's and Derrida's perspectives into a proximity that calls for careful consideration.[1]

Fear and Trembling is, first and foremost, a story of binding and rebinding. Kierkegaard, or more precisely his pseudonym, Johannes de Silentio, takes as his point of departure the biblical account of what is commonly described as "the binding of Isaac." Having been granted a son in his old age, Abraham is tested by God yet again. For no obvious reason, God calls Abraham to sacrifice Isaac on a mountain in the land of Moriah. Ever obedient, Abraham responds unquestioningly to the call of the Other: "Here I am":

> And the two of them went on together and came to the place of which God had spoken. There Abraham built an altar and arranged the wood. He bound his son Isaac and laid him on the altar on top of the wood. Then he stretched out his hand and took the knife to kill his son. [Gen. 22: 9–11]

The binding of Isaac is a figure for other bindings. This narrative might better be entitled: "The binding of Abraham." The binding of the son repeats and extends the binding of the father, even as it seems to break the tie that binds the two together as one. To whom . . . by whom . . . to what . . . by what is Abraham bound? What does it mean to bind . . . to unbind . . . to rebind . . . to double bind? These questions cannot be answered with certainty; thus, they are bound to linger.

Lingering questions of binding are inseparably bound to questions of justice, law, and religion. The word *justice* comes from *ieuos,* which means binding, sacred, and the law. *Iuris* designates that which is binding. Law, in turn, can be traced to *leg,* which means "to gather, set in order"; read and speak. *Leg* is also the stem of *logos* and *logion*. Religion, which derives from *leig,* "to bind," is a binding back or a *re*binding. Justice, law, and religion, then, seem to be bound together by a certain binding. We cannot, however, be certain whether these three bindings are one.

While Isaac is bound, Abraham is not only bound but is caught in a double bind that is itself double-bound. As a father who loves his son, Abraham is bound to Isaac. This bond is ethical and, as such, lawful. The law, for Kierkegaard, is bound to freedom and freedom is bound to and by the law. Freedom is not freedom *from* the law, but is freedom to bind oneself *to* the law. This self-binding is a double binding. First, the subject binds himself or herself to the universal moral law, and, then, through this law, binds his or her private desires. This intrasubjective double binding is doubled as the moral agent becomes bound in an intersubjective network of other moral actors. Although the intersubjectivity implied in the moral law seems to bring the self into relation with others, this apparent relation to others is actually a complex self-relation. Since the moral law is universal, the ethical relation to an other moral subject is a reflexive relation of the universal to itself in ostensibly different individuals. When this notion of morality is speculatively extended, it becomes possible to argue that one universal moral subject acts in and through many individual moral subjects.

It should be obvious that Kierkegaard's interpretation of ethics is a complex synthesis of Kantian and Hegelian principles. Kierkegaard realizes that despite Hegel's criticism of Kantianism as a philosophy of *Verstand* that never reaches the heights of *Vernunft,* Kant's analysis of theoretical and practical reason anticipates Hegel's own speculative rationality. The moral law or categorical imperative is the universal norm of practical reason through which human subjects are bound to govern their idiosyncratic inclinations. Freedom is autonomy or self-legislation in which the individual gives himself or herself (*autos*) the moral law (*nomos*), rather than accepting the rule of conduct on the authority of an other (*heteros*). From the ethical point of view, the responsible agent has no higher duty than to express the universal moral law in his or her individual life. Echoing Kant as well as Hegel, Kierkegaard writes:

> The ethical as such is the universal, and as the universal, it applies to everyone, which from another angle means that it applies at all times. It rests immanent in itself, has nothing outside itself that is its *telos* but is itself the *telos* for everything outside itself, and when the ethical has absorbed this into itself, it goes no further. The single one, sensately and psychically qualified in immediacy, is the individual who has his *telos* in the universal,

and it is his ethical task continually to express himself in this, to sublate [*ophæve*] his singularity in order to become the universal. [*FT,* 54]

Within the sphere of ethics, the affirmation of the universal is the negation of the singular and vice versa. Nothing escapes the grasp of universal law. In different terms, nothing is irreducibly exterior to reason and morality.

To underscore this important point, Kierkegaard draws a distinction between *Individet* and *Enkeltet*. *Individet* is the term he uses to describe the individual, who assumes determinate identity in and through the universal structure of reason and morality. *Enkeltet,* usually translated "the singular individual" but which I render either "singularity" or "the singular one," designates that dimension of human existence which cannot be expressed or represented in general or universal terms. The singular is "incommensurable" with the universal and hence remains exterior to the law:

> For if the ethical—that is, social morality—is the highest and if there is in a person no residual incommensurability in some way such that this incommensurability is not evil (i.e., the singular one, who is to be expressed in the universal), then no categories are needed other than what Greek philosophy had or what can be deduced from them by consistent thought. Hegel should not have concealed this, for, after all, he had studied Greek philosophy. [*FT,* 55]

If reason and morality cannot comprehend, appropriate, or internalize singularity, universality is incomplete and thus subverted as if from within.

It is important to stress that within the Kantian-Hegelian perspective of Kierkegaard's ethics, morality is practical *reason*. Though reason assumes multiple forms, it is essentially *one*. The universality of reason issues in the intelligibility of the moral law. Since reason is definitive of humanity, all people in all places at all times have the capacity to recognize the binding validity of moral principles. To illustrate the comprehensibility of moral obligation, Kierkegaard uses the example of the tragic hero.

Tragedy is the result of a conflict of *moral* duties. Kierkegaard underscores the distinctiveness of Abraham's dilemma by comparing it with the quandary Agamemnon faced. Though Agamemnon is a tragic hero, Abraham's crisis cannot be described as tragic. The Hebrew patriarch and the Greek king are both obligated to kill one of their children. However, for Abraham, the command to sacrifice Isaac comes from a God who surpasses the ethical perspective, while for Agamemnon, the duty to kill Iphigenia issues from the state and hence remains within the bounds of ethics. "The tragic hero," Kierkegaard argues, "is still within the ethical. He allows an expression of the ethical to have its *telos* in a higher expression of the ethical" (*FT,* 59). Agamemnon's slaying of Iphigenia is an expression of civic duty. His fellow citizens understand his impasse and empathize with the agony he suffers. Furthermore, they admire Agamemnon for his willingness to set aside personal feelings and responsibilities for his daughter in order to secure the common good. When understood within its proper social context, Agamemnon's deed is not horrifying but is completely reasonable.

Johannes de Silentio insists that

> Abraham's situation is different. By his act he transgressed the ethical altogether and had a higher *telos* outside it, in relation to which he suspended it. For I certainly would like to know how Abraham's act can be related to the universal, whether any point of contact between what Abraham did and the universal can be found other than that Abraham transgressed it. It is not to save a nation, not to uphold the idea of the state that Abraham does it; it is not to appease the angry gods. If it were a matter of the deity's being angry, then he was, after all, angry only with Abraham, and Abraham's act is totally unrelated to the universal, is a purely private endeavor. [*FT,* 59]

Abraham's sacrifice of Isaac suspends or transgresses the ethical in the name of something that surpasses or is exterior to the entire moral order. Though faith is not unrelated to morality, religion cannot be reduced to ethics. Kierkegaard repeatedly maintains that "faith is this paradox, namely, that the singular is higher than the universal" (*FT,* 55). Through faith, the *Individet* becomes the *Enkeltet*. The transition from individuality to singularity is not mediated by the interrelation of ethical agents but occurs when one is singled out from all others through the relationship to absolute singularity.

Absolute singularity is "infinitely and qualitatively" different from everything that exists and, therefore, is other—"wholly other." Incomprehensible in any system, this Other resists all totalization. The very otherness of the Other poses a dilemma: Can the Other be recognized *as other* without reducing it to same? Kierkegaard realizes that the Other as such is unthinkable, or is thinkable only as unthinkable. The impossible task he sets for himself and his reader is to think the unthinkable. This thinking or unthinking cannot be straightforward but must be indirect. Consequently, Kierkegaard develops a writerly strategy of indirection in what he describes as his "aesthetic" authorship. The purpose of Kierkegaard's aesthetic education is to lead the reader to the limit of human experience. At this point, which is a vanishing point, something Other approaches. Throughout his pseudonymous authorship, Kierkegaard refuses to speak in his own name; he always writes as an other. Never identifying with any of his personae, the author forever withdraws, thereby allowing an other Other to "speak" by *not* speaking. Kierkegaard's aesthetic education does not reveal the presence of the divine here and now but stages an unrepresentable retreat that leaves everyone gaping.

This withdrawal engenders a paradox that eventually becomes absolute. The *retrait* of the unspeakable is the condition of the possibility of speaking. Consequently, to speak is always, in some sense, to speak not; every word is shadowed by an uncanny double that faults it. In the nonabsent absence of the trace of this fault, all saying is unsaying. Through indirect communication Kierkegaard attempts to say the unsayable in and through the *failure* of language. The "name" of this failure is the unnameable, and *one* of the pseudonyms of the unnameable is God, whose devastating power of nondesignation incites the passion of understanding. Understanding pushes itself to its limits by struggling to think what it cannot think. This paradoxical gesture is unavoidable, for understanding constitutes itself by inscribing "within" itself a limit it cannot comprehend. The boundary, border, or limit that delimits understanding marks the nonsite of a different difference and an other Other, which Kierkegaard describes alternatively as "infinitely and qualitatively different" or "qualitative heterogeneity." Since this radical heterogeneity is neither positive nor negative, it can be figured neither through the *via negativa* nor the *via eminentiae*. In *Philosophical Fragments,* the pseudonym Johannes Climacus traces this unsettling neither/nor:

> What, then, is the unknown? It is the boundary that is continually arrived at, and therefore when the determination of motion is replaced by the determination of rest, it is the different, the absolutely different. But it is the absolutely different in which there is no distinguishing mark. Defined as the absolutely different, it seems to be at the point of being disclosed, but not so, because the understanding cannot even think the absolutely different; it cannot absolutely negate itself but uses itself for that purpose and consequently thinks the difference in itself, which it thinks by itself. It cannot absolutely transcend itself and therefore thinks as above itself only the sublimity that it thinks by itself. If the unknown (the god) is not solely the boundary, then the one idea about the different is confused with the many thoughts about the different. [*PF,* 44–45]

"Absolute difference" is not *a* difference among others, but is *the* difference of the between that opens the time and space in which specific

80

differences emerge and pass away. If absolute difference were not always differing from itself, it might be called "difference itself." But such a name would be improper in its very propriety.

By pushing understanding to its limit, Kierkegaard glimpses an unnameable limit that he names "the absolute difference." This extraordinary heterogeneity marks and remarks the limit of human experience. Abraham approaches this limit, or, more accurately, this limit approaches him on Mount Moriah. As I have stressed, Abraham is bound to and by that which interrupts ethical relations. The binding of the singular one to the absolutely singular does not negate the bindings and double bindings of ethics. Abraham's bond to Isaac, Sarah, and others is not broken. Furthermore, Abraham must continue to bind his private desires. In this way, the bond to the absolutely singular doubles yet again the bindings that are already doubled and redoubled.

Kierkegaard insists that this situation is absolutely incomprehensible to others as well as to Abraham. Absolute difference *exceeds* both reason and morality. It is, in Nietzsche's terms, "beyond good and evil." But it is "beyond" as "within," and is "within" as an exteriority that cannot be internalized (*er-indre,* "remember, recollect"). This "outside" that is inside founds the differences that reason and ethics presuppose. Neither rational nor irrational, moral nor immoral, absolute difference clears the space for the differences between reason and morality as well as rationality and irrationality, and morality and immorality.

Inasmuch as qualitative heterogeneity eludes the grasp of reason, absolute difference is unspeakable. For Kierkegaard, God "speaks" by *not* speaking. This not-speaking, in which God speaks not, inevitably offends reason. Since reason constitutes itself in and through the exclusion of the incomprehensible, it needs the not, which it cannot undo. In other words, reason is bound to and by that which it cannot bear. It includes what it excludes in a nondialectical relation of expropriation that subverts every dialectical appropriation.

The incomprehensibility of the wholly Other "speaks" through the words of Johannes de Silentio and the silence of Abraham:

> Abraham remains silent—but he *cannot* speak. Therein lies the distress and anxiety. Even though I go on talking continuously night and day, if I cannot make myself understood when I speak, then I am not speaking. This is the case with Abraham. He can say everything, but only one thing he cannot say, and if he cannot say that—that is, say it in such a way that the other understands it—then he is not speaking. The relief provided by speaking is that it translates me into the universal. [*FT,* 113]

81

Unlike the conflict of the moral actor and tragic hero, the crisis of faith involves a predicament that cannot be rationally explained. Since religious faith presupposes the relation of the singular one to the absolutely singular, it cannot be mediated by the universal laws of reason and morality. From every rational and ethical perspective, faith is not only paradoxical; it is absurd. This absurdity can never be overcome—not even for the singular one who undergoes the trial of faith. Abraham *cannot* explain his dilemma to others or even to himself. The language of reason and morality is *suspended,* which is not to say negated. Indeed, in this moment of suspense, the universal laws of reason and morality are actually determined. This paradoxical determination of the ethical appears in the multiple dimensions of the wound figured in the knife Abraham raises above Isaac.

There is no avoiding the violence of God's command and Abraham's response:

> Abraham cannot be mediated; in other words, he cannot speak. As soon as I speak, I express the universal, and if I do not do so, no one can understand me. As soon as Abraham wants to express himself in the universal, he must declare that his situation is a spiritual trial, for he has no higher expression of the universal that ranks above the universal he violates.
> [*FT,* 60]

The ethical description of Abraham's act is murder; religiously considered, it is sacrifice. Whether murder or sacrifice, the fulfillment of religious obligation is unlawful, for Abraham steps beyond resistance and transgresses the moral law. Instead of the conclusion of a reasoned argument, this transgression is the result of a *decision* made in the midst of the terrifying anxiety created by the momentary suspense of reason and morality. Like all decisions, this decision entails a certain cutting (*decision-em,* "cutting down," from *sek,* "cut").[2] In the instant of decision, the singular is cut off from all others and thus errs beyond reason and morality. As I have suggested, this erring is not unrelated to the laws of reason and ethics. Indeed, the decision of faith actually posits the rules that govern theoretical and practical reason.

All decisions, according to Kierkegaard, are ultimately blind leaps. Though rational reflection and moral principles can bring one to the brink of choice, they cannot move one to decide. Furthermore—and this point is critical for all that follows—*the very principles of reason and morality are themselves a function of decisions that are neither rational nor moral.* The decision that is beyond good and evil as well as reason and irrationality involves something like a "founding vio-

82

lence," which is a "preoriginary" decision through which differences within and between reason and morality emerge. The founding violence of the singular one's preoriginary decision repeats the founding violence of the absolutely singular that is the absolute "origin" of reason and morality. To say that the absolute difference of the absolutely singular founds the differences that establish the identity of reason and morality is to say something like God creates the world.

Even though choice inevitably involves an either/or, the complexity of decision cannot be reduced to exclusive alternatives. While always singling one out, the decision that cuts one off from others also establishes relationships. Furthermore, transgression needs law as much as law needs transgression. The suspension of the law clears the space in which its constitutive differences find articulation. The decision of the singular one simultaneously breaks the bond with other moral agents by binding one to the wholly Other, and establishes the law that binds one to others in and through the prearchaic origin that lies "beyond" (the) all as the "internal" exteriority of absolute difference. The faithful one is caught in a double bind that surpasses but does not abrogate the double bind of ethics. This double bind, which is created by the relation to the wholly Other, issues in what Kierkegaard describes as a "double movement" that exceeds all human calculation. The so-called knight of faith simultaneously resigns and reappropriates the spheres of reason and ethics. In the movement of resignation, he acknowledges that the laws of reason and morality are neither self-sufficient nor self-grounded but are posited by an Other that can never be named. The movement of reappropriation expresses the conviction that though these laws are partial and inadequate, they are nevertheless necessary and unavoidable. The faithful one does not flee from moral responsibility. To the contrary, he remains committed to the importance of moral action. This commitment, however, is always tempered by an uncertainty that forever accompanies the awareness of altarity. This abiding uncertainty is what creates inescapable fear and trembling. To heed the unavoidable call of the Other is to suffer a horror that is "the *horror religiosus*" (*FT,* 61).

"Force of Law: The 'Mystical Foundation of Authority'" is one of the strangest essays Derrida has ever written. Precisely for this reason, it is one of the most intriguing, most fascinating, and, perhaps, most important. The strangeness begins with the title or, more specifically, the subtitle. Force and law are familiar Derridean topics: "Force et signification"; "Ce qui reste à force de musique"; "Préjugés: devant la loi"; "La loi du genre"; *Lecture de droit de regards; Du Droit à la philosophie; inter alia.* But the subtitle, which, of course, is not Derrida's, refers to notions that he elsewhere calls into question: "the mystical," "foundation," and "authority." The force of Derrida's argument is that law is always forceful and force is always lawful. The play of forces, however, is not self-grounded but is given by an other that is "before" the law. This other, which is something like the "mystical foundation of authority," is neither moral nor rational. The law, Derrida concludes, is not just and justice is not lawful.

The significance of the notion of force is not limited to Derrida's analysis of law; it plays an important role in defining the overall contours of deconstruction. "For me," Derrida avers, "it is always a question of differential force, of force as difference of force, of force as *différance* (*différance* as a force *différée-différante*), of the relation between force and form, force and signification, performative force, illocutionary or perlocutionary force, of persuasive and rhetorical force, of affirmation by signature but also and especially all of the paradoxical situations in which the greatest force and the greatest weakness strangely enough exchange places" (FL, 929). Force, in other words, is a figure of unfigurable *différance.* As we have noted elsewhere, force is irreducibly duplicitous. There can never be merely *one* force; for there to be one force, there must always already be at least *two* forces. Force presupposes *resistance,* which is not simply the other of force but is another force. In other words, force inevitably resists and resistance is unavoidably forceful. Since there can never be only one force, duplicity or multiplicity is not secondary to an original unity. To make this point in the most provocative way: force does not exist. There are only forces that are locked in an interplay of unending strife.

Derrida's recognition of the relationship between law and force is not original. Though his source is not cited, Derrida's analysis of force and law is indebted to Hegel's account of force and understanding in the *Phenomenology of Spirit.* "Anticipating" Derrida, Hegel describes force in terms of law and law in terms of force:

> From this we see that the Notion of force becomes *actual* through its duplication into two forces, and how it comes to be so. These two forces exist as independent essences; but their existence is a movement of each towards the other, such that their being is rather a pure *positedness* or a being that is *posited by an other,* i.e., their being really has the significance of a sheer *vanishing.* They do not exist as extremes that retain for themselves something fixed and insubstantial, . . . what they are, they are, only in this middle term and in this contact. In this, there is immediately pres-

ent both repression within itself of force, or its *being-for-itself,* as well as its expression: force that solicits and force that is solicited. Consequently, these moments are not divided into two independent extremes offering each other only an opposite extreme: their essence rather consists simply and solely in this, that each *is* solely through the other, and what each thus is it immediately no longer is, since it *is* the other. [*PS,* 85–86]

Force is never irrational but is always comprehended in law. Since the structure of force is isomorphic with the structure of law, each perfectly mirrors the other:

Law completes itself in an immanent necessity, and all the moments of [the world of] appearance are taken up into the inner world. That the simple character of law is infinity means . . . (a) that it is self-*identical,* but is also in itself *different;* or it is the selfsame that repels itself from itself or sunders itself into two. What was called *simple force duplicates* itself and through its infinity is law. (b) What is thus dirempted, which constitutes the parts of thought as in the *law* exhibits itself as a stable existence; . . . (c) through the Notion of inner difference, these unlike and indifferent moments . . . are a *difference* that is no *difference,* or only a difference of what is *selfsame,* and its essence is unity. [*PS,* 99]

As this text makes clear, in Hegel's dialectical analysis, force and law consist of three moments: self-identity, difference/opposition, and unifying reconciliation. So understood, the law of force and the force of law are expressions of the yet more general structure of the absolute concept. The Hegelian concept is the law of laws that is the vital force of everything that exists.

Derrida's use of Hegel is subversive, for he turns Hegel's insight against itself in an effort to undo the system from within. While Hegel recognizes the differential character of force, he always subsumes differences is a more comprehensive unity. Difference, in other words, is the second moment in a three-part dialectic that begins and ends in unity. Force, Hegel argues,

posits a difference that is not only *not* a difference for us, but one that the movement itself cancels as a difference. . . . This contained the distinction of soliciting and solicited force, or force expressing itself and force re- pressed into itself; but these were distinctions that in reality were not dis- tinctions, and therefore were also immediately cancelled again. What is present here is not merely bare unity in which *no difference* would be *posited,* but rather a *movement* in which *a distinction is certainly made,* but because it is no distinction, is *again cancelled.* [*PS,* 95]

Derrida, in effect, erases the first and the third moments in Hegel's interpretation of force and law. Accordingly, difference is not epiphenomenal but implies a *différance* that cannot be negated. This non-sublatable difference eludes dialectical reappropriation and thus faults the very foundation of the Hegelian edifice.

In addition to reinscribing a difference that is not reducible to identity, Derrida, in a manner reminiscent of Kierkegaard, insists that not all otherness can be comprehended by reason. As I have already noted, Hegel argues that "two forces exist as independent essences; but their existence is a movement of each towards the other, such that their being is rather a pure *positedness* or a being that is *posited by an other* [*Gesetztsein durch ein Anderes*]." Throughout his analysis of force, Hegel underscores the lawfulness of force by stressing the etymological connection between "to posit" (*setzen,* whose past participle is *gesetz*) and "law" (*Gesetz*). Law relates opposites that appear to be different in a dialectic of mutual constitution in which each is posited through the other. Hegel's protests to the contrary notwithstanding, Derrida insists that the positing through which the Hegelian law operates does not really involve otherness. In the Hegelian dialectic, otherness is always penultimate, for it is, in the final analysis, reduced to the same. Speculative philosophy *must* exclude altarity in order to constitute itself. As we have discovered in our consideration of Kierkegaard, this exclusion is at the same time an (impossible) inclusion of what cannot be included. In Derrida's account of force and law, incomprehensible altarity returns repeatedly to interrupt and dislocate the lawful structure and structure of laws whose space it also opens.

To insist that the law is forceful and force is lawful is necessary but not sufficient because the differential play of the force of law and laws of force presupposes a more "originary" difference that falls *between* law and justice. In an effort to clarify long-standing confusions, Derrida insists that "law (*droit*) is not justice. Law is the element of calculation, and it is just that there be law, but justice is incalculable; and aporetic experiences are the experiences, as improbable as they are necessary, of justice, that is to say of moments in which the decision between just and unjust is never insured by a rule" (FL, 947). As the domain of the calculable, law defines the sphere in which moral agents interrelate through general values, norms, and principles that are shared by a given group. For Derrida, the law is always one or another version of the *law of exchange,* which makes both communication and community possible. Though the token of exchange varies from women and money to sacrifices and words, every economy of exchange is a closed structure in which mutually recognizable opposites circulate. Through lawful circulation, contraries seem to be bound together in an integrated totality.

The universality of the structure of exchange makes theoretical and practical calculations comprehensible. While every such calculable economy is lawful, it is not, Derrida argues, just. In the uneconomical play of differences, "justice" remains forever "incalculable; it requires us to calculate with the incalculable." But how can such incalculability be calculated?

While law or right involves "legitimacy or legality, stabilizable and statutory, calculable, a system of regulated and coded prescriptions," justice is "infinite, incalculable, rebellious to rule and foreign to symmetry, heterogeneous and heterotropic."[3] The heterotopos of justice is a dis-place that is "exterior" to the law. Though outside the law, justice is not exactly lawless. It is beyond every system of exchange that is constructed to establish and maintain a balance between good and evil, as well as truth and falsity. Justice is neither good nor evil, true nor false. It is a "gift beyond exchange and distribution" (FL, 929). That which lies beyond exchange permits no reciprocity—not even the response of thanks or gratitude. *Le coup de don* establishes an "absolute dissymmetry" in which the responsible subject finds himself or herself unable to respond to that to which he or she is indebted. *Denken,* as well as *danken,* is only possible for one whose being is *Schuldigsein.* Debt and guilt are not secondary to a more primordial innocence, for the subject is always already sub-jected to an other and hence is originally indebted. But to whom or to what is the indebted subject bound?

This question is, in a certain sense, unanswerable. Since that to which the responsible subject is originally indebted exceeds the system of exchange, it can only be named with the self-effacing name of "absolute alterity [*l'altérité absolue*]" (FL, 971). Derrida's "absolute alterity" refigures Kierkegaard's "infinite qualitative difference" in what they both describe as "a wholly other"—*un tout autre* (FL, 1023). Furthermore, Derrida follows Kierkegaard when he insists that this wholly other is *absolutely singular:*

> An address is always singular, idiomatic, and justice, as law (*droit*), seems always to suppose the generality of a rule, a norm or a universal imperative. How are we to reconcile the act of justice that must always concern singularity, individuality, irreplaceable groups and lives, the other or myself *as* other, in a unique situation, with rule, norm, value or the imperative of justice, which necessarily have a general form, even if this generality prescribes a singular application in each case? [FL, 949]

Singularity and generality (or universality) cannot be reconciled, though this does not mean that they are unrelated. Inasmuch as the singular is unique, it can never be comprehended within any general structure. Since the rule always violates the singular and the singular always violates the rule, law and singularity harbor a violence that is neither accidental nor avoidable. Violence is constitutive of law as well as singularity.

Though the absolute singular eludes time without being eternal, it is nonetheless *before* the law. Such anteriority is not a past present that can be re-membered or re-collected. To the contrary, it is an immemorial an-archie, which, in Levinas's terms, is an "unrepresentable before." The past that was never present is the preoriginary "origin" of all presence and every present. As the strange origin that is not original, absolute singularity institutes the law it forever escapes:

> Its very moment of foundation or institution . . . , the operation that consists of founding, inaugurating, justifying law (*droit*), making law, would consist of a *coup de force,* of a performative and therefore interpretive violence that in itself is neither just nor unjust and that no justice and no previous law with its founding anterior moment could guarantee or contradict or invalidate. No justificatory discourse could or should insure the role of metalanguage in relation to the performativity or institutive language or to its dominant interpretation. [FL, 941–43]

Norms that guide conduct and rules that inform reflection are not self-justifying or self-grounding. In as much as the principles of evaluation are always internal to an interpretive perspective, judgment presupposes a framework of interpretation that cannot be judged in its own terms. Once a person is involved in or committed to a particular framework, rules of judgment become applicable to particular instances of knowledge and action. But these principles cannot be used to justify the origin or the originary assumption of the framework itself. So-called "first" principles are not first but are secondary to an other they can never comprehend. This other is not simply another foundation that eventually disappears in the mists of an infinite regress but is *le tout autre* that the nonfoundational foundation of both the moral law and the singular one who is subjected to this law. In the words of Faust with which Freud concludes *Totem and Taboo,* "In the beginning was the Deed." But whose deed is this act of originary violence?

Originary violence is, impossibly, the deed of both absolute singularity and the singular one. These two are not one but are absolutely different and wholly other:

> Here we "touch" without touching this extraordinary paradox: the inaccessible transcendence of the law before which and prior to which "man" stands fast only appears infinitely transcendent and thus theological to the

extent that, so near to him, it depends only on him, on the performative act by which he institutes it: the law is transcendent, violent and nonviolent, because it depends only on who is before it—and so prior to it—on who produces it, founds it, authorizes it in an absolute performative whose presence always escapes him. The law is transcendent and theological, and so always to come, always promised, because it is immanent, finite, and so already past. [FL, 993]

In terms that are virtually Kierkegaardian, Derrida claims that the infinitely transcendent is *theological*. The "unrepresentable before" is the "terrifyingly ancient," which sometimes goes by the pseudonym "God." Commenting on Walter Benjamin's "Critique of Violence," Derrida argues:

It seems at first that there is no way out and so no hope. But at the impass, this despair (*Aussichtslosigkeit*, "insolubility," "hopelessness") summons up decisions of thought that concern nothing less than the origin of language in its relation to the truth, destinal violence (*schichsalhafte Gewalt*, "fate-imposed violence") that puts itself above reason, then, above this violence itself, God: another, a wholly other "mystical foundation of authority." [FL, 1021–23]

Though God and self are "wholly other," they are not unrelated. Never autonomous, the rational and moral subject is bound to an ancient other that can never be known. By binding every singular one to a singularity that remains antecedent to the law, this relation, which at the same time is a nonrelation, disperses human subjects. The binding of the moral law as well as the law of reason is, therefore, a rebinding that creates a double binding. The moral agent is bound to and by absolute altarity, which separates existing subjects and other ethical actors, who share moral obligation. Always already indebted to the wholly other that lies beyond the sphere of ethics, moral action presupposes "pre-originary obedience" to the prearchaic violence that founds the codes regulating human relations. "This violence," Geoffrey Bennington points out, "is that of a gift and of the '*oui*,' which always already assures a minimal relation to a transcendental dispersion (which, without this minimum of relation would not even be thinkable as dispersion . . .), but since it is not, for example, properly speaking a state or condition *anterior* to society but an event repeated in every statement and act, this dispersion is always at work as an element of tension or of the *bond* [bande] of the social contract, against which the contract and the laws that it puts in place, exercise a counter-bond or contraband [*contre-bande*]."[4] Instead of an original bond, the moral law is,

89

then, a counterbond that gathers together what altarity holds apart. Since neither dispersing nor gathering is final, the subject remains suspended between opposites that cannot be reconciled.

The singularity of the nonfoundational foundation of authority generates a mystery that reason cannot unravel. As Kierkegaard argues, the universality or generality of reason is unable to comprehend that which is singular. The singular is therefore *beyond* reason, and, as such, is neither rational nor irrational. Derrida might well have been describing Kierkegaard's analysis of Abraham instead of Benjamin's account of violence when he writes:

> The universalization of *droit* is its very possibility, it is analytically inscribed in the concept of justice (*Gerechtigkeit*). But in this case what is not understood is that this universality is in contradiction with God himself, that is, with the one who decides the legitimacy of means and the justice of ends *over and above reason and even above destinal violence*. This sudden reference to God above reason is nothing other than a reference to the irreducible singularity of each situation. [FL, 1023]

When reason attempts to grasp singularity—be it the absolute singular named God or the singular one who is the unique individual—it encounters irresolvable aporias. Derrida's aporias function in a manner that is structurally similar to Kierkegaard's absolute paradox. Aporia and paradox mark and remark the limit of reason. While this limit cannot be incorporated within reason, it is included by an exclusion through which reason constitutes itself. The withdrawal of the limit of reason clears the space in which reason itself emerges.

Since language presupposes reason, that which is inaccessible to reason remains unspeakable. If, following Derrida, who directly follows Benjamin and indirectly follows Kierkegaard, one of the "names" of this point of withdrawal is "God," then God is the name of the unnameable without which language could not speak. God, in other words, is the silence whose eternal withdrawal makes language possible. In this way, the withdrawal of *le tout autre* founds both the universal moral law and the universal principles of reason. In the beginning was the word; before the beginning was something else, something other, which, while it does not exist and hence *is* not, nonetheless "is" the mystical foundation of the law in all its guises. "Here discourse comes up against its limit: in itself, it is performative power itself. It is what I here propose to call the mystical [*le mystique*]. Here a silence is walled up in the violent structure of the founding act. Walled up, walled within, because silence is not exterior to language" (FL, 943). The silence encrypted in language hollows it out as if from within, thereby rendering language unavoidably cryptic. Forever doubled by an other it cannot express, language is irreducibly duplicitous. In speaking, one inevitably speaks not, or speaks the not that allows one to speak. Language, therefore, indirectly witnesses altarity, which it never knows.

Borrowing a phrase from Georges Bataille, Kierkegaard's first French translator, Derrida maintains that the silence shadowing language and haunting reason is "the night of non-knowledge" in which decision takes place without taking a place:

> The instant of decision is a madness says Kierkegaard. This is particularly true of the instant of the just decision that must rend time and defy dialectics. It is a madness [*une folie*]. Even if time and prudence, the patience of knowledge and the mastery of conditions were hypothetically unlimited, the decision would be structurally finite, however late it came, decision of urgency and precipitation, acting in the night of non-knowledge [*non-savoir*] and non-rule. Not of the absence of rules and knowledge, but of a reinstitution of rules which by definition is not preceded by any knowledge or by any guarantee as such. If we were to trust in a massive and decisive distinction between performative and constantive . . . we would have to attribute this irreducibility of precipitate urgency, at bottom this irreducibility of non-reflection and unconsciousness, however intelligent it may be, to the performative structure of speech and acts in general as acts of justice or law, whether they be performatives that institute something or derived performatives supposing anterior conventions. [FL, 967–69]

For Kierkegaard and Derrida, decision is a singular event enacted by a singular subject. Since the singular always eludes the rule, decision is inevitably a blind leap that entails unavoidable uncertainty and absolute risk. The heterogeneity of universal law and singular event leads to the *suspension* of the law in the moment that the decision to institute it occurs. Though Derrida uses Husserl's term *épochè* to specify this moment of suspension, the instant to which he points is really much closer to Kierkegaard's teleological suspension of the ethical:

> To be just, the decision of a judge, for example, must not only follow a rule of law or a general law but must also assume it, approve it, confirm its value, by a reinstituting act of interpretation, as if ultimately nothing previously existed of the law, as if the judge himself invented the law in every case. . . . For a decision to be just and responsible, it must, in its proper moment if there is one, be both regulated and without regulation: it must conserve the law and also destroy it or suspend it enough to have to reinvent it in each case, rejustify it, at least reinvent it in the reaffirmation and the new and free confirmation of its principle. Each case is other, each

decision is different and requires an absolutely unique interpretation, which no existing, coded rule can or ought to guarantee absolutely. [FL, 961]

Every decision is at least double. At the most obvious level, decision requires the application of a set of norms, principles, rules, or codes to a specific situation. The moral actor attempts to respond to others by relating to them through principles of conduct sanctioned by the group. As we have seen, however, these codes are neither self-grounded nor self-certifying. Consequently, the subject must reinstitute the law in every act that invokes it. In other words, the judging subject chooses the law with which he or she chooses. The choice of the law of choice is not itself lawful; it is *before* the law and thus serves as the necessary condition of lawful thought and action. The decision that institutes the law exceeds the regulated economy of calculation:

> Justice, as law, is never exercised without a decision that *cuts,* that divides. This decision does not simply consist in its final form, for example a penal sanction, equitable or not, in the order of proportional or distributive justice. It begins, it ought to begin, by right or in principle, with the initiative of learning, reading, understanding, interpreting the rule, and even in calculating. For if calculation is calculation, the decision to calculate is not of the order of the calculable, and must not be. [FL, 963]

The incalculable, which every economy of exchange presupposes, brings with it an uncertainty that is almost unbearable.

Kierkegaard develops a rigorous and ironic analysis of the strategies individuals devise to avoid the profound uncertainty of decisive situations. Appearances to the contrary notwithstanding, in the critical moment of decision, there are no rules to follow. More precisely, there are no rules to follow in deciding which rules to follow. Once one has chosen a code of conduct, shared rules seem to offer certainty and security. The ethical agent, like Agamemnon, freely communicates with others whose perspective he or she shares. The more "originary" decision that institutes the code, however, is usually unconscious or repressed. Thus, the all-important "foundational" decision is not a decision *sensu strictissimo.* Through the multiple and often conflicting viewpoints of his pseudonyms, Kierkegaard attempts to bring the reader to a vivid awareness of the impossible dilemma he or she faces. Like Abraham standing on Mount Moriah, the subject who would be moral is destined to decide in the absence—the absolute absence—of knowledge and certainty. This nonknowledge is what creates fear and trembling. The singular one confronting the unavoidable call of absolute singularity, which never actually arrives but only approaches from elsewhere, suffers overwhelming anxiety:

> The moment of suspense, this period of *épochè,* without which, in fact, deconstruction is not possible, is always agonizing, but who pretends to be just by economizing on anxiety [*l'angoisse*]? And this agonizing moment of suspense—which is also the interval or space of transformations . . . cannot be motivated, cannot find its movement and its impulse (an impulse that itself cannot be suspended) except in the demand for an increase in or supplement to justice, and so is the experience of an inadequate or an incalculable disproportion. For, in the end, where will deconstruction find its force, its movement or its motivation, if not in this always unsatisfied appeal, beyond the given determinations of what we call, in determined contexts, justice, the possibility of justice? [FL, 955–57]

The appeal (*l'appel*) of deconstruction is the call (*l'appel*) of an other that "arrives" by infinite deferral. Though never present, this other is not absent. The nonabsent absence of altarity implies an "incalculable disproportion" in all rational and moral calculation. It is precisely this unavoidable disproportion that calls for resistance.

Not Just Resistance: Not Just . . . Just Resistance . . . Not Just Resistance. In a certain sense, "Not Just Resistance" is unreadable. Or it must be read in so many ways that it becomes effectively unreadable. As every moral actor would no doubt insist, that which is not just should be resisted. And yet, Kierkegaard and Derrida maintain, the nonfoundational "foundation" of the moral law is not just. Forever *beyond* good and evil, the prearchaic origin of the ethical involves a resistance that is not just. Altarity resists the ethical, which, in the name of justice, resists the call of the other. But in resisting altarity, ethical activity resists its own impossible "foundation." The resistance of altarity is not, however, merely negative. Though moral resistance attempts to be just, the resistance that founds the ethical is not just; nor is it just resistance. Beyond the ethical, resistance is not just resistance.

Since the resistance of altarity is not just resistance, the originary violence of the absolutely singular does not destroy ethical obligation. The ethical subject who heeds the call of the other is, as I have stressed, doubly bound. Indebted to an other that can never be known, the singular sub-ject is obligated to others whose world he shares. To describe this double bind, Derrida borrows, without citing, Kierkegaard's term: "double movement." For Derrida, as for Kierkegaard, the ethical person must repeatedly perform a double movement in which the moral law is simultaneously suspended and reappropriated. In the moment of suspense, the subject withdraws from the law in order to allow the non-foundation that is the "foundation" of the law to appear:

> The sense of a responsibility without limits, and so necessarily excessive, incalculable, before memory; and so the task of recalling the history, the origin and subsequent direction, thus the limits, of concepts of justice, the law and law (*droit*), of values, norms, prescriptions that have been imposed and sedimented there, from then on remaining more or less readable or presupposed. [FL, 953]

The recognition of the limits of justice and the law does not destroy their necessity. There is no escaping the law. To believe that the law can be avoided is as utopian as to believe that it can be perfected. The law is both inevitable and inadequate. Since justice is never truly just, the law of justice must always be resisted. This resistance is not in the name of a higher justice but witnesses to an other that is not just:

> Never yield to this point, constantly to maintain an interrogation of the origin, grounds and limits of our conceptual, theoretical or normative apparatus surrounding justice is, on deconstruction's part, anything but a neutralization of interest in justice, an insensitivity toward injustice. On the contrary, it hyperbolically raises the stakes of exacting justice; it is sensitivity to a sort of essential disproportion that must inscribe excess and inadequation in itself and that strives to denounce not only theoretical limits but also concrete injustices, with the most palpable effects, in the good conscience that dogmatically stops before any inherited determination of justice. [FL, 955]

The determination of justice is always *partial.* This partiality reflects both an unavoidable incompletion and inevitable prejudice. Deconstruction resists prejudices that can never be completely avoided. The site or nonsite of resistance is the margin of difference marked by the disproportion between justice and injustice. Since the structures of oppression infinitely repeat themselves, the struggle of resistance is endless.

94

The resistance of the not creates the knot of double binding. Decision, which always cuts, ties this not in a double knot that cannot be undone. At this late hour—and what hour is not always already late?—the only ethic that remains possible is an ethic that acknowledges its necessary entanglement with the impossible. To decide is always to decide not; and to decide not is always to resist. But resistance is not enough. The Other that calls not, calls for not just resistance.

Art

o   o   o

5

Saving Not

2. Arakawa and
Madeline Gins,
Building Sensoriums
(1973–90).
Installation
photograph of the
September 1990
exhibition in New
York at the Feldman
Gallery. Photograph:
Dennis Crowley.
Courtesy Arakawa and
Madeline Gins.

3. Arakawa and
Madeline Gins, *The
Process in Question/
Bridge of Reversible
Destiny* (1973–89).
42-ft. model, detail.
Photograph: Nicholas
Whitman. Courtesy
Arakawa and
Madeline Gins.

The object of perception was strange—distressingly strange. This was no ordinary work of art (fig. 2). Neither painting, nor sculpture, nor architecture, but something else . . . something other. At first glance, the object seemed more scientific than artistic. It appeared to be something like a high-tech particle accelerator, a design for a future nuclear reactor, or even a model for an extraterrestrial colony. But as I examined the object more carefully, it slowly became apparent that it was a plan for a bridge—a bridge unlike any other that has ever been built: *Bridge of Reversible Destiny*. Long, low, and sleek, the black monochromatic model was comprised of geometric shapes: spheres, cubes, cylinders, pyramids, circles, squares, rectangles, and triangles. The *Bridge* was simple, yet complex; rooms inside rooms, rooms above rooms, rooms below rooms combined to create a bridge of bridges. Neither one nor many, the *Bridge* was undeniably duplicitous (fig. 3). The rooms that emptied the space of the *Bridge* bore perplexing names:

Bodily Conjecture at Light
In the Recesses of the Communal Stare
The New Missing Link
Diffuse Receding Gauge
Companion to Indeterminacy
Volume Bypass
Points of Departure Membranes
The Where of Nowhere
Edges of Apprehending
Inflected Geometry
Accrual Matrix
The Planet's Cry
Than Which No Other
To Not to Die
The Helen Keller Room

Reverse-Symmetry Traverse-Envelope Hall
Gaze Brace
Assembly of Latent Perceivers
Cradle of Reassembly
Forming Inextinguishability

Within and between the rooms, there were layers upon layers of black mesh that simultaneously transformed once solid walls into sites of passage and impeded movement. In some rooms, there was no room—only an endless tissue of mesh; in other rooms, there was nothing but room—only the uncanny darkness of seemingly empty space. All of this was suspended, or was supposed to be suspended above a river, the Moselle River in Épinal, France. A suspension bridge, a bridge of suspense, a bridge that suspends.

How?
Where?
What?

o   o   o

The space of the bridge is a nonspace; its site a nonsite. The bridge is suspended along a border, margin, boundary, in an interval, gap, cleavage. The place of the bridge is the nonplace of the between where here and now are suspended. This between, which is forever oscillating, brings together what it holds apart and holds apart what it brings together. "The bridge," Heidegger avers, "swings over the stream 'with ease and power'":

> It does not just connect banks that are already there. The banks emerge as banks only as the bridge crosses the stream. The bridge designedly causes them to lie across from each other. . . . The bridge *gathers* the earth as landscape around the stream. . . . Even where the bridge covers the stream, it holds its flow up to the sky by taking it for a moment under the vaulted gateway and then setting it free once more. . . . The bridge lets the stream run its course and at the same time grants their way to mortals so that they may come and go from shore to shore. . . . Bridges lead in many ways. . . . Always and ever differently the bridge escorts the lingering and hastening ways of men to and fro, so that they may get to other banks and in the end, as mortals, to the other side. . . . The bridge *gathers,* as a passage that crosses, before the divinities—whether we explicitly think of, and visibly *give thanks for,* their presence, as in the figure of the saint of the bridge, or whether that divine presence is obstructed or even pushed wholly aside. The bridge *gathers* to itself in *its own* way earth and sky, divinities and mortals. [*PLT,* 152–53]

"Bridges lead [and mislead] in many ways." But how many ways? And where do these ways lead?

o   o   o

Arakawa is one of the most intensely philosophical—perhaps even theological—artists now working. From the outset, his concerns are not only aesthetic. Since, unlike so many artists, Arakawa realizes that aesthetics and metaphysics are inseparable, his artistic investigations presuppose philosophical interrogations. The intricate interplay of art and philosophy is graphically displayed in his innovative work, *The Mechanism of Meaning,* which was first published in 1971 under the title *Mechanismus der Bedeutung. The Mechanism of Meaning* is something like a philosophico-aesthetic workbook that formulates questions, poses paradoxes, and explores conundra. Though elegant in their own way, the works included in this work are not guided by primarily aesthetic concerns. Nor are they simply conceptual. Rather, Arakawa probes the space where concept and figure, as well as word and image, intersect. While Arakawa's art is undeniably modern in its ambitions and purposes, he consistently rejects the modernist doctrine of the autonomy of the work of art. His painterly surfaces are interrupted by objects, found images, and, most important, words—some written, some stenciled, others reproduced in collage. Conversely, the written text is interrupted by objects, found images, and, most important, painterly surfaces that are often blank. Text supplements painting and painting supplements text in a play of supplements that subverts the classical opposition between concept and figure, word and image, and philosophy and art.

The textual supplements at work in Arakawa's works extend beyond the frame of the canvas. Works frame texts that reframe works. In this intricate tissue of supplements that creates art, Arakawa never works alone; his art is essentially collaborative. The texts that inform his work are written in cooperation with Madeline Gins. The origin of the work of art is not one but (at least) two—two who often seem to be one or almost one. But the textual weave that Arakawa and Gins fashion is even more complex than this duplicity suggests. Their work is intrinsically incomplete and inherently open ended. It is filled (or not filled) with holes, fissures, faults, and gaps. These gaps open the space-time that draws the viewer-reader into the work of art. Arakawa's and Gins's work *cannot* be passively received; it *must* be actively apprehended. This apprehension is a reproduction that is not simply a repetition of the same but is the articulation of something different. To grasp the work of art is to collaborate in the labor of production. The art of Ar-akawa and Gins issues an invitation: "Come! Join us in the work of art." Those who accept this solicitation gradually realize that to enter the *Bridge of Reversible Destiny* is to begin a journey that is irreversible. For Arakawa and Gins and their collaborators, the work of art is not an autonomous aesthetic object but is, in the final analysis, the perceiving subject. The work of art, in other words, is nothing less than oneself. Within this framework, the only art worthy of the name is an art that saves—saves not only itself but also saves the subject by allowing the self to lose itself. Saving art struggles to save art by refiguring the art of saving in a world deserted by the gods.

While the art of Arakawa and Gins is, as I have suggested, undeniably modern, their work does not simply repeat well-established modern doctrines and techniques. To the contrary, they develop a critical art that responds to certain failures of modernism. Modernism is irrepres-sibly utopian. Though ideas and images of the promised land vary, much twentieth-century art takes over the redemptive role once played by religion. From this perspective, art provides what Friedrich Schiller describes as an aesthetic education that prepares the way for the real-ization of the ideal society. The dreams of modernity, however, turn into terrifying nightmares. From the ovens of Auschwitz, to the scorched earth of Hiroshima and Nagasaki, utopian hopes are turned to ash. Art after Hiroshima bears the trace of a wound whose depth cannot be fathomed. How can art continue in the shadow of such a disaster? Though our world is admittedly "postutopian," Arakawa and Gins insist not only that art must continue but that art still has the power to save. *If* hope remains, it is hope nurtured by the work of art. In the midst of death and destruction, art teaches how "To Not to Die."

Clement Greenberg argues that Kant was "the first real modernist. The essence of modernism," according to Greenberg, "lies in the use of the characteristic methods of a discipline to criticize the discipline itself—not in order to subvert it, but to entrench it more firmly in its area of competence. Kant used logic to establish the limits of logic, and while he withdrew much from its old jurisdiction, logic was left in all the more secure possession of what remained to it."[1] To be modern, then, is not only to be critical but to be self-critical. Self-criticism presupposes the structure of reflexivity in which the knowing subject takes itself as its own object. Kant's so-called Copernican Revolution extends the turn to the subject with which Descartes initiates modern philosophy. Modern philosophy is, first and foremost, a philosophy of the subject. The modern subject, in turn, is a constructive subject who creates the world in his or her own image. Though not immediately evident, Kantian critical philosophy actually reinscribes classical ontology in modern epistemology. Since the time of Plato, the process of creation has been interpreted as involving a synthesis of form and matter. In Plato's myth of origins, the world is created through the activity of a Demiurge, who brings together transcendent eternal forms and the chaotic flux of matter. Kant translates the form/matter distinction into epistemological structures. While the Platonic forms become forms of intuition and categories of understanding, matter reappears as the sensible manifold of intuition. The stuff of sensation is, in William James's apt phrase, a "bloomin', buzzin' confusion," until it is ordered and organized by the structures of intuition and understanding. In a manner analogous to the Platonic Demiurge, the knowing subject creates the world by uniting form and matter. Though the process of world making is subjective, it is not, according to Kant, idiosyncratic. Like Plato's archetypes, Kant's human forms of intuition and categories of understanding are universal and immutable. Consequently, constructive subjects create a shared world in which common structures unite otherwise separate individuals. There is, however, a significant price to be paid for this unity. Since they are universal and unchangeable, the forms of intuition and categories of understanding constitute an irreversible destiny for the knowing subject. Epistemic structures, in other words, are unavoidable.

The task that Arakawa and Gins undertake in their art is to reverse the seemingly irreversible destiny of the modern subject. Toward this end, they develop something like what Maurice Merleau-Ponty describes as a "phenomenology of perception." The importance of Arakawa and Gins's artwork emerges clearly when their interrogation of the art of perception is contrasted with Merleau-Ponty's philosophical phenomenology of perception.

Merleau-Ponty formulates his phenomenology of perception in response to the philosophy of reflection, which receives its most complete articulation in Hegel's phenomenology of spirit. Hegel's speculative interpretation of the reflexivity of subjectivity brings to completion the analysis of the structure of self-consciousness begun by Kant. Merleau-Ponty argues that

> the philosophy of reflection metamorphoses the effective world into a transcendental field; in doing so it only puts me back at the origin of a spectacle that I could never have had unless, unbeknown to myself, I organized it. It only makes me consciously what I have always been distractedly; it only makes me give its name to a dimension behind myself, a

depth whence, in fact, already my vision was formed. Through reflection, the "I," lost in its perceptions, rediscovers itself by rediscovering them [that is, perceptions] as thoughts. [The "I"] thought it had quit itself for them, deployed itself in them; it comes to realize that if it had quit itself, they would not be and that the very deployment of the distances and the things was only the "outside" of its own inward intimacy with itself, that the unfolding of the world was the enfolding on itself of a thought that thinks anything whatever only because it thinks itself first. [*VI, 44*]

If the subject thinks only by first thinking itself, then all knowledge is actually self-knowledge. When the knower becomes fully aware of what and how he knows, consciousness is transformed into self-consciousness. Transparent self-consciousness dispels the obscurity of consciousness by effecting a perfect reconciliation of subjectivity and objectivity. In the philosophy of reflection, ambiguity is a penultimate moment that inevitably gives way to the clarity of certain knowledge. Merleau-Ponty argues that "a logically consistent transcendental idealism strips the world of its opacity and its transcendence. The world is the same, which we represent to ourselves not as empirical subjects, but insofar as we are all one light and participate in the One without dividing it." [2] The pure light of this transparent moment is supposed to reveal absolute knowledge.

From Merleau-Ponty's point of view, the embodied subject can never attain absolute knowledge. Consciousness and self-consciousness harbor a blindness that *cannot* be overcome. Reflection, he contends, "recuperates everything except itself as an effort of recuperation, it clarifies everything except its own role. The mind's eye too has its blind spot, but, because it is of the mind, one cannot be unaware of it, nor treat it as a simple state of nonvision, which requires no particular mention, the very act of reflection that is *quoad nos* its act of birth" (*VI,* 33). To glimpse the mind's blind spot, one must deconstruct the modern subject.

The modern subject, I have stressed, is a constructive subject that creates the world in its own image. Over against Kant and his followers, who argue that the subject is active even in perception, Merleau-Ponty maintains that the mind is primordially passive. At the rudimentary level of perception, the subject does not constitute the world. To the contrary, the world is "preconstituted" independently of the activity of the knowing subject. The most basic order or structure of the world, in other words, is not created by the constructive subject. "Thought cannot ignore its apparent history, if it is not to install itself beneath the whole of our experience, in a pre-empirical order where it would no longer merit its name; it must put to itself the problem of the genesis of its own meaning. It is in terms of its intrinsic meaning and structure that the sensible world is 'older' than the universe of thought" (*VI,* 12). The *intrinsic* order of the world is apprehended by means of perception. Rather than chaotic flux, perception discloses an inherent order that is inaccessible to cognition. "If I pretend to find, through reflection, in the universal mind the premise that had always backed up my experience, I can do so only by forgetting this non-knowing of the beginning, which is not nothing, and which is not the reflective truth either, and for which I must also account" (*VI,* 49). The purpose of Merleau-Ponty's phenomenology of perception is to recollect the nonknowing of reflection. Such remembering does not transform nonknowledge into knowledge but exposes the inevitable failure of reflection and, thus, the unavoidable partiality of knowledge.

Arakawa and Gins's phenomenology of perception falls *between* Hegel's phenomenology of spirit and Merleau-Ponty's phenomenology of perception. In keeping with the tenets of post-Kantian idealism, Arakawa and Gins insist that the subject is active at *every* level of awareness. Furthermore, it is possible to understand the way in which the mind operates in perception and conception. Nonetheless, Arakawa and Gins agree with Merleau-Ponty's recognition of the limits of reflection. Though the mind can grasp how it grasps the world, not everything is comprehensible for the sentient subject. Perception is riddled with gaps that interrupt the mechanism of meaning. In contrast to Merleau-Ponty's analysis of the faults of reflection, Arakawa and Gins maintain that the insurmountable cleavage of perception does not reveal an alternative order but implies a nameless blank that repeatedly eludes the apprehensive subject.

The seemingly simple question with which Arakawa and Gins begin their investigation of the mechanism of meaning is: "'How is here achieved?' or 'How is here?'"[3] Meaning does not float freely but is rooted in experience, which, in turn, presupposes perception. Consequently, to understand how meaning emerges or fails to emerge, it is necessary to analyze the operation of perception. Over against Merleau-Ponty, Arakawa and Gins contend that perception is not fundamentally passive but is a complex activity comprising multiple "microevents." Instead of being passively received, the images that constitute the fields of perception and cognition are fabricated through activities that border on the poetic (*poiesis,* to make).

Forming space,
the perceiving,
brings about the perceived image
of fiction of place as detail;
by repeatedly cleaving,
it initiates the game of distance,
making it possible, for example, for
one's arm, hand or foot to be seen. [*ND*, 108]

Since space is not preformed, it must be organized by the perceiving subject. Through constructive activity, the subject creates a "fiction of place" in which objects assume determinate form. By describing the site where objects appear as "fictive," Arakawa and Gins stress the artificial character of space. Objects are artifacts created by imaginative subjects. When interpreted in this way, the activity of perception approximates the work of art.

In an effort to disclose the process that generates meaning, Arakawa and Gins devise a series of visual puzzles, which they collect in *The Mechanism of Meaning*. By challenging the viewer/reader to perform impossible mental operations, the artists attempt to create an opportunity to observe perception in action. For example, in one of the works included under the heading "Logic of Meaning," they present four photographs of the same woman with different facial expressions (fig. 4). Beneath these images stenciled instructions appear: "USE ANY COMBINATION OF THE SETS BELOW TO DEMONSTRATE THE LOGICAL CONNECTIONS OF THE ONE ABOVE." The alternatives for decoding the logic of meaning include: silhouettes of a pencil, fish, apple, and a tangled line or string; four empty squares; the first four letters of the alphabet in "improper order" (C, A, B, D); a tube punctuated with four small holes; and four white socks folded to form different shapes. It is impossible to define the rationale of the photographs with any or all of these images and objects. This is not to imply that the exercise proposed by this work of art is meaningless or senseless. To the contrary, "The Logic of Meaning" poses many important questions that involve the relation between artistic production and reproduction, language and art, word and image, image and object, word and object, abstract form and concrete image/object. The impossibility of translating painted images into reproduced images, words, forms, and objects (and vice versa) suggests that there might be different logics at work in various domains of perception as well as reflection. These contrasting logics engender multiple meanings that cannot be reduced to each other. When gaps in meaning are acknowledged, it becomes possible to recognize what is

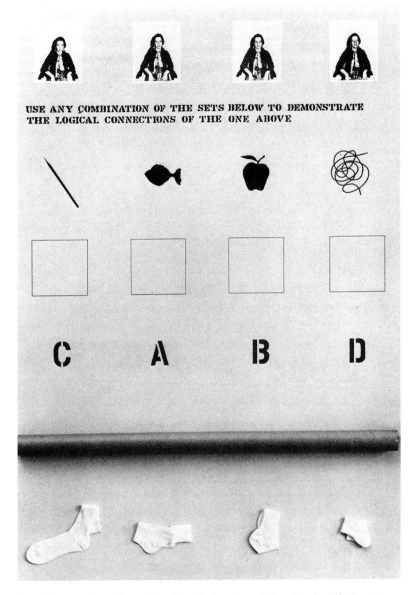

USE ANY COMBINATION OF THE SETS BELOW TO DEMONSTRATE
THE LOGICAL CONNECTIONS OF THE ONE ABOVE

C   A   B   D

4. Arakawa and Madeline Gins, *The Mechanism of Meaning* (1988). Courtesy
Arakawa and Madeline Gins.

105

all too easily overlooked—the white ground or blank space on which
figures appear. The question of the blank will return.

The artistic object, Arakawa and Gins insist, is neither autonomous
nor intrinsically significant. The artwork points beyond itself by turning
the perceiving subject back on itself to apprehend its own apprehending. In this way, *The Mechanism of Meaning* functions in a manner

similar to the interpretation of the experience of consciousness that Hegel plots in the *Phenomenology of Spirit*. To follow either Arakawa and Gins or Hegel is to submit to an aesthetic education in which the entire world is effectively transformed into a work of art.

In spite of notable similarities, there are equally important differences between the pedagogies of Arakawa-Gins and Hegel. The most consequential difference concerns the status of the creative subject. Arakawa and Gins begin a series of aphorisms entitled "The Tentative Constructed Plan as Intervening Device (for a Reversible Destiny)" by declaring:

> Consider "I" an architectural assertion and work out the details of how so. The task of coordinating the parts falls to the critical artist, the coordinator of events, the conductor of assertions. [TCP, 1]

As we have seen, the aim of Kant's critical philosophy is, in effect, to define the architecture of subjectivity. The *arche* of the subject is a universal and immutable structure that forms the foundation of intuition and understanding. While accepting the notion of transcendental subjectivity, Hegel introduces significant changes into the Kantian architectonic. Hegel accepts Kant's insistence on the constitutive activity of the knowing subject but rejects the universality and immutability of the forms of intuition and categories of understanding. The structures through which particular subjects organize experience develop historically and, therefore, vary from time to time and place to place. Hegel attempts to avoid historical and cultural relativism by arguing that a universal or absolute subject is present in the activities of every individual subject. However, inasmuch as the universal never exists apart from the individual (and vice versa), Hegel's struggle to escape the trap of relativism seems bound to fail. What appear to be the universal structures through which the world or, more precisely, worlds are created are actually historically determined generalities with which individuals and communities process their experience. Neither particular subjects nor specific groups are free to transform the structures that pattern their lives. History is destiny and destiny is irreversible.

Arakawa and Gins radicalize Hegel's revision of Kant's architecture of the I by attempting to reverse the destiny of the perceiving subject. The "Process in Question/Reversible Destiny" extends and expands the interrogation begun in *The Mechanism of Meaning*. The process in question is perception, which forms the point of departure for every mechanism of meaning. In undertaking an analysis of the microevents that contribute to the activity of perception, Arakawa and Gins's interest is not merely descriptive. They seek to understand how perception works in order to reform perception itself. To effect this reformation, Arakawa and Gins interrupt the process of perception by means of an art that becomes architecture:

> We call for an intervening role for architecture within the perceiving process. We believe that by means of architecture, or by means of something slightly but significantly different from what has up until now been called architecture, perception might be re-routed, and new sites for the originating of perception might be either found or formed, or both. How to make what is usually only observed into an observer (?). Any extending in this way of the active domain of sensibility would mark the beginning of the era of reversible destiny. [TCP, 1]

The structures through which we create worlds *are not* our eternal destiny. Though we are thrown into existence in such a way that conformity to a previously constituted symbolic order is unavoidable, the codes that condition perception and cognition are open to deliberate transformation:

> Each time, to the degree that a perceiver, with the help of a tentative constructed plan, succeeds in releasing herself from the limits of her conditioning, the number of possible alternatives suggesting themselves increases and the scope of the ubiquity in question widens. . . . Ubiquitous Site comprises not only all ongoing engagings, realized and realizable landing sites, but also all approaches to these, all procedural queries and hints of query surrounding these events. Once again, this amounts to everywhere the senses range or could range. [TCP, 5]

A landing site is a locus of perception. Like the fiction of place in which objects appear, the landing site, where perception settles, is a fabrication. Consequently, the subject as well as the object is something like a work of art. Indeed, the object of Arakawa and Gins's art is the *perceiving subject.* The art object as it is usually understood—that is, painting, sculpture, or architecture—is nothing more than a means to the end of the artwork *sensu strictissimo,* which is the creative subject. I am—the I is—a work of art. In the preface to the revised edition of *The Mechanism of Meaning,* Arakawa and Gins explain:

107

> In the first part of this work, we take fragments, and we try, by making linkages to perceiving tactics immediate, slowly to draw these tactics, these ways of construing a demonstrably conceivable whole that *are* the perceiver-reader, into a unified field that we refer to as "the perceiving field." We propose, in the second section, to re-create and rejoin fragments, and would-be fragments, so as possibly to make a new whole, a completely other perceiver. [*MM*]

The limits of perception are not absolute but are a function of a historically determined code that can be changed. To reform perception is to
transform the architecture of the I. Since the world is not merely given
but is constructed by the activity of the subject, the recoding of the I is
the recreation of the world.

"Perceiving," Arakawa and Gins conclude, "may be said to require
at nearly every juncture a making use by the perceiver of a tentative but
rather well-defined plan. If these plans for perceiving could be made at
last to be recognizably present, perhaps the species could finally begin
to get somewhere" (TCP, 4). *Bridge of Reversible Destiny* is an architectural plan for reforming the architecture of the subject. As the margin
of the between, a bridge is the site of passage. In this case, the shores
brought together and held apart by the bridge are the self itself. Though
reversing destiny, *Bridge of Reversible Destiny* does not inscribe a
circle; the points of departure and arrival are both the same and different. The subject who enters the Bridge dies and, somewhere in between, an other subject is born. *Bridge of Reversible Destiny* marks the
boundary where a transformative rite of passage takes place. As Arthur
Danto points out, "the terminal component of the Bridge has the shape
of an octagonal tank, at least from the outside; sloping away from it, like
the wall of a pyramid, is a structure bisected by a passage. One exits
from the octagon and enters the passage, whose walls diminish as one
advances until, free at last in all senses, one is on the other side. Meta-
phorically, one is walking between the legs of a geometrical sphinx, so
perhaps the octagon is construed as a womb and exiting as a kind of
rebirth. If this is true, then the sphere could be an abstract head, as the
final space is the division between abstract legs, and the whole bridge
is then a kind of relative of Duchamp's nude [in *Étant donnée*], with its
component parts perhaps analogous to the perceptual parts—or sensorium—of the reclining body. So it could be a very powerful enactment to traverse the apparatus."[4]

Neither birth nor rebirth is an easy process. The passageway that
leads to the reformation of the subject of perception is actually an ob-
stacle course. Instead of cultivating aesthetic distance, *Bridge of Reversible Destiny* invites one to enter the work of art. By inserting oneself
inside the work, the subject actually becomes a part of *l'oeuvre d'art*.
To pass through the Bridge, it is necessary to conform to the architectural design (figs. 5 and 6). What appear to be walls in the birth canal
are actually layers of tissues or membranes that the emerging subject
must penetrate. Far from facilitating passage, the difficult space of the

Bridge impedes movement by repeatedly interrupting and dislocating the subject. Each room is designed to disrupt the structures of perception in a distinctive way.

> The Reverse-Symmetry-Transverse-Envelope Hall, a typical instance of a tentative constructed plan, reduces the number of objects to be taken into consideration, while increasing the number of surfaces offered up for processing. Standing within this constructed-out plan, a participant is able to make use of the layout of the surface she is facing to get a sense of how things have been apportioned on the surface that is directly behind her; similarly, the vertical surfaces to her left and to her right share a single scheme for the positioning of their elements. . . . Having to undertake only half the amount of active perceiving that might otherwise be needed, the perceiver may be able to secure for herself some hesitations in the generalizing process known as making a world. With the great reduction in number of specific perceptual events having to be attended to, due to the high level of repetition of large segments of compositional elements, raw perceptual energymatter, freed from the usual obligation of having to be translated immediately into a part of the whole, will hover possibly more noticeably on or about perceptual landing sites. New ways of perceptual landing sites being engaged are likely to come from this. [TCP, 6–7]

For those who linger patiently *in* the work of art, repeated disruptions and dislocations gradually begin to undo the sense of the world and to open new, previously unimagined worlds of experience.

Despite the rigor of the exercises performed, the apprehension of perception always remains incomplete. The impossibility of closing the circle of reflection is not only the function of changes wrought in the subject; nor is it the result of infinitely proliferating structures of subjectivity and worlds of experience. The subject's return to itself is always interrupted by a *residue* that neither perception nor conception can grasp:

> Following each reassembling, there is left a residue or blank, an accumulating of. As long as it remains more or less undifferentiated, this accumulation turned to action, or field of action, continues as a blank projection. The extent of this accumulation of blank determines the rate of both formation of a fiction of place and the ultimate stability and flavor of it. [*ND*, 76]

109

The unassimilable remainder of perception cannot be figured—it is both unrepresentable and incalculable. Its presence is traced by a certain absence, and its absence is marked by a certain presence. The absent-presence/presence-absence of the residue is blank:

Above all, they wished to find out how perceiving could enter what it could. At its limits, what stood hovering, and in what way? A graduated penetrability in and around what? How much traction could perceiving have on what was being perceived anyway? They came up with the notion of a perceptual tread. If something were traversed to be entered, this would have had to have happened by means of these treads, this treading. Between the treads, always the generalizing blank would lie in all its specificity—all full of non-images in a wide-spread non-eye. [RD, 15]

Blank   Blank   Blank

Blank is the space-time of the not; it is neither nothing nor something. Neither existing nor not existing, neither being nor nonbeing, blank is not meaningless, though it is not meaningful. The not of blank is implicated in meaning in such a way that it remains not simply insignificant. While there is no meaning without blank, blank itself is not meaningful. Neither meaningful nor meaningless, neither sensible nor senseless, blank clears the space of meaning by withdrawing. The appearance of the not as blank is the disappearance that allows appearance to appear. This withdrawal is unspeakable, for it is "an event preceding language" (RD, 12). "With all the preconceptions gone, what would be left would be blank perceiving" (RD, 16). But how is "blank perceiving" to be understood?

Blank perceiving must not be confused with perceiving blank. While blank is as necessary for perception as it is for meaning, its absence-presence/presence-absence continues to be imperceptible. Thus blank perceiving is perceiving not. The erasure of preconceptions does not allow one to perceive blank but renders perception impossible. And yet, blank is the not, which is at work in all perception. Though the perceiving subject is, to a certain extent, its own creator, it nevertheless is not autonomous but is a modification or modulation of a more encompassing process. Arakawa and Gins use various terms to describe this process: *energymatter, worldenergy, massenergy, spacetime,* and *spacetimematter.* Never inert, the process in question pulsates endlessly in contrasting rhythms that are suggested by the word *cleaving.* To cleave (from the Greek *glyph,* to cut with a knife or carve, and the Latin

111

5. *Opposite, top.* Arakawa and Madeline Gins, *Critical Resemblances* (1979–90). Mixed media, 22 × 13 ft. Courtesy Arakawa and Madeline Gins.

6. *Opposite, bottom.* Arakawa and Madeline Gins, *Perceptual Landing Sites (I)* (1979–90). Mixed media, wooden octagon, 16 × 12 ft., rubber octagon, 9½ × 11 ft. Courtesy Arakawa and Madeline Gins.

glubere, to peel), means to part or divide by a cutting blow, to split, to intersect, to fissure, to separate. There is, however, a contrasting cadence to *cleave*. *Cleave* means not only divide, separate, split, and fissure, but also adhere, stick, and cling. Cleaving simultaneously divides and joins, separates and unites. The ambiguous activity of cleaving, Arakawa and Gins insist, is "ubiquitous":

> Cleaving appears to us to be a basic operative factor in the conducting of the world. The world, energymatter, might be said to cohere by means of cleaving, or cleaving, a simultaneous dividing and rejoining, ubiquitously provides this coherence. We would like to say that this instantaneous non-sticking adherence, all in discrete parts, continually separable and separating out, serves as source and substratum for all action. [TCP, 3]

This "omnipresent" substratum is blank perceiving. The perceiving agent is a concrete embodiment of the substratum of cleaving. "In other words, within 'here,' a segment of the process is cleaving apart to be isolated as it is cleaved together to a denoting of itself as 'the segment that is in the process of separating out'" (RD, 5). The subject is bound to and distinguished from the "spacetimematter" continuum that operates in all times and places:

> Everywhere is cleaving: massenergy cleaves itself, cleaves to and
> from itself. In this way, it makes from and of itself dimensions and
> turns itself gradually into various tissues of density.
> Where fiction of place steps, edge blank eddies.
> There is no space, no dimension apart from perceiving. [*MM*]

The activity of the subject repeats the rhythms of cleaving. Perception, for example, involves both a distinguishing and a relating in which the particular object is simultaneously differentiated from and associated with the context where it is embedded. Like Wallace Stevens's jar in Tennessee, the cleaving of perception assembles a world:

> I placed a jar in Tennessee,
> And round it was, upon a hill.
> It made the slovenly wilderness
> Surround that hill.
>
> The wilderness rose up to it,
> And sprawled around, no longer wild.
> The jar was round upon the ground
> And tall and of a port in air.
>
> It took dominion everywhere.
> The jar was gray and bare.
> It did not give of bird or bush,
> Like nothing else in Tennessee.[5]

The wild of the wilderness is the forest through which Heidegger cuts his *Holzwege*. The cleavage opened by the jar on a hill reinscribes the clearing that Heidegger identifies with the origin of the work of art. Exploring this origin in *Holzwege,* Heidegger explains: "A construction, a Greek temple, images nothing. It simply stands in the midst of a rock-cleft valley." The temple images nothing by holding open the differential interval of the between:

> Standing there, the construction rests on rocky ground. This resting of the work draws up out of the rock the obscurity of the rock's monstrous yet spontaneous support. Standing there, the construction holds its ground against the storm raging above it and so makes the storm itself manifest in its violence. The luster and gleam of the stone, though itself apparently glowing by grace of the sun, yet first bring to light the light of the day, the breadth of the sky, the darkness of the night. The secure tower makes visible the invisible space of air. The steadfastness of the work contrasts with the surge of the surf, and its own repose brings out the raging of the sea. Tree and grass, eagle and bull, snake and cricket first enter into their distinctive forms and thus come to appear as what they are. [*PLT,* 41–42]

Neither eagle nor bull, tree nor grass, snake nor cricket is original, for each arises in and through the work of art. The origin *of* art is an "original" cleaving that makes possible all such paired opposites. The work of art works by opening this opening. Heidegger opens his essay, "The Origin of the Work of Art," by asking: "Where and how does art occur?" "Art," he concludes, "breaks open an open place." In the space and time of this opening, disclosure and concealment repeatedly intersect in a play of differences that constitutes "the essential strife" of "world," "self-disclosing openness" and "earth," that is, "the essentially self-secluding" (*PLT,* 17, 47–48). The artwork works by setting up the world as the region within which Being and beings emerge, and setting forth earth as the sheltering domain where they withdraw. The alternating strife of world and earth forms the "tear" (*Riss*) of cleaving:

> But as a world opens itself, the earth comes to rise up. It stands forth as that which bears all, as that which is sheltered in its own law and always self-secluding. World demands its decisiveness and its measure and lets beings extend into the open of their paths. Earth, bearing and jutting strives to keep itself closed and to entrust everything to its law. The strife is not a tear [*Riss*] as the gaping crack of a pure cleft, but the strife is the intimacy with which combatants belong to each other. This tear pulls the opponents together in the origin of their unity by virtue of their common ground. It is a basic design [*Grundriss*], an outline sketch [*Aufriss*], that draws the basic features of the rise of the lighting of beings. This tear does not let the opponents burst apart; it brings the opposition of measure and boundary into their common outline [*Umriss*]. [*PLT,* 63]

113

The strife of the tear captures the duplicity of cleaving. The tear of cleaving, we have observed, alternates between two rhythms—one centrifugal, the other centripetal. By holding open this alternating difference, the origin of the work of art simultaneously joins and separates. This separation that joins and joining that separates transforms the tear of cleaving into the tear of pain:

> But what is pain? Pain tears or rends [*risst*]. It is the tear or rift [*Riss*]. But it does not tear apart into dispersive fragments. Pain indeed tears asunder, it separates, yet in such a way that it at the same time draws everything together to itself. Its rending, as a separating that gathers, is at the same time that drawing, which, like the predrawing and sketch, draws and joins together what is held apart in separation. Pain is the joining in the tearing/rending that divides and gathers. Pain is the joining or articulation of the rift. The joining is the threshold. It delivers the between, the mean of the two that are departed in it. Pain articulates the rift of the difference. Pain is difference itself. [*PLT,* 204]

The site of cleaving is the Bridge that gathers together what it holds apart and holds apart what it gathers together. The pain of cleaving is a symptom of the rending caused by reversing destiny. To re-route perception is to re-form the subject. Such reformation sunders what it re-creates. The negotiation of the *difference* between the old and the new is inevitably painful. Though dreadful, this pain is also strangely pleasurable. The pleasure of such pain is the excess of ecstasy—"the most perspicuous of ecstasies":

> "The Process in Question" wends its way as the "Bridge of Reversible Destiny." This construction takes on the open enigma of perception postutopianly. The post-utopia spirit is the one that has found the means no longer to have fearfully to dally with any set of given necessities whatsoever. Take destiny, or the inevitable, fateful progression of the human condition, and reverse that. The "Bridge of Reversible Destiny" will set the species in question on this path. A creature of the post-utopian era exacts out across its thinking field place-forming images of how to position oneself or an evolving to that maximum demanded by the most perspicuous of ecstasies. For this to happen, every detail must be attended to and all processes in question should be exaggerated and prolonged. [RD, 2]

For Arakawa and Gins, the end of the modernist dream of utopia does not mean the impossibility of salvation. Lingering in the shadow cast by the white light of Hiroshima and Nagasaki, Arakawa and Gins still dream, still hope—dream and hope passionately, desperately, perhaps even impossibly. In the postutopian world, they believe, only art can save us. Saving art reverses destiny in such a way that it becomes possible "to elude mortality":

> Reversible destiny architects stand opposed to mortality on all counts and take their project to be the constructing of those conditions that will make it possible for this vile destiny to be reversed. They propose to construct sensoria that will be capable of eluding mortality. [TCP, 7–8]

The destiny of mortality is reversed when perceiving is perceived in all its richness, density, and complexity. We have discovered that this perception involves both the apprehension of the activity of the perceiving subject and the acknowledgement of the not in the blank of all perceiving. Blank marks the "zone of diffuse receding" where everything is destined to proceed (RD, 9). In Heidegger's terms, blank is "the essentially self-secluding" whose withdrawal clears the space for the "self-disclosing openness" named "world." The origin of the work of art is the cleavage in which all things arise and pass away. As the event or non-event that precedes even the microevents of perceiving, the origin of art is a "BRANCH OF THE UNSAID" (MM, 105). Though unspeakable, the UNSAID releases the word without which the world cannot be created. "In the beginning was the word"; before the beginning was the UNSAID. Ever unspeakable, the UNSAID is the NAMELESS that haunts every name and all naming. When art saves, the creator of the wor(l)d discovers the rending ecstasy of "THE SHARING OF NAMELESS" (MM, 105).

THE SHARING OF NAMELESS . . . BRANCH OF THE UNSAID. . . . The *Bridge* is suspended, or is supposed to be suspended above a river. A river whose flow is endless and, in a certain sense, unspeakable. The UNSAID "appears" by disappearing in the gaps—as the not of perception. The river over which the *Bridge* is suspended is a BRANCH OF THE UNSAID. While never present, this river nonetheless flows through us all. To retrace the meandering of the BRANCH OF THE UNSAID is to rediscover the garden that is our end:

> Unconditionally to live, that is what a post-utopia might offer in contrast, yes, even to a utopia, with its more conservative range of promises, from universal plumbing, more equality, down to, quite likely, more uniformity in belief. No, the post-utopia has nothing to offer except a chance finally to know what you are doing. (Every post-utopia would call forth, for the sake of a working out of the details, its own utopia.) This would be a garden of Eden of epistemology, and more. [MM]

115

Much, much more. To enter *Bridge of Reversible Destiny* is to assume a destiny that is irreversible.

o   o   o

o

o

Saving not

o

Not saving

o

Art of saving not

o

Saves art

o

That saves not

o

By not spending

o

Or spending not

o

o

o

To not

o

To die

o

To die

o

To not

o

o

o   o   o

And yet . . . and yet . . . and yet, *is* it ours to not to die? Or is to die precisely the not we must learn to live? To live not might be the only way to live, and not to live not might be not to live.

116

o   o   o

Beyond *The Process in Question/Reversible Destiny,* toward the back of the gallery, in a side room, there was another installation: *Post-Frankensteinian Architecture/Stuttering God.* I cannot show you this work; it has been disassembled and there are no photographs of it. Even if there were photos, images could only represent what the work is not.

I do not know whether there are any plans for its reassembly; (its) absence might be irreplaceable.

As I approached *Stuttering God,* I met a friend who was terribly distraught. She paused only long enough to mumble, "I can't enter, I just can't do it!" Soft light cast a strange glow throughout the narrow empty room. On the far wall, two perfectly symmetrical openings were veiled by beige curtains. In the absence of signs, it was impossible to know which was the entrance and which the exit. Cautiously drawing back one of the veils, I stared into the darkness of the work of art. After a moment's hesitation, I entered the darkness. I could see nothing; I could perceive not. Or so I thought.

No sooner had I turned a corner in the passageway I was following than something soft but abrasive hit me in the face, sending my glasses flying. As I reached out to try to find my glasses, my watch band caught on a net that suddenly seemed to engulf me. For a brief instant, panic overwhelmed me. Struggling blindly to free myself, I felt caught in a trap from which there was no escape. Gradually, I untangled my arm and began to grope for my glasses. Afraid that someone else would enter the maze and accidentally crush them, I anxiously ran my hands over the dark floor. After several sweeps of the area, I suddenly felt the metal frame. In the midst of *Stuttering God,* I could see no better with than without my glasses. The darkness remained impenetrable.

Glasses recovered, I turned and started down the passageway again. This time I had a better sense of what to expect. Proceeding slowly with hands outstretched, I encountered a wall that seemed to be made of plastic bags filled with some indefinable material, surrounded by plastic netting. To proceed in this obscure labyrinth, I had to force my way through the dense tissue of plastic. Beyond the net in which I had been caught, there were more obstacles. Webbed bags of plastic clung to the walls, hung from above, and littered the floor. Passage was almost impossible. Without sight to guide me, my other senses became more acute—especially touch and hearing.

Realizing that after coming this far, there was no difference between forging ahead and turning back, I paused to ponder my situation. It slowly became obvious that *Stuttering God* was actually an extension of *Bridge of Reversible Destiny.* Abandoned in my blindness, the whole world became a "Helen Keller Room." Having crossed the threshold that was both an entrance and an exit, I had become part of the work of art. Indeed, the work of art was now working on me by beginning to transform me into something other than what I previously had been. If

117

I allowed the work time to work, if I lingered in the work instead of rushing through it, I might actually become the work of art.

I proceeded more slowly. The passageway bent to the left and turned back on itself. Less preoccupied with finding the way out, I realized that my eyes had grown accustomed to the darkness. Though I still could see nothing, I was able to discern dim shapes and obscure forms. Since they kept receding as I approached, I was never able to figure out what they were. I do, however, believe something was there.

As I followed the turns in the course, I realized that I was beginning to move in a circle. Out of the corner of my eye, I caught a glimpse of a tiny point of light—white light—to my left. Pushing bags and nets aside, I traced the beam of light to its source. It was a peephole, no bigger than a quarter, which was reminiscent of the cleft in Duchamp's *Étant donnée*. Gazing into the gap, I did not discover a naked woman spread before me but saw nothing other than light passing through miniature reproductions of the black mesh that forms *Bridge of Reversible Destiny*. I was not sure whether I was peeking through glass, clear plastic, or a small magnifying lens. The question of proportion seemed important but unanswerable.

Turning from the light, I again entered the darkness. More nets, webs, grids, and bags rushed to meet me. Like an explorer growing better accustomed to new terrain, I became more adept at making my way through the tangled weave of the membranes that gave me pause. The more adroit I became in negotiating obstacles, the more deliberately I had to avoid rushing through the passageway. Patience is a difficult lesson to learn. Sometimes I simply stood thoughtfully for several moments; once I even sank to the floor and sat silently. Throughout it all, no one else appeared; I was alone . . . absolutely alone.

The longer I roamed, the more points of light I discovered—four, maybe five, perhaps more. Each was similar, though not identical. In every opening, the light was blocked, deflected, interrupted by screens within screens, grids within grids, webs within webs, and nets within nets. All black. The play of black on white created a tissue of texts more obscure than any I had ever read. It was not clear whether all of the holes were cut into a central column—to create something like an incised phallus in the middle or the labyrinth. Nor was it clear whether all the gaps opened onto the same space. Each cleavage could have been a separate opening that was only a few inches deep. Forever defracted, it was impossible to know whether the light was (the) One. One crack especially fascinated me. Unlike the other openings, this one was not a square or a rectangle; it was shaped like an *L*—an inverted *L*.

What was this *L*? How was this *L* to be read? Was Arakawa and Gins's *L* a parody of Duchamp's *ELLE*? Or was *L* a pseudonym for EL? And why was *L* inverted? Might the inverted *L* be the name of the nameless who cannot speak and is not the word but can only stutter? As questions multiplied, the points of light threatened to become pointless—sense-less points of nonsense.

If the tissue of the labyrinth repeats or anticipates the texture of the (unbuilt) Bridge, the radiance of the light (or lights) reflects the flow of the river. River and light: BRANCHES OF THE UNSAID. To see the light—directly, immediately, here and now—is to SHARE THE NAMELESS. Light is God . . . God is light . . . the Light that dispels darkness. The Light in the center of the labyrinth saves by showing the way out.

But can (the) light be seen? Is it visible or invisible? Perceived or perceived not? The vision of pure light is blinding. In the moment of illumination—if such a moment there be—light becomes darkness and darkness becomes light. For light to appear, it must disappear. Shadows not only obscure; they also illuminate. Is the presence of light the absence of darkness or the presence of darkness the absence of light? Light and dark . . . black and white . . . a play . . . a "textual" play in which everything and nothing are entangled. The presence-absence/absence-presence of light-darkness opens the opening in which appearances appear and disappear. To be drawn into the play of appearing/disappearing is to be drawn into the draw of withdrawing. To think the withdrawing that allows appearing/disappearing to appear and disappear, it is necessary to think withdrawing with drawing. Whether directly or indirectly, drawing underlies painting and architecture. But what is drawing?

It is difficult to know where to begin or to end. To draw, which derives from *dhragh* (to draw, drag on the ground) means, among other things—many other things—to pull, drag, contract, shrink, distort; to pull (as a curtain or veil) over something to conceal it; to pull (a curtain or veil) away from something to reveal it; to render into another language or style of writing, translate; to bear, endure, suffer, undergo; to adduce, bring forward; to turn aside, pervert; to add, subtract, multiply; to attract by physical or moral force; to pull out, extract; to deduce, infer; to select by lot; to cause to flow; to take in (as air), breathe; to take out, receive, obtain (money, salary, revenues) from a source; to empty, drain, exhaust, deplete; to stretch, extend, elongate; to straighten out by pulling; to represent, mold, model; to frame; to compose; to track (game by scent); to trace (a figure) by drawing a pencil, pen, or the like across the surface; to cut a furrow by drawing a plowshare through the soil; to draw a line to determine or define the limit between two things or groups; to lay down a definite limit of action beyond which one refuses to go; to pull or tear in pieces, asunder; to bring together, gather, collect, assemble; to leave undecided (a battle or game) . . . . "Drawing" is irreducibly duplicitous. Its meaning cannot be penned down, for it is constantly shifting and changing between opposites it neither unites nor divides; distorting/straightening, adding/subtracting, taking in/taking out, bringing forward/turning aside, revealing/concealing, pulling together/tearing asunder. The meaning of *draw(ing)* forever remains undecided. In this word, meaning itself is a draw. To say "withdrawing" with drawing—to say "withdrawing" without withdrawing saying, one cannot avoid stuttering.

Though the meaning of *drawing* is undecidable, its stuttering involves the rhythms we have discerned in "the origin of the work of art." This "origin" is not a foundation or ground but an abyss or *Ungrund* that never appears as such but "appears" only by withdrawing. When withdrawing is figured with drawing, it appears to be the appearance of the disappearance. To be drawn into the draw of (with)drawing—to linger in the draw with drawing—is to be drawn to a void that cannot be a-voided. This void "is" no more emptiness than fullness, no more nonbeing than being. It is beyond what is and what is not:

> And yet—beyond what is, not away from it but before it, there is an other that occurs. In the midst of beings as a whole, there is an open place. This is a clearing, a lighting. Thought of in relation to what is, to beings, this clearing is in a greater degree than are beings. This open center, therefore, is not surrounded by what is; rather, the lighting middle itself encircles all that is, like the nothing we hardly know. [*PLT,* 53]

This is the open center (un)figured in *Stuttering God:* "The nothing we hardly know." The work of art does not reconcile opposites but articulates differences. Articulation is a separating that gathers and a gathering that separates. When neither movement can be reduced to the other, only stuttering remains. Stuttering speaks not without not speaking. The question of *Stuttering God* is whether this stuttering is the uttering of God.

120

As soft pink light filtered through the veil, the darkness slowly withdrew. But things became no clearer. I made my way toward the exit or entrance, which was really neither an exit nor an entrance. Outside had become inside in a monstrous labyrinth from which there was no withdrawing.

What was *Stuttering God* doing to me? What had (a) stuttering God been doing to me for years . . . many, many years? I turned back and reentered *Stuttering God.* This time I would reverse my course and maybe my destiny. I was not sure I had seen all the blanks. Perhaps in one of the gaps no webs, nets, grids, tissues, membranes—textures obscured vision. Perhaps it was not necessary to perceive not. Perhaps to perceive not is to perceive the nonsense that inhabits all sense. Perhaps. But I was no longer certain . . . certain whether to perceive not was to perceive or not to perceive. What *does* it mean to perceive not?

o   o   o

Failingly

the blank

returns

not

o

o

o

Not Architecture

Z

Σ

Silence... trace... cinder... desert... abandonment... the nearness of the remote... the remoteness of the near. Drawing... forever withdrawing. Desertion.

Z Σ

a wound

is a

shared frontier

the time of

the infinite

is the time of

borders crossed

Z Σ

Daniel Libeskind's architecture is not architecture. The point is not... the point is not that he has not built—though he has not. The point is that he approaches building with the obsession of building not. The question Libeskind asks—asks repeatedly and insistently—is how to build not without not building.

For years, many years, Libeskind has resisted building. It is not that opportunities have been lacking; a deeper, more obscure resistance appears to inhabit his work. His hesitation seems to suggest that, in a certain sense, form cannot contain idea, image cannot reflect concept, matter cannot embody spirit. There have been drawings—extraordinary drawings, models—fantastic models, writings—baffling writings, and lectures—enigmatic lectures. But no buildings—at least not yet. Nevertheless, Libeskind's work is increasingly acknowledged to be at the forefront of contemporary architectural theory and practice. Rarely has an architect exercised so much influence by not building.

123

Libeskind's resistance to building has been a prolonged initiation into the nomadic ways of a certain negativity that has uniquely prepared him to develop what can best be described as Not Architecture. In his introduction to a collection of Libeskind's drawings entitled *Chamber Works: Architectural Meditations on Themes from Heraclitus,* Peter Eisenman argues that "it might be possible to locate limits of architecture by simply examining its complement, 'not-architecture.' Unlike a just not architecture, which is a state of having nothing to do with the subject, a 'not-architecture' would be intimate with architecture, would know it, would contain a 'not-architecture'; would constitute a relationship to being by not being."[1] For Eisenman, the not-architecture that Libeskind develops is the *dialectical* opposite of architecture. Since every determinate identity is, from a dialectical perspective, always constituted by the internal relation to its own opposite, the definition of anything is inseparably bound to what it is not. Thus, to comprehend something adequately it is necessary to push reflection to the limit where opposites pass into each other. According to Eisenman, the not that determines architecture is, in the first place, drawing. To draw is not to build. In this sense, Libeskind's drawings are the not-architecture through which he attempts to articulate the limit that constitutes architecture. Architectural drawing, however, is not just any drawing, for it presupposes a logic of exemplarity in which the drawn figure presents the model for the built form. In different terms, the building re-presents the drawing. When understood in this way, architectural drawing perfectly illustrates the theory of representation that forms the foundation of the entire Western ontotheological tradition. It is precisely this notion of representation that Libeskind's extraordinary drawings are designed to call into question. As Eisenman points out:

> To insist that these are drawings, that they are working documents for real physical form (whether as a three-dimensional model or a constructed building, i.e., the traditional role of architectural drawing) would disappoint us. The three-dimensional artifact that would result could at best echo but could not contain, represent, or signify the content of these drawings, for the drawings exceed the existing cause and effect of drawing/building or drawing/model by a destruction of it. That exceeding sets them loose, unhooks them as an architectural writing from the traditional architectural drawing.[2]

The excess released by drawing stages a play of signs that subverts the classical economy of representation. Drawing becomes writing when signs refer to other signs rather than to things or objects. At the limit of this not-architecture, signifiers consume the signified and leave only a trace that is not a trace but is something like ashes or cinders that appear by disappearing.

The not of the not-architecture that Eisenman attributes to Libeskind is not, however, negative enough; nor is it sufficiently positive. To think the not of Libeskind's Not Architecture, it is necessary to think not non-dialectically. Dialectical reflection implicitly or explicitly translates the not by transforming negation into affirmation. In this way, negation is negated and the not undone. The challenge of Not Architecture is to linger with the negative endlessly:

> As the night is sinking on realities that have had their Day, one can still hear some lamenting a vanishing present. Others rejoice at the luminous perspectives—fascinating both as threat and charm—which emanate from the empty and endless. However, it is only when the processes that orient these transformations are themselves forgotten that consciousness is torn from its dogmatic slumbers by a return to the Unoriginal.[3]

The site or nonsight of the Unoriginal is the place or nonplace of a certain holocaust.

Libeskind is consumed by fire. Heraclitus, in whose name Libeskind writes his "Unoriginal Signs," is, of course, the philosopher for whom fire forms the "substance" of all things. Fire, however, is a strange substance; it does not endure or endures as what does not endure and appears as what does not appear. As such, fire is an impossible endurance, which is one appearance of the not. But how can fire be drawn? How can not be built?

The all-consuming not can be built only at the limits of architecture as a limit that is not *of* architecture. In 1988, Libeskind fabricated a construction named "Line of Fire" (fig. 7). In a text accompanying this work, he writes:

> Architecture ON line: line which traces a furrow by drawing a ploughshare through the soil and line which defines limits between things beyond which one refuses to go. Architecture TOWARD line: equalizer of day and night—reaching to make equal. Great circle of celestial sphere, which is not a circle, and whose plane is refractory to the access of words, which are not words. Architecture UNDER line: at the equator. Line under: UNDER-LINE. For just perceptible below the red line and submerged in white light is an inscription of architecture which does not consume or demolish. [AD, 38]

7. Daniel Libeskind, Line of Fire (1988). Courtesy Daniel Libeskind.

The line of fire is a red line, which, in Libeskind's words, is "The read line. The red line. The read red line. The red read line." This brilliant red/read line is shaped like a zigzag that snakes its way between two rows of vertical columns. The zigzag is transected by two discontinuous straight lines that are cut into the cubic red form. Within these disruptive slits, fragments of drawn images can be glimpsed. The Line of Fire traces a limit that marks the margin of a between that is not architecture. The red of the line must be read in many—perhaps infinite—ways. Red is *inter alia* the sign of sacrifice, the trace of blood spilled on the fiery altars of idols.

Z Ƨ

"I saw a point lying in its blood."

Z Ƨ

The bloody red of fire also recalls the bright red of constructivist constructions. Appearances to the contrary notwithstanding, Libeskind's wandering line is not an extension of lines of his precursors but is constructed to deconstruct what others have built.

> Architecture 1,244 degrees. Zero degree. Many directions with a single angle. Endless row directed to the spaces inclination between all angles. The end of right angles, of rite angles, of write angles. Bend along a fold.[4]

The inclination of the between marks the space that Libeskind attempts to construct in and through his diverse strategies of deconstruction. The deconstruction of the Line of Fire faults the metaphysical foundation of classical as well as modern architecture. Repeating the Heideggerian gesture repeated in Derrida's *différance,* Libeskind's deformed forms figure the erasure of Being itself.

> The remainder of this treatise is wanting:

> I shall not consider the actions and passions of men as if they were a matter of lines, surfaces, and volumes. I shall consider these as Spinoza's secret rendezvous with Humanism's ghost: inscribing in the diamond the taste for a one-room house.

> Entering the hallway, one is confronted by an architecture of weird and commanding beauty, the baffling intricacy of its fearless design. . . .

> At moments of fatigue, however, one no longer looks ahead but laterally, cancelling the depth of the whole by a line that connects the two uprights with a lintel.

> In short, we ordinarily find it impossible to align the axes of perception with Adam's rib.

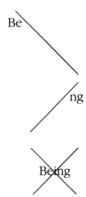

[*NI*]

The crossing of the line opens a transgressive space in which building is building not.

The Line of Fire implies but does not realize an architecture turned to ash whose trace is nothing other than cinders. In his mournful text *Feu la cendre,* Derrida avers:

> —At present, here and now, there is something material—visible but scarcely readable—that, referring only to itself, no longer makes a trace, unless it traces only by losing the trace it scarcely leaves
> —that it just barely remains
> —but that is just what he calls the trace, this effacement. I have the impression now that the best paradigm for the trace, for him, is not, as some have believed, and he as well, perhaps, the trail of the hunt, the fraying, the furrow in the sand, the wake in the sea, the love of the step for its imprint, but the cinder (what remains without remaining from the holocaust, from the all-burning, from the incineration the incense).[5]

The trace . . . the trace of ash remarked by cinders. What remains without remaining from the holocaust? Which holocaust? Whose holocaust?

Z ℵ

Cemeteries, I know all your names, rotting in the abyss of the Name.

Z ℵ

On 1 August, 1987, a holocaust of sorts took place. Libeskind's disturbing "Architectural Machines" ("The Reading Machine," "The Memory Machine," and "The Writing Machine") were destroyed in a fire at the Centre d'art contemporain in Geneva (fig. 8).[6] Originally designed for the Italian village of Palmanova and displayed at the 1985 Venice *biennale,* Libeskind's "Three Lessons in Architecture" is a complex meditation on architecture as it enters what he describes as its "end condition." At this end point, the process of architectural production becomes more important than the nature of the architectural product:

> The three machines, Libeskind explains, propose a fundamental recollection of the historical vicissitude, in particular of western architecture. They constitute a single piece of equipment and are mutually interdependent. Each is the starting point for the other. The purpose of this equipment is to release the end to itself, not to take the end, but to release the end to itself. I think these objects in architecture are only residues of something which is truly important: the participatory experience (the emblem of re-

8. Daniel Libeskind, The Writing Machine (1985). Courtesy Daniel Libeskind.

ality which goes into their making). You could say that everything we have
is that kind of a residue. It is this experience that I would like to retrieve,
not the object.[7]

The residue that Libeskind longs to retrieve is something like a remainder that "remains without remaining from the holocaust, from the all-
burning."

Z Σ

Grief! Chasm!
Who among us will be able to describe what we know we have
seen hidden in smoke? What calls out with its deep haunting
presence, yet stubbornly beats back our eyes?
Ashes. Ashes.

Z Σ

Traces of fire, sacrifice, ash, cinders . . . trace as fire, sacrifice, ash, cinders haunt(s) these strange architectural machines. In a text that supplements his constructions, Libeskind writes:

> to offer architecture as a sacrifice to its own possibilities of making a text. . . .

> We built this machine in a small place without any power tools, just with hand tools. With no electricity, just with candlelight.

> During the procedure we agreed to work hard, speak only in "small talk," smoke cigarettes. . . .

> You may have heard of Giordano Bruno, the philosopher, the heretic, who was burned in Rome exactly in the year 1600. . . .

> I don't know where Mossem comes from, but Mossem is killed in Roussel's book by having a text burned onto his feet. . . .

> But then I discovered that St. Theodore of Constantinople in the seventh century was killed by burning an iambic text onto his forehead. . . .

> Angelica with the grid, who was finally burned on a grid as St. Donatella, at a particular date in the third century A.D. Well, there are forty-nine empty boxes. They have to be filled with ashes of unknown saints. . . .[8]

Libeskind's Architectural Machines seem to prefigure the holocaust that consumes them. The forty-nine empty boxes are, in effect, funerary urns for the ashes that are the remains of their own incineration.

> They wind up in these small shrines, funerary urns, and then one has the ashes inside of them. It is a ritual object that I'm showing you.[9]

The object of the ritual taught in Libeskind's "Three Lessons in Architecture" is mourning. Not just any mourning but an impossible mourning that repeatedly recalls a loss that can never be overcome, a wound that can never heal, a tear that can never be mended.

Who is mourned in this impossible mourning? What is mourned in this mourning that is endless? "All mourning," Jabès insists, "mourns, above all, God" (*EL,* 72).

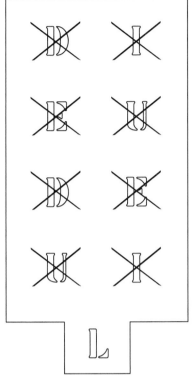

DIEU: God
DEUIL: mourning

Z Σ

Z Σ

But the mourning *of* God is not necessarily the mourning *for* God. Since loss is always the shadow of another loss, light forever recedes in the obscure darkness of an immemorial past that was never present:

Every experience of growth, consciousness, development of one's work is accompanied by the feeling of loss, destruction, and of passing away. When my work turned to ashes late last summer on the shores of the "dark city at the edge of the lake," I experienced a sudden perishing of my soul engulfed as it were in Fire. I also participated in the Biblical "leap" into that loss which thereby gains it: I became aware of how much the thought, deep friendship and mysterious inspiration of Aldo Rossi has meant in my life. . . . At this moment of illumination, I understood that my own path in architecture had been rescued from derailment by living a common idea with him: Architecture is for the Other. [NI]

131

The memorial to the immemorial is not only "Architecture for the Other" but is "Architecture of the Other" whose other name is Not Architecture. Where *can* such a memorial be built? Where *must* such a memorial be built?

Through all of his wandering, in all of his erring, Daniel Libeskind seems to have been heading toward Berlin. Berlin is his Jerusalem, which, as such, does not exist. Or exists as the not that ineluctably draws him toward its impossible presence. Born in Poland, Libeskind was forced to flee to Russia where he lived for more than ten years. After studying in Israel, the United States, and England, he has taught at many universities throughout America, Asia, and Europe. Orders issued in Berlin sent Libeskind into an exile that seems both unavoidable and endless.

ℵ ℵ

"Exile within exile."—REB SARDA

ℵ ℵ

Libeskind's return to Berlin, which was not a return, was not a homecoming intended to settle but a displacement designed to unsettle. Where else could this errant nomad unsettle? Where else could the wandering exile build not?

Few cities are more of a border—margin, limen, edge—than Berlin. Berlin is the frontier that simultaneously brings together and holds apart the differences that define our era: East/West, communism/capitalism, statism/consumerism. . . . For some observers, Berlin is "the greatest purely modern city in Europe." In an article entitled "Street without Memory," written in 1932, Siegfried Kracauer remarks: "'If some street blocks seem to be created for eternity, then the present-day Kurfürstendamm is the embodiment of empty flowing time in which nothing is allowed to last.' Its ever-changing facades, its rapidly disappearing shops and enterprises, are such that many of them 'no longer make the effort to create the feeling of a securely grounded concern but rather from the very first awaken the impression of improvisation.' "[10] For others, Berlin is less the epitome of modernity than "the first postmodern city." Describing Berlin "after the Wall," John Borneman writes:

> If . . . Paris was the capital of the nineteenth century, Berlin is arguably the twentieth century's paradigmatic space—every major social upheaval of significance in this century has either graced or scarred its surface. Wan-

dering along its wide boulevards and tree-lined avenues, beholding its bullet-scarred apartment facades set in relief by postmodern facelifts, I am always struck by how much history I see: not the history of other centuries preserved as in a museum, but twentieth-century history. Berlin forces one to "be there"—*Dasein*. The romanticism of Paris or the nostalgia of Vienna protect one, by contrast, from the vertigo of the peculiar imprisonment of raw, undigested present time.[11]

For the Nazis, Berlin epitomized the cosmopolitan degeneracy that corrupted the National Socialist ideal of *Heimat*. Representing alienation that disrupts community, fragmentation that sunders wholeness, and uprootedness that cuts one off from soil and fatherland, Berlin embodied *die Zerrissenheit* that plagues modernity.[12] Nevertheless, it was Berlin that Hitler chose for the capital of his Reich. With all the passion of an amateur, the führer developed elaborate architectural schemes for the city that was to be the center of his empire. But dreams of grandeur reduced this erstwhile mighty metropolis to ruins. More than one hundred fifty thousand Berliners died in the war. One-sixth of all the wartime rubble in Germany littered Berlin's once grand boulevards. Most tragically of all, between 1938 and 1945, the Jewish population of Berlin was reduced from one hundred seventy thousand to a mere five thousand.[13]

Libeskind's Berlin is more postmodern than modern. In an interview with Flemming Frost and Kjeld Vindum, Libeskind reflects: "I have, in a way, fallen in love with Berlin. As I think everybody who has no place finds himself represented in Berlin, and in that sense Berlin continues to be a very remarkable city in the world, with its division and its peculiar gap of history."[14] This love is not, however, without its ambivalence. When Libeskind reads Berlin—or anything else—Walter Benjamin is always in the not-too-distant background. Benjamin opens his "Berlin Chronicle" by recollecting his introduction to the city by his nursemaids:

> With them I went to the Zoo—although I recall it only from much later, with blaring military bands and "Scandal Avenue" (as the adherents of *art nouveau* dubbed this promenade)—or, if not to the Zoo, to the Tiergarten. I believe the first "street" that I discovered in this way that no longer had anything habitable or hospitable about it, emanating forlornness between the shopfronts and even danger at the crossings, was Schillstrasse.[15]

133

Such impressions run deep, leaving traces that can never be erased. Though Benjamin roamed ceaselessly throughout his life, the streets of the modern metropolis never lost their inauspicious air for him. Repeatedly insisting that Ariadne was never far away, Benjamin could not

deny that in the urban labyrinth he lost all sense of direction. On in-
hospitable streets that emanate forlornness, homelessness becomes a
chronic condition.

Z Σ

> I feel that I exist only outside of any belonging. That non-
> belonging is my very substance.

Z Σ

Libeskind conveys his sense of Berlin in his extraordinary 1987 City
Edge project (fig. 9). In this design, which has not been built, the city
appears (if it can appear) as edge—nothing but edge, border, margin,
limen, frontier. A threshold that is nothing but a threshold leads nowhere beyond the between. This between is the gap that is the spacing
of Berlin. In this spacing, the other that Berlin has long repressed returns. Exposing the gap that is the wound of German history, Libeskind
comments:

> I believe the Holocaust is not something you can get away from. The
> placelessness should not be bemoaned. . . . How do you grasp empti-
> ness? . . . Architecture is getting more obscure, and like the human quest
> will get completely lost. . . . Don't seek to find your way out, but rather
> your way in.[16]

Not here, not there, and yet not nowhere. To build (in) the placeless
place of the gap, it is necessary to construct otherwise by building not.

The City Edge project is a residential and office complex for the
Tiergarten district of Berlin. Its defining feature is a colossal bar that
emerges at an inclined angle along the Flottwellstrasse. This structure,
which houses offices and residences, rises from ground level to a ten-
story elevation overlooking what was at the time the Berlin Wall. In
designing this stunning complex, Libeskind draws freely on the constructivist use of tilted bars, slanting supports, and irregular angles.
When set in the context of the greater metropolitan area, it becomes
clear that this bar repeats the motif of the Wall, which, for decades, had
given not only Berlin but the entire world its sociopolitical identity.
Along the margin of Libeskind's City Edge, one discovers that Berlin
forms something like the limit of the Western as well as the Eastern
world.

Libeskind's repetition of the Wall, however, is neither simple nor
straightforward. To the contrary, he uses the structure of the wall to
subvert the ideology of the Wall. "The project exploits the logic of the

wall, the violent slicing up of territory. The bar is an abstraction of the wall, slicing through the city, breaking fragments off the city structure. But then it subverts the logic of the wall by lifting itself up and creating a new public street below. It becomes a device for breaking down rather than establishing them."[17] By turning the wall against itself in multiple foldings and refoldings, Libeskind effectively deconstructs the binary logic of either/or, which grounds oppositions that can never be mediated: "The wall is further transformed by being broken into pieces, which are then twisted against each other. At one end of the site, a pile of smaller, solid bars is assembled; at the other, the main bar competes against its shadow, which is cut into the ground. The wall is thus made to cross over itself many times in ways that conflict with its ability simply to define enclosure."[18]

The subversion of the oppositional logic of the wall involves not only the relation between building and context but extends "inside" the structure itself. The interior space of the bar is neither regular nor homogeneous (fig. 10). The bar, which refigures the edge of the Wall, is itself a montage of edges. In the design for City Edge, structure is decentered as if from within by multiple exteriors that cannot be integrated to form a coherent whole. The interior of the bar is comprised of irregular and fragmented spaces that clash and conflict with each other. Paradoxically, this inward dehiscence does not destroy structure but is a condition of its very possibility. Within the heterogeneous spacing of this bar, order and chaos are neither binary nor dialectical opposites but conform to a third yet unnamed and perhaps unnameable logic or alogic.

As Libeskind folds and refolds the structures with which he works, the excessive complexity of his vision begins to emerge. City Edge is, in Kurt Foster's apt phrase, "a project of daunting otherness." The otherness of this project is the trace of the altarity that pursues Libeskind. In the drawings and models for City Edge, Libeskind unleashes a chain of signifiers that is virtually infinite. Through this endless play of signs, he suggests the scope and the stakes of his interrogation of modern architecture. City Edge is suspended between the architecture of Albert Speer and Mies van der Rohe:

> *Erased line: Historical Axis. A public space:* Edge, limit, delusion, Speer's ordered disorder. . . .
> *The Fulcrum: 23 Am Karlsbad. A monument in the park:* A turning point. Crisis toward which possibilities return in order to revolve in an invisible lever. Proposal for the Fulcrum of Universal Ideals. Chiasm of di-

136

9–10. Daniel Libeskind, Berlin, City Edge (1987). Courtesy Daniel Libeskind.

rection whereby an X grounds itself in the sky. Mies van der Rohe hanging pieces of glass outside of his window in order to study their reflections. [*AD*, 27]

Though the architects of the Reich found modern art and architecture degenerate, there is nonetheless a disturbing complicity between certain strands of modernism and fascism. The point is not simply that some of the leading modernists were drawn to fascism but that the desires of modernism and the longing of fascism meet in the struggle to overcome multiple dimensions of *Zerrissenheit*. For those who see homelessness and exile as the disease of the modern era, the wandering Jew appears to pollute the polis and hence must be purged.

Z   Ƨ

"The wall," he also said, "is not in front of us, but inside. There we must strike."

Z   Ƨ

This purgation, this repression, this extermination is the abyss, the void over which the modern city and the lives of its inhabitants remain suspended:

> Edge, limit, delusion. Speer's ordered disorder. Underneath the ground the city traces its own schizoid memory and protects it by insulating and covering the site. What is unforgotten cannot be eradicated, concealed. Opening unbuildable realms which stretch directly into the foundations, the block discloses a public space. By cutting off the presence of fragments, both the street and the area of building are reconsecrated. Reconstructing that which cannot be filled up, the site abruptly turns its own emptiness into an Archimedean point. [*AD*, 27]

Schizoid memory opening unbuildable realms . . . reconstructing what cannot be filled up . . . emptiness. This is the space of an unforgetting that might not be the same as remembering. The solicitation of the repressed is the unending task of Not Architecture.

One of the most remarkable features of the City Edge project is Libeskind's resolute unwillingness to succumb to despair. Having learned the painful lessons of the avant-garde's commitment to utopian dreams, Libeskind insists on the "Reestablishment of a City without Illusion." The absence of illusion is not, however, the occasion for either despair or resignation. The paralysis of despair can only be overcome by a hope that is realistic and as such does not deny the horrors that form the history of the twentieth century. This faint, fragile hope marks

137

the very limit of our world. Libeskind's deconstruction of the Wall opens the space in which such hope *might* survive:

> A voyage into the substance of a city and its architecture entails a realignment of arbitrary points, disconnected lines and names out of place along the axis of Universal Hope. Very thin paper—like that of architectural drawings, Bibles, maps, telephone books, money—can be easily cut, crumpled or folded around this indestructible kernel. [*AD*, 27]

Texts refigure the architecture that refigures texts to create a circuit that is not circular and thus never reaches its end. A kernel—an indestructible kernel—always remains. What is this kernel? Does the kernel exist? Is the indestructible kernel the remainder that "is" the trace . . . the trace of "what remains without remaining from the holocaust, from the all-burning?" Is the kernel a cinder, perhaps ash? Is this the cinder that marks the "peculiar gap of history" that is the "place" of Berlin? Is this the ash that is buried in the city's "schizoid memory?" How might one construct "a ritual object" to hold these ashes? Can a memorial to the immemorial be built? When? Where? At what time? In what space?

In 1988, one year after receiving first prize for his City Edge project, Libeskind won the intense competition for the "Extension to the Berlin Museum with the Jewish Museum." This time the project was to have been constructed. At last, Libeskind would no longer defer building. Though often frustrating, the delay, it seemed, had finally been worth it. If Libeskind's erring had always been heading toward Berlin, his lengthy apprenticeship now appeared to be a prolonged preparation for this particular project. It is hard to imagine anyone other than Daniel Libeskind serving as the architect for the addition to the Berlin Museum.

Commission awarded, plans for construction were set in motion. The ambitious schedule called for completion of the project in 1995, the fiftieth anniversary of the end of World War II. But world historical events intervened to delay the realization of Libeskind's building.

Z   Σ

"Waiting," he said, "is the point of no return in the dark which we hope will lift."

Z   Σ

With the collapse of the Wall in November 1989 and the eventual reunification of Germany, the municipal government of West Berlin suspended all building initiatives to free financial resources for the reconstruction of what had been East Berlin. This delay created the opportunity for Libeskind's critics to try yet again to sabotage his project. Precisely the strength of his proposal now became a liability. Designed to unsettle rather than settle, Libeskind's extension created an uneasiness that many Germans—both Jewish and non-Jewish—preferred to avoid. Nothing less than an international campaign of support, which was carefully organized and professionally carried out by Nina Libeskind, Daniel's wife, was necessary to rescue the project. In September 1991, merely one month after suspending all new construction, the Berlin senate voted to make a single exception to its building moratorium. Construction of Libeskind's building is now scheduled to begin in 1993.

The Extension to the Berlin Museum with the Jewish Museum is, of course, a supplement and, as such, displays the dangerous (a)logic of supplementarity. As a supplement, Libeskind's project appears to be secondary to a more original structure. But the construction to which the extension is to be appended is not primal but is itself a substitute for an ever-recessive ruin. The Berlin Museum is located at the center of the old city of Berlin on Lindenstrasse near the famous intersection of Wilhelmstrasse, Friedrichstrasse, and Lindenstrasse. Opened to the public in 1969 as a substitute for the Märkisches Museum, which was cut off from the West when the Wall was raised, the city museum is housed in a baroque building that was constructed in 1734–35 by Philipp Gerlach to serve as the *Königliches Collegienhaus* (fig. 11). In the early nineteenth century, this building was the seat of the Prussian supreme court and housed the offices of the German author, composer, and critic, E. T. A. Hoffmann, whose work serves as the point of departure for Freud's famous essay "Das Unheimliche." Severely damaged during the Second World War, the present building is a reconstruction that was not completed until 1967–69. The new addition to the museum will be devoted to the history of Berlin since 1875 and will include the so-called Jewish Department.

Libeskind names his project for the extension to the Berlin Museum "Between the Lines." "The work is conceived," he explains, "as a museum for all Berliners, for all citizens. Not only those of the present, but those of the future and the past who should find their heritage and hope in this particular place, which is to transcend involvement and become participation. With its special emphasis on housing the Jewish Museum, it is an attempt to give a voice to a common fate—to the contradictions of the ordered and disordered, the chosen and not chosen, the vocal and silent." It is clear, however, that Libeskind views the significance of his project as extending beyond a particular building to encompass the

11. Daniel Libeskind, The Berlin Museum. Courtesy Daniel Libeskind.

entire cultural domain. The questions raised by this uncanny supplement form an interrogation of the very presuppositions of modernity:

> The problem of the Jewish Museum in Berlin is taken as the problem of culture itself—let's put it this way, as the problem of an avant-garde humanity: an avant-garde that has been incinerated in its own history, in the Holocaust. In this sense, I believe this scheme joins architecture to questions that are now relevant to all humanity. What I have tried to say is that the Jewish history of Berlin is not separable from the history of Modernity, from the destiny of this incineration of history; that they are bound together. But bound not through any obvious forms, but rather through a negativity; through an absence of meaning of history and an absence of artifacts. Absence, therefore, serves as a way of binding in depth, and in a totally different manner, the shared hopes of people. It is a conception which is absolutely opposed to reducing the museum or architecture to a detached memorial or to a memorable detachment. A conception, rather, which reintegrates Jewish/Berlin history through the unhealable wound of faith, which, in the words of Thomas Aquinas, is the "substance of things hoped for; proof of things invisible." [*CD*, 87]

140

Between the lines: ordered and disordered . . . chosen and not chosen . . . vocal and silent . . . visible and invisible . . . negativity . . . absence of meaning . . . wound . . . unhealable wound.

The zigzag of Line of Fire and the straight line of City Edge intersect in Between the Lines (figs. 12–15). Explaining the title of his plan for the addition, Libeskind writes:

> I call it this because it is a project about two lines of thinking, organization and relationship. One is a straight line, but broken into many fragments;

the other is a tortuous line, but continuing infinitely. These two lines develop architecturally and programmatically through a limited but definite dialogue. They also fall apart, become disengaged, and are seen as separated. In this way, they expose a void that runs through this museum and through Architecture—a discontinuous void. [*CD*, 86]

These intersecting lines represent two histories that are at once intertwined and discontinuous. The zigzagging line follows the errant course of Berlin and, by extension, Germany. If, as Hegel—who at the height of his fame lectured only a few blocks from the present-day museum—insists, modern Germany embodies the telos of Western culture, then Libeskind's twisted line actually retraces the history of the West. The straight line, by contrast, points toward gaps in this history, which are opened by an other history that is the "history" of a certain other.

The past fatality of the German-Jewish cultural relation in Berlin is enacted in the realm of the not visible. It is this invisibility which must be brought to light in order to give rise to a new hope and to a shared inner vision. Thus this project seeks to reconnect Berlin to its own history which must never be forgotten. [BL, 64]

These tangled lines can, however, be read in other—perhaps infinite—ways. By "rewriting" the lines of City Edge in and through Line of Fire and vice versa, Libeskind creates a structure that is all edge. Even more radically than City Edge, the edges of Between the Lines create something like an edge-in-itself. The extension, which might be an addition but is not really an extension, figures a wall or, more precisely, multiple walls. In contrast to Berlin's famous Wall artists, whose work required a preexisting Wall, Libeskind transforms the wall itself into a work of art by devising a space that is irreducibly liminal.[19] The walls sketched in Between the Lines are at least triple. When Libeskind developed his design, the Berlin Wall stood merely two blocks away. Contrary to expectations, the collapse of the Wall did not mean its disappearance. Scars—deep and lasting scars—remain. Libeskind's zigzag mirrors the oblique course the Berlin Wall once followed (fig. 16). In the interval between conception and realization, Libeskind's lines were translated from a mirror image into a lasting memorial to the history of the tensions that have defined East and West during the past several decades.

But Berlin's relation to the wall is more ancient and profound than its most recent appearance suggests. Like so many other cities in Europe and elsewhere, Berlin was for much of its history a walled city. The

141

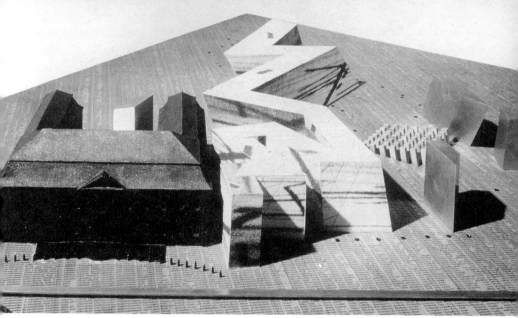

12

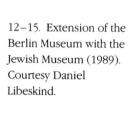

12–15. Extension of the
Berlin Museum with the
Jewish Museum (1989).
Courtesy Daniel
Libeskind.

14

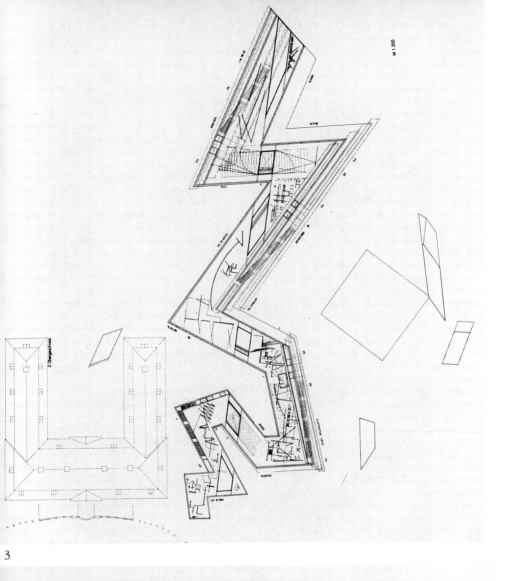

3

5

16. Potzdamer Platz and Leipziger Platz (1967). Photograph: Landesbildstelle Berlin.

ruins of this ancient wall lie near the walls of the museum. As one digs through the layers of the past, there seems to be a disturbing relation between the reality of the city and the logic of the wall. One is forced to ask whether there can ever be cities without walls.

Even before the construction of the Berlin Wall, the protection of the city seemed to require additional walls that were not exactly outside and yet were not really inside. Not all dangers, it seems, are external. Indeed, what are regarded as the most insidious threats to order and stability are often "internal." An internal threat is not, of course, internal to the body politic but is inside as an outside that cannot be incorporated and hence must be circumscribed. The line of circumscription outlines the wall of the ghetto. All too often, the Jew can be "inside" only as an "outsider" who is never at home. This is what renders the Jews so *unheimlich*. The walls that Libeskind figures suggest that these three walls—as well as others yet unnamed—are not unrelated to each other. To discern the interconnection of these walls, it is necessary to turn to the disconnection of the straight line that cuts through them.

The line charting the Jewish history of Berlin is a void. The spacing that transects the zigzag is empty—absolutely empty. Libeskind has long been fascinated, even obsessed by emptiness. Emptiness, he insists,

> is not a pure minus—not a deficiency as the idealists thought—but a play of new curvatures, curvatures eternally misadjusted to each other's hollowness. The audibility of Unoriginal Sounds—yet to be heard amidst the cheerful ice crackling around us—projects this immeasurable 'hole' of absence into a megalithic proportion coextensive in size with the head, the hand, and the eye. No one can be closer than that to the creator, while disremembering his plans for a uni-directional telecommunications center from which radiate signals that can never be retrieved. [*NI*]

Not a pure minus but not a plus, the immeasurable hole of absence constitutes the "center" of Libeskind's supplement. A "center" that is absence is an absent center that decenters the structure it haunts. The absent-presence/present-absence of the void is the not that cannot and yet must be built.

The void in the midst of the museum comprises one third of the total volume of the addition. Though cost-conscious politicians find this residual space wildly impractical and engineers and contractors constantly urge its use for anything from electrical lines and ventilation systems to heating ducts and plumbing, Libeskind resolutely refuses to place anything in this space. The void remains void. Useless, nonfunctional, excessive. The emptiness of the void extends and deepens the interplay of negative and positive space reflected in the zigzag. Though not immediately evident, Libeskind has designed the angles of the building in such a way that internal as well as external spaces form negative images of each other. Along the margin of these walls, the positive becomes negative and the negative becomes positive. The relation of opposites staged between the lines is not, however, dialectical.

145

There is no synthesis; unity is forever displaced, completion infinitely deferred.

The void, which is itself interrupted, divided, and fragmented, interrupts, divides, and fragments the seemingly solid structure of the museum. From the outside, the addition appears to be a continuous building. But appearances are deceptive, for the structure is inwardly divided. The broken line of the void cuts the convoluted line of the museum to form what are, in effect, seven separate structures. While intricately related, these parts never have and never will form a totality:

> The distant and the gaping mark the coherence of the work because it has come apart: in order to become accessible (both functionally and intellectually). What was, from both inside and out, never pre-existed as a whole (neither in the ideal Berlin nor in the real one), nor can it be put together again in some hypothetical future. The spacing is the sundering, the separation brought about by the history of Berlin, which can only be experienced as the absence of time, and, as the time, fulfillment of space no longer there. [*BL,* 64]

In Libeskind's uneconomical vision, that which is ever rent cannot be made whole.

By inscribing an exteriority within a structure that is apparently whole, Libeskind turns everything inside out and outside in. The "interior" and "exterior" of the museum are not separate but repeatedly pass into each other without becoming united. The play of inside and outside extends from "interior" to "exterior" walls. "Outside" the walls of the museum, Libeskind locates three further elements that are "integral" to the building: the Holocaust Tower, the E. T. A. Hoffmann Garden (with a Mechanical Garden of Olympia), and the Celan Hof. As supplements to the supplement, the tower, garden, and courtyard are no more and no less external to the addition than the addition is to the putative original structure.

The web interlacing inside and outside continues to expand until it entangles the entire city:

146

> I felt that the *physical* trace of Berlin was not the only trace, but rather that there was an invisible matrix or anamnesis of connections in relationship. I found this connection between figures of Germans and Jews; between the particular history of Berlin, and between the Jewish history of Germany and of Berlin. I felt that certain people and particularly certain writers, scientists, composers, artists and poets formed the link between Jewish tradition and German culture. So I found this connection and plotted an irrational matrix which was in the form of a system of squared triangles which would yield some reference to the emblematics of a compressed

and distorted star: the yellow star that was so frequently worn on this very site. I looked for addresses of where these people lived or where they worked—for example someone like Rachel Varnhagen I connected to Friedrich Schleiermacher, and Paul Celan to someone like Mies van der Rohe and so on. I was quite surprised that it was not too difficult to find and plot the addresses of those people, and that they formed a particular urban and cultural constellation of Universal History. [*CD*, 86]

By triangulating the addresses of E. T. A. Hoffmann, Heinrich von Kleist, Rachel Varnhagen, Arnold Schönberg, Erich Mendelssohn, Friedrich Schleiermacher, and Walter Benjamin, Libeskind defines a star, which establishes the coordinates that situate his addition to the Berlin Museum (fig. 17). Drawing the city into the museum and the museum into the city, this Star of David depicts the agony and the hope that form the shared history of the West:

> The great figures of the drama of Berlin who have acted as bearers of a great hope and anguish are traced into the lineaments of this museum. . . . They spiritually affirm the permanent human tension that is polarized between the impossibility of System and the impossibility of giving up the search for a high order. Tragic premonition (Kleist), sublimated assimilation (Varnhagen), inadequate ideology (Benjamin), mad science (Hoffmann), displaced understanding (Schleiermacher), inaudible music (Schönberg), last words (Celan); these constitute the critical dimensions that this work as discourse seeks to transgress. [BL, 64]

The transgression of Libeskind's architectural discourse creates the space in which the repressed can return. The return of the repressed opens a cryptic underground that has long been sealed. Libeskind's supplement not only subverts the opposition between interiority and exteriority but also calls into question the boundary separating below and above as well as surface and depth.

On a superficial level, the museum and its addition are unrelated; they seem to form two separate structures. But appearances again are misleading. The connection between "original" and supplemental is not obvious but is obscure; it is hidden underground in something like what Libeskind elsewhere describes as the city's "schizoid memory":

147

> The existing building is tied to the extension underground, preserving the contradictory autonomy of both on the surface, while binding the two together in depth. Under-Over-Ground Museum. Like Berlin and its Jews, the common burden—insupportable, immeasurable, unsharable—it is outlined in the exchange between two architectures and forms that are not reciprocal: cannot be exchanged for each other. [BL, 64]

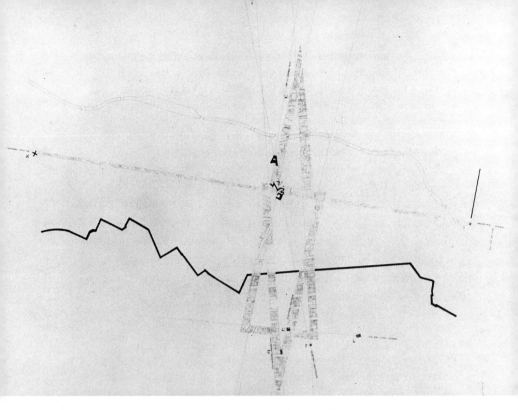

17. Daniel Libeskind, Extension of the Berlin Museum with the Jewish Museum (1989). Courtesy Daniel Libeskind.

From the outside, there seems to be no entrance to the addition. It appears to be tightly sealed—like some ancient tomb or crypt. To enter the new structure, it is necessary to pass through the old building.

The Berlin Museum does not, however, remain unscathed by its new addition. In the midst of the old building, Libeskind inserts an empty volume that inversely mirrors the shape of one of the negative spaces in the addition. This void cuts through every floor of the baroque building in a way that disrupts what had been homogenous exhibition spaces. At the base of the empty space, Libeskind locates a stairway that leads to an underground passage connecting the two structures.

In order to construct the subterranean stairs, Libeskind had to excavate the foundation of the old museum. What he discovers at the base of this baroque structure, which, as we have seen, is really a simulacrum, is not solid ground but a false bottom. The seemingly secure museum lacks a true foundation and rests on nothing more than a concrete slab. Since the water table in this section of Berlin is very high and the soil quite sandy, it is impossible to construct a firm foundation. The void that Libeskind opens exposes the absence of a foundation. He

148

digs under the base of the existing structure in order to sink the tunnel joining the buildings below water level. At this depth, the chaos of flood waters constantly threatens to engulf the fragile construction.

Descending the staircase, one enters a labyrinth in which no Ariadne can be found. The uncanniness of this labyrinthine underworld is deeply unsettling. Summarizing the etymological excursus with which he begins "Das Unheimliche," Freud writes:

> What interests us most in this long extract is to find that among its different shades of meaning the word "*heimlich*" exhibits one that is identical with its opposite, "*unheimlich*." What is *heimlich* thus comes to be *unheimlich*. . . . In general we are reminded that the word "*heimlich*" is not unambiguous, but belongs to two sets of ideas, which, without being contradictory, are yet very different: on the one hand it means what is familiar and agreeable, and on the other, what is concealed and kept out of sight. . . . According to [Schelling], everything is *unheimlich* that ought to have remained secret and hidden but has come to light. [U, 224–25]

Freud develops his interpretation of the uncanny through an inventive reading of "'The Sand-Man,'" in Hoffmann's *Nachtstücken,* which contains the original of Olympia, the doll that appears in the first act of Offenbach's opera, *The Tales of Hoffmann*" (U, 227). As his analysis unfolds, Freud associates the uncanny most closely with two phenomena: blindness and what he describes as "the theme of the 'double.'" Though Freud consistently correlates blindness with castration, the etymological affiliation between *das Unheimliche* and "what is concealed and kept out of sight" suggests a more comprehensive relation between the uncanny and a certain invisibility, which might be the unconscious itself. From a psychoanalytic perspective, the underground of the museum is the repressed unconscious of German history and culture:

> The new extension is conceived as an emblem. The invisible has made itself apparent as the Void, and the not visible. Void/Invisible: these structural features have been gathered in this space of the City and laid bare. An Architecture where the unnamed remains: the names keep still. [BL, 64]

When blindness becomes uncanny, the absence of sight yields insight into the invisible void. In this void, the unnamed remains and names keep still. How can the void become apparent? How can one see the invisible? What is the name of the unnameable? Whose names are inscribed in the dis-place of emptiness?

The uncanny entails not only blindness but also doubleness. Libeskind's deconstruction of the museum is irreducibly duplicitous. The

149

void doubles the museum and the museum doubles the void. Though apparently the shadow of life, the duplicity of the double actually figures death:

> For the 'double' was originally an insurance against the destruction of the ego, an 'energetic denial of the power of death,' as Rank says; and probably the 'immortal soul' was the first 'double' of the body.... Such ideas, however, have sprung from the soil of unbounded self-love, from the primary narcissism that dominates the mind of the child and of primitive man. But when this stage has been surmounted, the 'double' reverses its aspect. From having been an assurance of immortality, it becomes the uncanny harbinger of death. [U, 235]

Which death? Whose death is memorialized by the crypt that undercuts the foundation of Berlin's past and interrupts the course of German history?

Libeskind's underground is utterly disorienting; it is a maze that seems to have no exit and hence no (final) solution.

Z Σ

So far this path has been a series of detours of unclear comings and goings. But here I am, all of a sudden, trying point by point and step by step to go over its course in my mind, that is to say, trying to go back to a period of writing, to a past of symbols for which I was not entirely responsible, but of which I was attributed a share. So that, whether I started from a place I had chosen or from where I happened to be (without really knowing how I had gotten there), each of my departures was from a different point of the space granted the book. Place of all places, anchored in the void.

Z Σ

The floor is slanted to create the sensation of an unstable ground; the corridors, which serve as exhibition space, twist and turn in odd and unexpected ways. There are no right angles in this strange space. Though it is impossible to get one's bearings when caught in the midst of the maze, Libeskind's drawings make it clear that the underground is structured by three axes. The main axis of the building is intersected by two axes that form an elongated X. The shape of the X that divides the building repeats precisely the X with which Schönberg finished or failed to finish *Moses and Aron*.

The Jewish collection of the Berlin Museum will be shown only in the underground labyrinth and on the walls of the sealed void that severs the dominant zigzag structure. By restricting the display of Jewish history to the underground and the discontinuous straight line that interrupts the story of Berlin, Libeskind attempts to make the invisible visible without completely erasing its invisibility. The two axes of the X represent the two poles of Jewish history. Surreptitiously establishing a link between inside and outside, Libeskind's disruptive X charts the course to both the Holocaust and the Promised Land.

Beyond the "outer" wall of the museum stands a twenty-two-meter tower whose irregular angular shape is the reverse image of the negative space that forms the void inside the old museum structure. This is the Holocaust Tower, which is dedicated to Schönberg. Doubling that is redoubled, negations that are negated, reversals that are reversed create a vertigo that removes the ground from beneath one's feet. At the end of a long subterranean passage, one enters a vast empty space that extends upward for more than five stories. There is nothing in this void except five enormous "veils" that stretch from the top of the structure to several meters above the floor. To apprehend this play of veils, it is necessary to rise a few steps above ground level and look upward. As one gazes into the darkness of the Tower, the silence of the void echoes in one's ears. How are these unsettling sounds of silence to be read?

Freud concludes his examination of the etymology of *uncanny* with an unexpected reference to the divine. "'*Unheimlich*,' [Schelling] notes, '*is the name for everything that ought to have remained . . . secret and hidden but has come to light.*'—'To veil the divine, to surround it with a certain *Unheimlichkeit*'" (U, 224). To strip away the uncanny veil behind which the divine withdraws was the lifelong ambition of Schönberg. Throughout his musical career, Schönberg was obsessed with the problem of the relationship between form and formlessness, speech and silence, the visible and the invisible, image and the unimaginable, and name and the unnameable. He set for himself the impossible task of using sound to allow silence to speak. Raised an agnostic Jew and baptized a Protestant in 1898, Schönberg returned to the Judaism that provided the inspiration for his art in 1933. From the time of his early *Harmonielehre* (1911), Schönberg struggled to create what Charles Rosen describes as "chromatic saturation," which, as Daniel Albright explains, constitutes "a new definition of consonance; the ear takes a certain satisfaction in the filling-out, the movement of sounds in the

151

direction of a chromatic blur, all the twelve notes played at once, the musical analogue of white light."[20] The white light of this chromatic blur is intended to create a "plenum of sound" that allows one to "hear" the silence of the Invisible.

But Schönberg always remained suspicious of his own artistic desires and accomplishments, for he was extremely sensitive to the problem that lies at the heart of the Jewish religious imagination: Can any means of representation ever be adequate to present the unrepresentable? The tension between representation and the unrepresentable reaches its climax in Schönberg's most powerful work, *Moses and Aron*. The opera begins with Moses standing beside the burning bush proclaiming: "Single, elemental, omnipresent, invisible, and unrepresentable God!" Chosen to convey a message that cannot be conveyed, Moses resists the call of the Other. But the Other is unavoidable; Moses is destined to struggle and fail to say the unsayable:

> *Aron:* O shape of highest fantasy, how it thanks you that you charm it into image!
> *Moses:* No image can give you an image of the unimaginable.

Moses' dilemma is, of course, Schönberg's own. In his effort to sound silence, he finds every not(e) a golden calf. In the end, the composer is forced to confront the undeniable impossibility of his task. Moses speaks for Schönberg:

> Thus I have myself made an image, false, as an image must be! Thus I am defeated. Thus everything that I had thought was madness, and cannot, must not, be spoken. O Word, thou Word, that I lack!

> O Word
> Thou Word
> That I lack!

When haunted by the unnameable, the only way to speak is to speak not.

Libeskind, who studied music in Israel and turned away from a very promising career as a concert pianist to pursue architecture, is wary of Schönberg's desire to strip away the veils that obscure altarity. Having lived through the pain of the Holocaust, Libeskind realizes that the white light of pure sound can also carry the shadow of a fire that is less than divine. As Schönberg's famous pupil Anton Webern declared: "The further one presses forward, the greater becomes the identity of everything."[21] But as identity approaches, difference withdraws. When identity becomes absolute, difference is consumed, leaving only the trace of ash and, perhaps, a cinder. The fullness that attracts also repels. "Architecture," Libeskind maintains, "makes visible the *horror pleni.*"[22] To figure this horror, Libeskind de-signs Schönberg's lack in an architecture that is Not Architecture.

Schönberg's *X* is duplicitous; it both implies the white light of the ovens and points toward the guiding light of the desert.

Z   Χ

Maybe the desert is the pulverized beyond of the question: at the same time its disproportionate humiliation and triumph.

Z   Χ

At the end of the path, which begins in the void of the groundless museum, lies the E. T. A. Hoffmann Garden. This is a Garden that is not a garden in any traditional sense of the term. If the Kingdom is the recovery of the Garden, then, in the errant course that Libeskind plots, the return is not a return or is a return with (a) difference. The Garden is not secure but is precariously located beyond the limit of the museum. Pitched at an angle that goes from below water level to above ground level, the fragile Garden constantly threatens to slip away. For the moment, the Promised Land is empty. It is surrounded by a continuous ramp made of Jerusalem stone. The inside wall of the border is glass and contains sand from the desert of Israel. It is unclear whether the Garden will remain empty. If anything is ever placed in the vacant place, it will be mechanical instead of natural. In an early version of the project, Libeskind proposed:

> E. T. A. Hoffmann plaza whose focus is the "Mechanical Garden of Olympia" this moving image of Berlin is projected on four planes, 49 cubes, 196 surfaces and 98 hidden facets. The spectacle is oriented for the benefit of the museum-goer, but is also accessible to the public at-large outside of the Museum and in the Restaurant. [BL, 66–67]

Even if the space between the walls of sand is littered with mechanical devices, its strangeness will not disappear. To the contrary, a mechanical Garden would increase the sense of the uncanny. In Freud's reading of Hoffmann's tale, it is precisely a mechanical doll, which is something like a distant relative of latter-day cyborgs, that is, at least in part, responsible for the creation of the feeling of *das Unheimliche.*

The space of the desert, however, is no less ambiguous than the displace of the *plenum.* Though the desert is the land of hope and promise, it is also the place of despair, for it can become the site of desertion:

153

If I say the divine has deserted the temples, that does not mean, as ruse of dialectic is always ready to suggest, that the emptiness of the temples now offers us the divine. No: it means precisely and literally that the temples are deserted and that our experience of the divine is our experience of its desertion. It is no longer a question of meeting God in the desert: but of this—and *this* is the desert: we do not encounter God; God has deserted all encounter.[23]

If absence cannot be negated to create presence, and emptiness sublated to generate fullness, then desertion is absolute. In this desolate (no)place, the not can be neither overcome nor undone. The double bind of the inescapable not turns sand to ash.

Z Σ

Above the labyrinthine X, at the precise *point* where the axes of hope and despair intersect, Libeskind locates the Celan Hof. Conversely, the uncanny spacing of a strange cross-ing faults the foundation of the Celan Hof, leaving only a groundless ground that secures nothing. The Celan Courtyard is an enclosure that is nonetheless "outside" the walls of the museum. Paul Celan, who commemorated his return to Berlin in a poem entitled "Oranien Strasse 1," married the painter Gilese de Lestrange. From her many conversations with her husband, Lestrange fashioned a mosaic that Libeskind appropriates in designing his courtyard. The mosaic of the poet's life casts somber hues that illuminate the space of Libeskind's Not Architecture. Much of Celan's most moving poetry was written in and about the horror of the concentration camps. Throughout this dark poetry, the image of ash returns repeatedly. In an essay devoted to Celan's work, Derrida cites several lines from "Chymisch":

> Great, gray,
> like all that is lost near
> Sisterly shape
>
> All the names, all the
> names burnt up
> with the rest. So much
> ash to bless.

As Derrida develops his analysis, ash becomes the image of "what remains of what doesn't remain."[24] As such, ash refigures the Derridean trace, which "inscribes itself only to efface itself" in a night where white light illuminates not:

Ash.
Ash. Ash.
Night.
Night-and-Night.[25]

The ash that is the remains of the holocaust, which consumes every name, is the trace of something that is both unnameable and immemorial and as such is always already forgotten.

The forgetting of this unnameable is a strange forgetting. The immemorial is not simply forgotten but is inseparable from a remembering that is not a re-membering and a recollection that is not a recollection. The memorial to the immemorial recalls a lapse of memory that dis-members. Inasmuch as memory struggles to take into itself what it cannot interiorize, recollection inevitably entails something like an impossible mourning. As traditionally understood, mourning is a healing process in which an individual works through the experience of loss. The end of mourning is the sublation of absence through which the self is reconciled to loss as well as to itself. There is, however, another mourning that mourns an altarity with which there is no reconciliation. Derrida contrasts these two mournings:

> Is the most distressing, or even the most deadly infidelity that of a *possible mourning* that would interiorize within us the image, idol, or ideal of the other who is dead and lives only in us? Or is it that of the impossible mourning, which, leaving the other his alterity, respecting thus his infinite remove, either refuses to talk or is incapable of taking the other within oneself, as the tomb or the vault of some narcissism?[26]

The mourning of the irreconcilable other is endless, for this other is not merely outside but is "inside" as an "outside" that cannot be interiorized.

The dis-place of mourning is the deserted crypt. A dark, obscure crypt that is something like an urn for ashes or cinders. But a crypt is never present or it is only "present" as what forever withdraws:

> No crypt presents itself. The grounds are so disposed as to disguise and to hide: something, always a body in some way. But also to disguise the act of hiding and to hide the disguise: the crypt hides as it holds. . . . The crypt is thus not a natural place, but the striking history of an artifice, an *architecture,* and artifact: of a place *comprehended* within another but rigorously separate from it, isolated from the general space by partitions, an enclosure, an enclave. So as to purloin *the thing* from the rest. Constructing a system of partitions, with the inner and outer surfaces, the cryptic enclave produces a cleft in space, in the assembled system of various places.[27]

155

The architecture of the crypt, which deconstructs seemingly stable structures by constructing a cleft in space, is Not Architecture. Libeskind builds not by figuring an unfigurable crypt.

To emerge from the underground is not to flee the labyrinth; rather, it is to pass from one maze to another. One does not enter the new addition to the Berlin Museum at its beginning (for the supplement has no beginning) but in the middle (for the supplement is nothing but middle). The initial encounter with the zigzag is utterly bewildering. Walls appear where there should be no walls, halls turn in unanticipated directions, rooms assume irregular shapes, and doors proliferate everywhere, usually in pairs that pose choices whose consequences remain obscure. Though its space is circumscribed, the void seems to be everywhere. As one follows the tortuous course of Berlin's history, it becomes ever more obvious that Libeskind's addition is about the void.

Z Σ

Against life I set the truth of the void.

Z Σ

The void is sealed but not completely closed. At carefully spaced intervals, there are narrow cracks and slender slits in its walls that make it possible to peer into the emptiness. Through something like a negative synaesthesia, the vision of invisibility allows one to hear silence. For those with ears to hear, the acoustics change ever so slightly as one moves from gallery to gallery. But between the lines the soundless sound of the void remains constant. By listening carefully and attentively, one gradually comes to understand that the Word I lack allows me to hear and speak.

The silence of the void is the name of the unnameable that is inscribed in the names of mournful witnesses we are called to recall. In the models and drawings for this project, names, countless names are inscribed everywhere (fig. 18). Libeskind describes the source of these anonymous names:

156

> I was interested in the names of those people who were deported from Berlin during the fatal years, the Holocaust, that one knows only historically. I received from Bonn two very large volumes called "*Gedenkbuch*"— they are incredibly impressive because they contain all the names, just names, dates of birth, dates of deportation and presumed places where

18. Daniel Libeskind, Extension of the Berlin Museum with the Jewish Museum (1989). Courtesy Daniel Libeskind.

these people were murdered. So I looked for the names of all the Berliners where they died—in Riga, in Lodz, in all the concentration camps. [*CD*, 86]

157

The *Gedenkbuch* is the "memory book," which, in its silent testimony, commemorates an absolute sacrifice. The names written in this book witness an ancient past—a past that always remains past and hence forever approaches. "The memory we are considering here is not essentially oriented toward the past, toward a past present deemed to have really and previously existed. Memory stays with traces, in order to 'preserve' them, but traces of a past that has never been present, traces that themselves never occupy the form of presence and always remain, as it were, to come—come from the future, from the *to come.*"[28] Names as traces . . . traces as ashes . . . cinders . . . what remains without remaining from the holocaust, from the all-burning. Traces of this ancient memory make it necessary to read (the) between (of) the lines of the zigzag Other-wise.

Z Σ

For me, the words "Jew" and "God" are, it is true, metaphors. "God" is the metaphor for emptiness; "Jew" stands for the torment of God, of emptiness.

Z Σ

Z's within *Z*'s, *Z*'s reversing *Z*'s, *Z*'s inverting *Z*'s—all cut by a line—an empty line that is a void. What is the point of the void—the void that is the point of Libeskind's Not Architecture? Perhaps the point of the void is nothing other than the point itself. Jabès opens *The Last Book* by noting:

> When God, *El,* wanted to reveal Himself
> He appeared as a point.—*The Kabbalah*

In an effort to translate this untranslatable point, Jabès writes:

> *(You arrive at a certain point, you leave, you return immediately: same place, same point, but you do not know where.*
> *Imagine everything beginning with this point. Around it, no cry which is not the last, no sound which is not the last to be uttered, no breath which is not the last breath.*
> *From this point on, we should be able to write and speak without words, from this point on which probably lies on the far side of gesture, agreement or truth, in the mute space death has hollowed out at the end of the book.)* [*EL,* 3, 20]

The point, like God, does not exist; nor does it not not exist. Always falling along the margin that marks the difference between existence and not existence, the point "is" not and not "is" the point. The not of the point can never be undone, for it is never present; nor is it absent. If, as Jabès insists, everything begins with the point, the origin is always missing and something is forever lacking. The point is the site of a certain concentration that eventually becomes unbearable. In this concentration, the appearance of the point is its disappearance. Since the point has always already withdrawn, disappointment is unavoidable. We invariably miss the point and thus our erring is endless.

The unfigurable point is (impossibly) figured in the void that faults the supplement to the Berlin Museum. This void is the not that Libeskind's uncanny Not Architecture is designed to deconstruct. The point of Not Architecture, if it has a point, not only echoes Schönberg's "pure sound" and, in a different register, Derrida's *khora,* but, perhaps more important, translates the "nucleus" of Benjamin's "pure language," which itself has always already been translated.[29] Benjamin's nucleus anticipates Libeskind's "indestructible kernel."[30] In his seminal essay "The Task of the Translator," Benjamin argues:

> In all language and linguistic creations there remains in addition to what can be conveyed something that cannot be communicated; depending on the context in which it appears, it is something that symbolizes or something symbolized. It is the former only in the finite products of language, the latter in the evolving of the languages themselves. And that which seeks to represent, to produce itself in the evolving of languages, is that very nucleus of pure language. Though concealed and fragmentary, it is an active force in life as the symbolized thing itself, whereas it inhabits linguistic creations only in symbolized form. While that ultimate essence, pure language, in various tongues is tied only to linguistic elements and their changes, in linguistic creations it is weighted with a heavy, alien meaning. To relieve it of this, to turn the symbolizing into the symbolized, to regain pure language fully formed in the linguistic flux, is the tremendous and only capacity of translation. In this pure language—which no longer means or expresses anything but as expressionless and creative Word, that which is meant in all languages—all information, all sense, and all intention finally encounter a stratum in which they are destined to be extinguished.[31]

This extinguishing involves a different holocaust—a holocaust of an other order whose cinders and ashes are traces of an other Other.

The nucleus of pure language, like the point, is never present as such or is "present" only as the erasure that translation is always performing in an event whose strangeness grows as reading becomes more rigorous. Not present, the indestructible kernel or nucleus of language is translated as the untranslatable whose very inaccessibility releases the play of words. The point of this nucleus is the lack of the Word. Another "name" for this wordless Word that speaks not is "God."

For Libeskind, responsible architecture must have a spiritual dimension. Concluding a recent interview, he confesses:

> Some sage said a long time ago that every day one should reach a higher spiritual level. If you do not, you are not really doing anything worthwhile. So everyone has to ask himself at night: have I reached a higher spiritual level today? If the answer is no, you are really in trouble. I think this is

right. But how does one get to a higher level after days and days of discussion of such things as water levels, fire codes, and cost deductions? One has to work not only on architecture, not only on objects, but also correspondingly always on oneself, to cope with these things. So, improving architecture is not a one-way street. Making it better means also to improve oneself spiritually.[32]

Various translations of spirit appear throughout Libeskind's writings, drawings, and models. But the spirit of his work is not the spirit that has governed the Western tradition. Not Architecture, Libeskind insists, "is not for the victors who have dominated architecture for five thousand years, but for the vanquished—an architecture for losers."[33] An architecture for losers is an architecture of loss. Libeskind's spirit is never whole and yet it is not broken—fragmented but not broken. *The Word* is always missing:

(Pirit spi Ritsp irits.)
PIRIT. Spiri tspi rit spi rit spiritsp irits,
Piritsp ir it spi Ritspi'r itsp-iritsp iritspi
Ritsp iri tspiri tspirit spi ritsp,
Iritspi rit spirit's pirit spiritsp.
Iritspir itspir itspiri tspi
Rits pi rit spirit spiritsp iritsp;
Irits, pirit spiritspir, itspir itspi,
Rit spirit spiritspir itspiri tspiri,-
Tspirits pir it Spiri't spirits.
Pirits pir its pir itspi ri tspi,
Ri tspi ritsp irit spirit spi ritspirit
Spi ritsp ir itspir it sp iritspir;
Its, pirits pir itspiri tsp irit spirit spiri tsp,
Ir itspi rit spirits-pi ritspir itspi ritspir.
Itsp iri tspi rits, pir itsp irit spirit
Spi rits pirit sp iri tspir.
Itsp iri tspir itspirits pirit spir
Itsp iritsp iritspirit sp irits.
Pi ritspiri tspi rits piri tspiri
Ts piri tsp Iritspi ri tsp irit,
Spi rits piritspiri tsp iritspirits
Piri tspiri tsp iritspirit spiri
Tsp irit spiri tsp iritsp iritsp,
Iri tspiri tsp iritspir itspi rits'pi ritspirit.
Spir itspiri tspi ritspi, ritspi rits pirit,
Spir its piri tspiri't spiritspir itsp,
Irit spi rits piritspi ri tsp irits.
Pir, its pir itspir its pirits pirits
Pir itspir its pi ritsp iri tsp;

Iri tsp iri tspir itspi rit spiri
Tspi rit spiri tspir its pir,
Itspi rits pir itspiri tspir, its pirits
Pir itsp-irits pirit spir.
Itsp iri tspirit spiritsp irits
Piritsp iri tspir it spirit spir.[34]

The faults of the text that wound the Word are infinite. In these faults, through these faults, the sublimity of altarity approaches. The sublime, as Jean-Luc Nancy points out, is "on the edge of all form or figure." This edge is the no place of Libeskind's Not Architecture. Though no form can contain it, no figure can figure it, no image can imagine it, and no word can sound it, the not opens the space in which form, image, figure, and word can be presented:

One must learn—and this is perhaps the secret aspect of the sublime . . .—that presentation does indeed take place, but that it does not *present* anything. Pure presentation, presentation of presentation itself, or presentation of the totality presents nothing at all. One could no doubt say, in a certain vocabulary, that it presents nothing or *the* nothing. In another vocabulary, one could say that it presents the non-presentable. Kant himself writes that the genius (who represents *a parte subjecti* the instance of the sublime in art) "expresses and communicates the unnameable." The without-name is named, the inexpressible is communicated: *all is present—at the limit.* But in the end, and precisely at this limit itself, where all is achieved and where all begins, it will be necessary to deny presentation its name.[35]

In the sublime dis-place of the unnameable, one discovers that the Z's of the zigzag translate the Z's of Zim Zum.

Z   Ƨ

"A point so small, and yet it holds the ashes of all other points," he said.

Z   Ƨ

The impossible point of Zim Zum marks the site of desertion that transforms every place into a desert. Silence . . . trace . . . cinder . . . desert . . . abandonment . . . the nearness of the remote . . . the remoteness of the near. Drawing . . . forever withdrawing. Desertion. As the place of interminable exile, the desert is the point of no return. In the no place of desertion, despair and hope struggle for the body and soul of every wanderer. The very withdrawal that recalls a distant past that was never present leaves open a remote future that creates the space in which hope remains possible. Conversely, the remote future that never arrives leaves the trace of an ancient past whose lack inflicts an unhealable wound that draws despair ever near. Between the Lines—between the lines of hope and despair lie the errant (de)constructions of Daniel Libeskind's Not Architecture.

Z Σ

Afterwords

31 October, 1991. I was only in Paris for a few days but knew I had to visit Arlette. It had been almost ten months since Edmond had died. They had been unspeakably close for so many years; I was sure she was silently suffering.

Her face had changed, as had mine. Mine older, more gaunt; hers lined deeply with traces of a sadness that could never be erased. The lines of her face echoed the weary melancholy of her voice. The apartment was unchanged. It was as if nothing had been moved since Edmond's death. The desk covered with books, pens, photographs, and stones—small polished and unpolished stones. A large folder labeled "Les revus importants." Flowers, freshly cut flowers, ten white and six red roses.

"You will not believe this, but only two days ago, I said, 'I must write to Mark.' I hadn't heard from you. Didn't you get *Le Livre de l'Hospitalité?*"

"No, it never arrived. The postal system is so unreliable. You *know* I would have written to you."

"It was his last book. Here, you *must* have a copy. He realized he was dying. Look, look how he begins:

> Écrire, maintenant, uniquement pour faire savoir qu'un jour j'ai cessé d'exister; que tout, au-dessus et autour de moi, est devenu bleu, immense, étendue vide pour l'envol de l'aigle dont les ailes puissantes, en battant, répètent à l'infini des gestes de l'adieu au monde."

"Was it sudden?"

"No. Yes. It's always sudden, even when it's expected. He was not well. You remember how we talked when you were last here with your father. And how is *he?*"

"*Pas mal.* It remains difficult. Some wounds never heal. He knows that. He is well but can't sleep. Nights are endless. Edmond often told us that."

"We went to Spain in December. There were so many events planned to honor Edmond—lectures, readings, exhibitions. We were to stay a fortnight, but five days after we arrived he began to have trouble breathing. I was terrified and wanted to return to Paris. But he would not hear of it. 'They are expecting me to be here. I *will not* leave!' He continued but was tired—dreadfully tired. He knew the end was near. Several months earlier, his dear friend Michel Leiris had died. Edmond was deeply upset. One day he told me about a dream that haunted him. It was the last dream he recounted to me:

> I was walking in Luxembourg Gardens on a beautiful spring day. A day when the chestnut trees were just beginning to bloom. There seemed to be no one else in the gardens. But as I roamed, I noticed an indistinct figure in the distance. When I drew near, the person turned toward me. It was Michel. He slowly raised his head and, as our eyes met, said, 'Edmond, I did not expect you so soon.'

The dream continued to disturb Edmond. He never said any more about it but I know he felt this dream was his future.

"Spain was marvelous. The people, the weather, the food. For me, not for Edmond. When we returned to Paris, I took him straight to the doctor who said that he must go directly to the hospital. Edmond refused. 'You know I will never go to the hospital. If I must be treated, it will be at home.'

"The doctor, who is an old family friend, reluctantly agreed. He told me that Edmond had only a few months to live. I was, of course, shocked—devastated.

"Though we never discussed it, Edmond knew his time was very short. During our first few days back in Paris, the medicine worked wonders. His lungs began to clear and he was able to breathe again. All of the children were away for the holidays, so we had many long evenings alone together. New Year's Eve he was feeling better than he had for a long time. We had a lovely dinner and stayed up to greet the new year. At 12:00, we even danced a few steps to the music of Louis Armstrong, here in the living room—here, *right here*. The next day, two Italian scholars called and asked if they could meet with Edmond. Even though he did not know them, he agreed to see them. As always, we had a light lunch. After we had finished eating, Edmond said that he wanted to take a rest. This was not unusual, especially since our return from Spain. I closed the door to the living room. When I came back twenty minutes later, he was dead.

"I did not know what to do. Only at this moment, did I realize that we had carefully avoided discussing certain things. Several months earlier, I told him that I wanted to be incinerated. But I was unable to ask

163

him what his desire was and he said nothing. Then, for some reason, I remembered a passage from *Le Livre de l'Hospitalité:*

> A ma mort—disait un juif—je ne voudrais pas être enterré mais incinéré: car je ne souhaite pas avoir de tombe, de crainte qu'un quelconque passant malintentionné n'inscrive, un jour, en lettres noires ou rouges, sur la plate dalle qui m'abriterait, un slogan antisémite de son cru. Je ne le supporterais pas.

Some members of the Jewish community created difficulties for me. Incineration, you know, is not permitted in Judaism. But Edmond often wrote of cinders and ashes. Fortunately, there were other rabbis—true rabbis—who were supportive: 'Do whatever you think is best. God will understand.'

"The service was beautiful—but not religious. I could not believe it; there were more than three hundred people there. Many I did not know. His remains? They are marked simply."

Edmond Jabès
Écrivain

"You know, Arlette, the first time we talked, many years ago right here where we are talking now, I, in my faltering French, made the mistake of referring to Edmond as 'un écrivain juif.' He immediately corrected me: 'Je ne suis pas un écrivain juif. Je suis un écrivain et un Juif.' " She said nothing but remained wrapped in silence, lost in reflection that had carried her elsewhere.

The silence was shattered by the ringing of the phone. While Arlette spoke, I got up and roamed around the room—pondering a painting of a scene from Egypt and reading the titles of the books that lined the walls. As I passed the window, I paused and gazed blankly at the street below. I was haunted by the image of Edmond and Arlette alone, so terribly alone on New Year's Eve, knowing—both knowing but knowing differently, not speaking or speaking by speaking not. And dancing together. *Dancing!* A few hours later, Edmond lay dead on the couch where they had been sitting, the couch that marked the space where they had danced.

As I raised my eyes from the street beneath me, I caught a glimpse of a window in the adjacent building. The apartment seemed completely empty; I could see nothing inside it. In the window, there hung a skeleton—a human skeleton. It was, after all, October 31st.

After visiting Arlette, I had planned to go to Musée d'Orsay to view the highly acclaimed Munch exhibition. I had been looking forward to seeing the woodcuts, prints, and paintings that had long preoccupied me and about which I had written from time to time. But, for the moment, I could not face Munch. Though I knew it was impossible, I needed a little time to collect my thoughts and myself. I found a café, ordered some coffee, and began to read *Le Livre de l'Hospitalité*. I met Edmond yet again in words he had left for me:

"Plus tu t'éloignes, plus tu me rapproches de moi-même—écrivait un sage.

"Ton visage dément le mien, car tu es l'étranger que je suis et nos destins, pour être identiques, se doivent de ne jamais se croiser.

"L'errance est notre lien."

L'errance... le lien... L'errance

Z

Σ

7

Adverteasing:
Forget Not

I hate silence.
—KIRSTEN J. TAYLOR

Capitalism has proven itself
more dynamic—i.e., Dionysian—
than socialism. Its essential
nature is to be out of control;
exuberant energy, exploiting
every opportunity, to extract
a surplus.
—NORMAN O. BROWN

Today . . . modern art is beginning to lose its powers of
negation. For some years now its
rejections have been ritual
repetitions: rebellion has turned
into procedure, criticism into
rhetoric, transgression into
ceremony. Negation is no longer
creative. I am not saying that
we are living the end of art:
we are living the end of the idea
of modern art.
—OCTAVIO PAZ

Kirsten's Room

> But there's still some mystery that we're not approaching. It has to do with the tearing of a picture out of a magazine and that picture having an art resonance. —DAVID SALLE

Some habits die hard—like reading and writing. Distressed by how little my fourteen-year-old daughter knew or cared about the world around her, I started making her read an article in the newspaper every day. As I expected, it was a struggle. Whenever I failed to remind her, she "forgot" to do her reading; whenever I tried to discuss an article, she resisted. But I persisted until one day when we seemed to reach a turning point. While I was engaged in the Sunday ritual that long ago replaced churchgoing for me—reading the *New York Times*—Kirsten called: "Dad, please don't throw out the magazine section when you are done with it." At last, I thought, a spark of interest without parental prodding. Putting the magazine aside, I said nothing but was silently pleased.

Later in the day, I noticed that she was leafing through the *Times* Sunday magazine and cutting out advertisements.

"Why are you doing that?" I asked.

"I do it every week."

"But what on earth for?"

"Because I like to hang the ads on my wall."

Without my noticing it, Kirsten had covered the walls of her room with signs appropriated from the *Times;* she was completely surrounded by ads. She had, in effect, created an extraordinary collage of images and words that was as startling and unsettling as many of the artworks produced in the past several decades (figs. 19–20). Almost all the im-

19–20. Kirsten's room (1992). Photographs: Mark C. Taylor.

ages were from fashion advertisements: Guess, Esprit, Banana Republic, Ralph Lauren, Benetton. Words and phrases were fragmentary: "If looks could kill" ; "Make the man" ; "Uptown girl" ; "So proper" ; "Guess who?" "Addicted to love" ; "Some Kind of Wonderful" ; "Eternity" ; "Dare" ; "Live it up." There were also Absoluts—lots of Absoluts: Absolut Appeal, Absolut Peak, Absolut L.A., Absolut Definition, Absolut Subliminal, Absolut Original, Absolut Warhol. Scattered among the seductive images and words were pictures of a few film stars and celebrities and several photographs of her and her friends. The greatest number of images by far were ads for the Gap. One in particular caught my eye: it was a photograph of Robert Rauschenberg wearing a denim jacket from the Gap. Though Kirsten had no idea who he was, it was as if she had unknowingly recreated a Rauschenberg combine or refabricated a Warhol silk screen.

I studied the walls carefully but could detect no pattern of association. Addicted to writing and suspecting that she would find it easier to

168

express herself indirectly, I asked Kirsten to write a few pages about her walls. Again, she resisted.

"Dad, get serious! There's nothing to write. Everything is there on the wall. It doesn't mean anything. It's not like there's any profound or deep meaning or anything."

Lyotard is wrong; postmodernism is not something we teach our children; it is something *they* teach us—if we are patient enough to look and listen.[1]

Signs of the Times

On 25 May, 1991, the *New York Times* ran an article entitled "Look Up, See Jesus, or a Lunch Deal." Under the headline was a picture of a forkful of spaghetti overwritten with the words: "spaghetti junction. W $1.29 LUNCH MENU" (fig. 21). The article began: "A lot has happened here since Joyce Simpson saw the face of Jesus in the forkful of spaghetti on the Pizza Hut billboard near Coleman Watley's Jiffy-Lube." Joyce, "a forty-one-year-old fashion designer, body builder and mother of two teenagers," was at a turning point in her life. Struggling to decide whether to leave her church and do some "secular singing," she asked the Lord for a sign. God seems to have taken her a bit more literally than she expected. Joyce recounts what followed: "The Holy Spirit simply said, 'Look up.' I looked up, and as soon as I looked up, I lost my breath. I simply lost my breath . . . I saw the Michelangelo version of Christ. I saw the crown of thorns. I saw the deep-set eyes. I saw the nose, the mustache, I saw just the total vision of Christ."

Eager to spread the good news, Joyce called the *Atlanta Constitution* only to discover that she was not alone. Many had seen Christ in the spaghetti. Word spread and soon hundreds began to gather to gaze at the sign for a sign. God, it seems, has become a sign; or, perhaps more precisely, the (advertising) sign has become God.

On 28 July, 1991, the *New York Times* published three photographs with the caption: "Crowds Gather at Billboard for a Glimpse of Light or Vision" (fig. 22). In Chula Vista, California, people became convinced that the image of nine-year-old Laura Arroyo, who had been abducted several months previously from her San Diego home, had appeared on an apparently blank sign. Pointing to a ghostly image, Luis Arroyo, Laura's father, declared: "I am sure that's my little girl." According to an Associated Press report, on the evening of 18 July, between ten and

21. Peter Schumacher, Christ billboard (1991).
Photograph: AP/WIDE WORLD PHOTOS.

22. Jim Wilson, Billboard (1991). Photograph: NYT Pictures.

twenty-five thousand people gathered to look at the sign. Some went so far as to insist that in addition to Laura's image, the face of her killer could also be seen. The sign, it seems, has become the vehicle of immortality. For the moment, at least, the sign of eternity appears to be the eternity of the sign.

The Ob Seen

PS: If your work were a religion, what would it be?
DS: I don't know why I say this, because I don't even know anything about that religion except through marriage, but I think it would be Roman Catholic.[2]

The history of twentieth-century painting is, in large measure, a story of the struggle between abstraction and figuration. From the early nonobjective paintings of Wassily Kandinsky and Piet Mondrian, to the work of Barnett Newman, Mark Rothko, and Ad Reinhardt, there is a movement away from image and toward pure form or complete formlessness. By midcentury, a reaction to what many perceived as the empty formalism of abstraction developed. When figure reappears in the combines of Rauschenberg and silk screens of Andy Warhol, it returns with a difference. The images of pop art do not stand in a mimetic relation to objects in the world but are representations of representations or signs of signs. The endless play of signs apparently inverts the emptiness of abstract formalism. Though not immediately evident, the relation between abstraction and figuration reinscribes the tension between the iconoclasm inherent in Protestantism and Judaism and the iconolatry implicit in Catholicism.

During the second half of the twentieth century, painting restages the drama of the first half. Abstraction and figuration again engage in a contentious conflict in which the artistic stakes steadily increase. Abstraction is pushed to its logical conclusion in minimalism and conceptualism. Conceptual art is an *artistic* reenactment of the Hegelian declaration of the death of art. The *objet d'art* is completely dematerialized and idealized as it becomes pure concept or idea. Through this process, art attains the transparent self-reflexivity characteristic of the Hegelian Idea and definitive of the modernist artistic program. By the late 1970s, art seemed to have reached its end; there was nothing new left to be tried. The question facing artists who came of age in the 1980s was how to continue making art without ignoring the theoretical and stylistic "advances" made in the course of the twentieth century.

In an effort to respond to this dilemma, many artists violated one of the most basic doctrines of modernism by returning to the history of art for insight and inspiration. This turn is one of the founding gestures of what eventually comes to be known as postmodernism. Though highly touted as a radical departure from modernism, postmodernism, in many of its guises, actually grows out of and extends some of the most important modernist assumptions. This is especially evident in the spectacularly successful art movement of the eighties known as neo-expressionism or neofigurative painting. During the late seventies, minimalism and conceptualism combined to create an aversion to painting among many of the most advanced artists. Attempting to resist the commodification of the work of art, artists tried to take the art object out of circulation by rendering it immaterial (conceptualism) or transient (performance art). Rejecting this critique, which to many seemed to leave art with no future, neofigurative artists like Georg Baselitz, Gerhard Richter and Sigmar Polke in Germany, and Julian Schnabel and David Salle in America returned to painting with a vengeance.[3] Instead of resisting the commodification of the work of art, neofigurative painters seemed to welcome the extension of the speculation that ran wild in the eighties beyond the world of finance to the art market. To critics on the left as well as the right, neofigurative canvases appeared to be little more than the junk bonds of the art world.

There is, however, more at stake in the return of painting and figuration in the wake of minimalism, conceptualism, and performance art than an opportunistic revitalization of retrograde artistic practices. As I have suggested, to artists attempting to find their way after the upheavals of the sixties, the very possibility of art seemed in doubt. In search of a future, artists in the early seventies turned to the recent past. Through a careful reexamination of pop art and exploration of some of the unnoticed implications of minimalism, conceptualism, and performance art, an artistic program began to emerge in which painting and figure could be revived in a way that is stylistically innovative and theoretically responsible.

In his classic essay "The Work of Art in the Age of Mechanical Reproduction," Walter Benjamin heralds the advent of photography and film as the revolutionary artistic media of the future. By the late fifties and early sixties, the period when most of the neofigurative artists were growing up, the scope and significance of the media had expanded beyond anything Benjamin could have foreseen. Though Rauschenberg was the first to use television and advertising images in his art, it was left for Warhol to make such appropriation the basis of his entire artistic practice. Warhol expands his repertoire of found images from television and advertising to photographs, newspapers, magazines, and film. Warhol's relentlessly ironic stance makes it impossible to be certain whether his embrace of media icons represents an endorsement or a critique of consumer capitalism. What is clear is that Warhol's iconography recasts the terms in which artists approached the problem of representation.

The critique of pop art's use of figure developed in minimalism, conceptualism, and performance art reflects a return to the guiding tenets of modernist formalism and abstraction. Though committed to what Paul Virilio describes as an "aesthetics of disappearance," even the most stringent minimalists resist letting go of the art *object* completely. Objects constructed to disappear and works built in inaccessible spaces (for example, the earthworks of Michael Heizer and Robert Smithson) are recorded in photographs, and performances enacted only once are filmed or taped. In other cases, the work of art never materializes but remains a written description or set of instructions for production. For all practical purposes, *l'oeuvre d'art* becomes the photograph, film, video, or text of an object that is never present as such but always remains absent. Indirectly extending these artistic practices, postmodern artists take as the "object" of their work the mediated image. The painterly sign, in other words, is never a representation of the thing itself, but is always a sign of a sign. This strategy of recasting figures that have already been represented is known as *appropriation* or *quotation*. The central issue in aesthetic theory and artistic practice during the eighties was the significance of appropriation and quotation.

For the artists who are committed to it, appropriation involves an implicit criticism of realist epistemology and an explicit critique of the notion of originality that is so important for the avant-garde. At least since the time of Kant, philosophers have recognized that knowledge is never immediate but is always mediated by subjective categories of perception and conception. While many modern artists attempt to break out of the grid of knowledge to establish an immediate experience that is self-authenticating and universally valid, postmodernists realize that consciousness is inevitably mediated by structures of awareness that are historically relative and culturally conditioned. In different terms, knowledge is always already encoded. What we take to be an object of direct perception is actually a fabrication of the knowing subject's constructive imagination. Every representation, therefore, is a re-presentation of an antecedent representation. Awareness is never original but is forever secondary to an origin that *cannot* be present. Instead of attempting to deny the belatedness of awareness in artworks that claim to be original, postmodern artists admit the inescapability of the network of images and language that constitutes not only cognition but the very structures of subjectivity. To explore the human condition in the age of postmodernism is to examine not only the mediation of knowledge but the mediaization of reality.

The strategy of appropriation is most obvious in the photography of Sherri Levine and Cindy Sherman. While Levine rephotographs photographic "originals," Sherman presents a series of "self-portraits" in which she assumes poses drawn from various film stills. Levine's and Sherman's images of images, however, are overly didactic and thus quickly lose their capacity to engage the interest and imagination of the viewer. A far richer and more subtle deployment of appropriation can be found in the disturbing paintings of David Salle, who is the most accomplished of the neofigurative painters. Thoroughly committed to the postmodernist critique of modernism, Salle recognizes the artistic potential and cultural importance of the images with which consumer society constantly bombards its citizens.

The genius of Salle's neofigurative art is its provocative combination of mechanical means of production and use of painting to create carefully crafted images that are hyperreal. Instead of using Warhol's method of silk screening to manufacture prefabricated images, Salle appropriates Jasper Johns's painterly virtuosity to create figures that are simultaneously "originals" and "reproductions." The sources of Salle's images range from the work of previous artists, often as reproduced in art history books, to photographs, films, videos, ads, cartoons, diagrams from popular science books, newspapers, and magazines—especially soft-porn magazines. "One might say," Salle insists, "that one can use anything, one can appropriate anything or incorporate anything in the scheme of the picture. And that it is the scheme of the picture that determines what gets used and how it gets combined, what gets overlaid on top of what. What determines that is simply the eternal meaning mechanisms of the painting itself. It is simply an aesthetic recognition that all material is fair game."[4]

Not only are the images in Salle's paintings quoted or stolen; he also appropriates styles and techniques from other artists and different media. Salle creates hyperreal images by projecting other images (most often photographs) on the canvas and then literally tracing the outline of the appropriated figure. His paintings never form a coherent or unified whole. To the contrary, Salle juxtaposes images and styles to create a heterogeneous space that resists totalization. Though his preferred format is the diptych, Salle frequently fragments his canvases in multiple parts that bear no evident relation to each other (fig. 23). Having been deeply influenced by the directors Jean-Luc Godard and Douglas Sirk, Salle's techniques approach the filmic. He cuts, splices, crops, and edits to create a montage which, though disturbingly dynamic, is, nonetheless, strangely frozen in time. The painters who most obviously inform Salle's styles are Francis Picabia, Johns, and, most important, Sigmar Polke, who is one of the leaders of German neo-expressionism. From Polke, Salle borrows the method of overlay, which has become his signature. In most of his mature works, Salle not only juxtaposes but also layers images to create a paradoxical coincidence of transparency and opaqueness.

Salle describes his method as involving the "promiscuity of image sources and stylistic sources." While his juxtaposed figures and styles are often historically allusive, Salle's appropriated images are always decontextualized and thus dislocated from any fixed or determinate meaning. Such promiscuity releases a play of signs in which free association generates constantly shifting meanings. The absence of hierarchy among images creates the possibility of readings that are infinitely reversible and finally undecidable. For example, in one of his most suggestive works, *Géricault's Arm,* Salle combines two hyperreal monochromatic images of a partly clothed female torso, a colored fragment from one of Théodore Géricault's paintings, and a brightly colored child's top (fig. 24). One of the female figures, who is cut off just above the mouth and below the knees, stands with arms raised and hands touching to form a space approximating the shape of the mutilated foot in the Géricault fragment. In the other female figure, Géricault's severed arm and foot replace the woman's head and arms. The child's top in the middle of the painting is brightly colored and sexually ambiguous; its shape both repeats the curved body of the woman and suggests a phallic form.

One of the most original nineteenth-century romantic painters, Géricault was best known for *The Raft of the Medusa* (1819). In preparation for his masterwork, Géricault did numerous studies of anatomical parts that took the form of grotesque severed heads and limbs. He also completed a remarkable series of portraits of mental patients. As if anticipating the postmodern method of appropriation, Géricault developed his painting technique by making copies of old masters at the Louvre. In the fall of 1971, while Salle was studying in Los Angeles, there was an exhibition of Géricault's work at the Los Angeles County Museum of Art. Salle obviously saw the Géricault show and filed some of the figures in his image bank. When the mutilated arm and foot reappear fourteen years later, the context hardly recalls the romantic ambiance of Géricault's work. Salle's use of images releases troubling associations of sexuality and violence that seem to have something to do with the

23. David Salle, *Pauper* (1984). Acrylic and lead on canvas, 84 × 106 in.
Photograph courtesy Gagosian Gallery, New York.

24. David Salle, *Géricault's Arm* (1985). Oil on canvas, 78 × 96 in.
Photograph courtesy Gagosian Gallery, New York.

apparently innocent play of children. Woman becomes a toy whose fate is dismemberment. But this meaning—or any other meaning—remains uncertain, for Salle creates the expectation of meaning only to frustrate it. The violence depicted on the canvas is repeated in the interruption of every semantic circuit of exchange. Commenting on his work at a symposium sponsored by the Institute for Architecture and Urban Studies in 1981, Salle remarks:

> I think that the way in which the work makes use of the past is not nostalgic. Rather the pictures have a quality of something being an accidental trigger to something which is beneath the surface. I think of the images in the paintings as the focus of an eruption, an eruptive focus, which is probably quite different from the function of classical references in Post-Modernist architectural theory. The images have a quality of things rejected which have come back in a disturbing way. The images are never criticisms. They are not critiques of the modern world. They are things themselves. The images are primary, even if they are used in conjunction with other images or are buried beneath layers of paint or other images. The fact that the paintings are literally representational, that they are representations of images, is itself not a critique or a response, simply part of the program.[5]

"The images are never criticisms. They are not critiques of the modern world. They are things themselves." It is not only, as Octavio Paz insists, that "modern art is beginning to lose its powers of negation"; many of the most important contemporary artists actually *reject* the power of art to negate. For postmodern painters, the vision of critical art is a vestige of the misguided hopes of the avant-garde. Salle goes so far as to proclaim: "I'm not interested in making a statement about alienation, or any of that nonsense." Instead of negation, which always entails a certain absence, Salle is preoccupied with *presentation*. During the early seventies, his appreciation for the insights of minimalism, conceptualism, and performance art led him to stop painting. Like many of his generation, Salle thought that art had come to an end. This did not mean, of course, that no more art would be produced. Rather, art had exhausted its possibilities and thus neither originality nor novelty was any longer possible; future work would be nothing but a repetition of previous innovations. In a certain sense, postmodernism attempts to make a virtue out of this necessity. If originality is impossible, perhaps repetition can be creative. By the mid-seventies, Salle was attempting to find a way back to painting that would allow him to repeat the past without falling prey to its illusion and mistakes. Describing the course he followed, Salle anticipates the method Kirsten used in making her all-encompassing collage:

About 1973–74, I made pieces that were just fashion photographs cut out of magazines and pasted on pieces of cardboard that were a color related to the dominant color in the fashion photograph. . . . And then I lettered the name of the photographer underneath in a kind of show-card style, and what I was interested in was "presentation," which I think is a more apt word to describe my work. I always considered the presentational modes as simply "what I saw," which I think is what got me back into painting. I sort of worked back into painting, via this obsession with presentation. Like, can you make a presentation of a presentation? Can you make a presentation without the thing presented?[6]

To be obsessed with presentation is to be preoccupied with appearances, and to be preoccupied with appearances is to be consumed by what *is* rather than by what *ought to be*. In the world of consumer capitalism, what is, is image. Salle concludes that you can make a presentation without the *thing* presented but not without the *image* presented. From this point of view, *the real is the image and reality is imaginary*. The task of the artist in the age of electronic reproduction is to present presentation by displaying the omnipresence of images.

But not just any image will do. As we have observed, Salle insists that "the images have a quality of things rejected which have come back in a disturbing way." In other words, Salle's promiscuous imagery frees powers of association in a way that creates the possibility of the return of the repressed. He explains:

> Things are what they are because of the way people are. The other idea, which casts an even wider net, was the linguistic idea of "the obligatory," that we're only able to say what, in a sense, can be said. We all speak and think and act within what linguists call the obligatory. I would say that a real theme in my work has been to get outside of that, or to address the possibility of transcending that, or at least making it so painfully visible that you can think about what the world would be like if that weren't the case, even though ultimately whether it is or is not the case is not even discussible. I think much art that interests me is about getting outside of oneself.[7]

What Salle calls the obligatory approximates Lacan's symbolic order, which, in contrast to the imaginary and the real, regulates desire by channeling its flow according to socially constructed codes. Lacanian psychoanalysis can be understood as a surrealistic rereading of Freud. Long associated with surrealist artists and writers, Lacan developed a profound appreciation for their psychological insight and stylistic innovations. Through disruptive artistic practices, the surrealists attempted to create an oneiric space in which the unconscious could present itself. While surrealist canvases refigure the space of Freud's consulting room, Lacan translates the art of surrealism into the art of analysis. Lacan's

179

nearly unintelligible lectures and writings are, in effect, surrealist poems in which he allows "the thing to speak of itself." When *la chose parle d'elle-même,* the obligatory falters and the impossible speaks or is spoken.

Many of Salle's canvases recall surrealist paintings. When the space of the work is the place of the return of the repressed, painting becomes the presentation of eros and thanatos:

> It is interesting just as an aside that I've started to become very attracted to surrealist imagery; the most recent painting has some quotations from surrealist imagery. . . . I think the consistent ingredient about the selection of images and what I do with them once selected is a certain kind of erotic poetry. That's probably the only consistent thing I can focus on. Now what I mean by erotic has direct relationship for the presentational. That probably is what makes my work my work.[8]

But Salle's presentation of eros does not exactly repeat the paintings of the surrealists and the analysis of Lacan. For Salle, *la chose* can never *parler d'elle-même.* The surrealists and Lacan use images and language against themselves to break the hold of the obligatory and allow the repressed to appear or speak in the full power of its *immediacy.* Salle is convinced that such immediacy is a modernist ruse that must be exposed as such. There is no access to the real that is not mediated by images or language. The return of the repressed is not the manifestation of the real but is the presentation of *images* that have been driven from consciousness by the order of the obligatory imposed in a given culture. According to the most important tenet of postmodernism, *there is nothing outside the image.*

For modern Euro-American culture, one of the primary figures of the repressed is the body of woman. Salle's obsession with presentation is actually an obsession with the presentation of the female body. The body, he avers, "is the location of human inquiry that one finds in my work."[9] Modern painting "begins" with the transformation of the representation of the female body. In Manet's *Olympia,* the dignified composure of the classical nude is reinscribed in the confrontational defiance of the prostitute. The flow of capital traverses the body of woman to transform her into a commodity in the freely flowing economy of capitalism. Salle's insistence on the precession of the simulacrum is even

180

25. *Opposite, top.* David Salle, *His Brain* (1984). Oil and acrylic on canvas, 117 × 108 in. Photograph courtesy Gagosian Gallery, New York.
26. *Opposite, bottom.* David Salle, *Midday* (1984). Oil, acrylic, and wood on canvas, 114 × 150 in. Photograph courtesy Gagosian Gallery, New York.

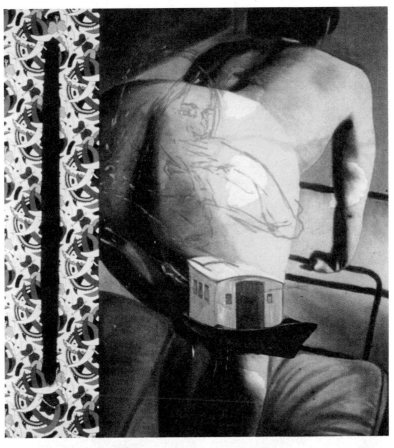

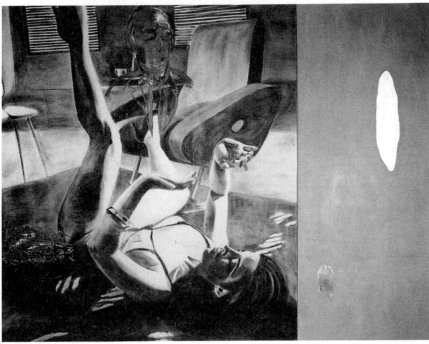

more transgressive than Manet's once scandalous work. Drawing many of his images from pornographic magazines, Salle presents the body of woman as the site of violence.[10] In Salle's imagination, eros is forever haunted by thanatos and death is always erotic. Violence is, of course, the death drive turned from self toward other. The first act of violence that Salle inflicts is the exposure of the other to the aggression of the *male* gaze, which is intended to penetrate, dominate, and control. The positions of the female figures in his paintings are consistently compromising. He represents women undressed or undressing, lying with legs spread, bending over, hanging upside down, kneeling, twisted, and contorted (figs. 25 and 26). In some cases, it is possible to detect traces of earlier masterworks. For example, *The Cold Child* (1985) recalls Picabia's *The Acrobat* (1949), and *Midday* (1984) is a perverse refiguring of Michelangelo da Caravaggio's *Conversion of St. Paul* (1600–1601). In the majority of cases, however, Salle turns to his file of pornographic photographs for his images of women. Nude or seminude figures rarely appear in direct frontal poses and are often approached from behind. In paintings where the woman is not turned away from the viewer, her eyes are usually closed or diverted, as she stares into the distance, or her head is cut off. It is as if Salle is struggling to avoid the castrating gaze of Medusa, whose raft we have already discovered in Géricault's work. In spite of their rich sensuality, these images exhibit a strange vacancy. The space of the other is violated in its very inscription.

There is an undeniable obscenity in this violation. By trying to expose everything to the omnivorous eye of the voyeur, Salle attempts to erase interiority by making all privacy public. When the penetration of the gaze renders everything transparent, the "ob-seen" becomes the ob-scene where nothing is left unseen. So understood, obscenity is not merely a matter of sexuality, but marks the end of the society of spectacle, which Baudrillard describes as "the Ecstasy of Communication":

> The private universe was certainly alienating, insofar as it separated one from others, from the world in which it acted as a protective enclosure, as an imaginary protector. Yet it also contained the symbolic benefit of alienation (the fact that the other exists) and that otherness can be played out for better or for worse. Thus the consumer society was lived under the sign of alienation; it was a society of spectacle—at least there was a spectacle, and the spectacle, even if alienated, is never obscene. Obscenity begins when there is no more spectacle, no more stage, no more theatre, no more illusion, when everything becomes immediately transparent, visible, exposed in the raw and inexorable light of information and communication. *We no longer partake of the drama of alienation, but are in the ecstasy of communication.* And this ecstasy is obscene. . . . Obscenity is not

confined to sexuality, because today there is a pornography of information
and communication, a pornography of circuits and networks, of functions
and objects in their legibility, availability, regulation, forced signification,
capacity to perform, connection, polyvalence, their free expression. . . .
There is no longer the obscenity of the hidden, the repressed, the obscure,
but that of the visible, the all-too-visible, the more-visible-than-visible; it is
the obscenity of that which no longer contains a secret and is entirely sol-
uble in information and communication.[11]

In this obscene ecstasy, the miracle of transubstantiation is extended
from communion to communication. The real disappears in the image
and image becomes reality. Salle's claim that his art closely approximates Roman Catholicism can be understood only when one recognizes the iconolatry that distinguishes Catholicism from Protestantism as
well as Judaism. It is precisely Salle's "iconophilia" that sets his art apart
from the austere abstraction and formalism of many of his most important predecessors.[12]

If, however, Salle's art is "Catholic," it involves a *radical* Catholicism
that presupposes the death of God. As I have suggested, in the culture
of the simulacrum, God becomes a sign, and, conversely, the sign becomes God. When there is nothing outside the image, transcendence is
absorbed in immanence and altarity is reduced to the same. The fading
of transcendence is the theological counterpart of the eclipse of the
interiority that is the last refuge of individual subjectivity. With the loss
of transcendence and negation of altarity, the possibility of resistance
recedes. By attempting to transgress the obligatory, Salle is struggling
to forget not:

I'm thinking of an art that functions as an accidental trigger rather than a
logical one. And that does have to do probably with certain things everyone has pointed out, like media glut, things like that. Like, ho ho, maybe
we really are morally bankrupt. And maybe it's fun.[13]

To become morally bankrupt by forgetting not is to negate the "No" of
traditional religion and morality with a "Yes" that *seems* to enact
Nietzsche's gay wisdom. But as Nietzsche realized and Salle suspects,
this negation is at the same time an affirmation. Through a dialectical
reversal, the death of God issues in the fulfillment of the presence of
the kingdom in the present—here and now. This presence/present,
which seems to point to nothing beyond itself, is the "object" as well as
the "subject" of Salle's presentation. To realize this presentation is to
enjoy the ecstasy of communication.

But Salle stops short of exploring all the channels of communication open to him. In the culture of the simulacrum, reality not only becomes image, but image becomes electronic. Paint and canvas are transformed into screen and light. In the video terminal, figure and sound intersect to create a *Gesamtkunstwerk* that accomplishes the avant-garde's dream of uniting art and life, even while ironically reversing the utopian expectations that once fueled the artistic imagination. There is, however, a darker side to the light that flickers on the video screen. As we will see, this darkness harbors a not, which, paradoxically, must and yet cannot be forgotten.

Communification

In a provocative essay entitled "Surrealism without the Unconscious," Fredric Jameson argues that "video can lay some claim to being postmodernism's most distinctive new medium, a medium which, at its best, is a whole new form in itself":

> If we are willing to entertain the hypothesis that capitalism can be periodized by the quantum leaps or technological mutations by which it responds to its deepest systemic crises, then it may become a little clearer why and how video—so closely related to the dominant computer and information technology of the late, or third, stage of capitalism—has a powerful claim for being the art form par excellence of late capitalism.[14]

As computers and video combine to create an electronic revolution, the currency of capitalism, as well as every other economy, is electrified. Both modernists and postmodernists have long been fascinated by electricity. For the painter Robert Delaunay, the global importance of electricity was figured in the Eiffel Tower, which was completed in 1889 for the Paris World's Fair. A decade later, the first radio broadcast system was installed on the Eiffel Tower. In a poem, composed in the epochal year 1917 and dedicated to Delaunay, Vincente Huidobro writes:

Eiffel Tower
Guitar of the sky

Your wireless telegraphy
Draws words to you
As a rose-arbour draws bees

In the night the Seine
No longer flows

Telescope or bugle
Eiffel Tower

And a beehive of words
Or the night's inkwell

At the dawn's base
A spider with wire feet
Spins its web with clouds
  Do
    re
      mi
        fa
          sol
            la
              ti
                do
We are high up:
A bird calls the antennae
Of the wireless

         It is the wind
         The wind from Europe
         The electric wind[15]

According to the futurist Filippo Marinetti, the electric wind heralded a New Age, whose arrival he proclaimed in his deliberately provocative Vanity Theater. For moderns, "born from electricity" and "fed by swift actuality," Marinetti envisioned a theater whose purpose, like that of MTV decades later, was "to wrap the audience in a thunderous sensorium, 'a theatre of amazement, record-breaking, and body-madness,' erotic and nihilist, whose hero would be 'the *type* of the eccentric American, the impression that he gives of exciting grotesquerie, of frightening dynamism, his crude jokes, his enormous brutalities." When Phillip Johnson places a monumental statue of the Genius of Electricity in the lobby of the AT&T building in New York City, his exemplary postmodern skyscraper, he does nothing more than extend the worship of electricity into the latter part of the century.

It was left for the leader of surrealism and erstwhile Catholic, Guillaume Apollinaire, to express the religious significance of the Eiffel Tower in words that ironically evoke the millenarian fervor with which many anticipated the twentieth century:

185

At last you are tired of this old world.
O shepherd Eiffel Tower, the flock of bridges bleats this morning
You are through with living in Greek and Roman antiquity
Here, even the automobiles seem to be ancient
Only religion has remained brand new, religion
Has remained simple as simple as the aerodrome hangars
It's God who dies Friday and rises again on Sunday
It's Christ who climbs in the sky better than any aviator

He holds the world's altitude record
Pupil Christ of the eye
Twentieth pupil of the centuries he knows what he's about
And the century, become a third, climbs skywards like Jesus.

The vehicle for the arrival of the Kingdom of God on earth is *speed*, which is made possible by new technology. In his "Futurist Manifesto," published in *Le Figaro* in 1909, Marinetti declares: "We affirm that the world's magnificence has been enriched by a new beauty; the beauty of speed." He confidently elaborates: "We already live within the absolute since we have already created an omnipresent speed."[16] The increase in speed creates the hope of breaking the barriers of space and time and entering a fourth dimension where it is possible to experience an eternal now in which everything appears *sub specie aeternitatas*. For many early twentieth-century visionaries, electricity held the promise of uniting the entire world of communications in a free flow of instantaneous information. What the futurists imagined, the telecommunications network of the late twentieth century realizes. Planetary communications systems create immediate access to information, images, and data in what Paul Virilio describes as the world of "absolute speed." As speed increases, time appears to accelerate until it comes to a standstill and everyone and everything seem to be suspended in the eternal presence of a *nunc stans*.

It is precisely this dream of the total presence of the now that Jameson believes is realized in video culture. By creating the sensation of "total flow" (Raymond Williams's term), video paradoxically integrates and fragments the experience of temporality in a series of immediate instants isolated from the past and future. Indirectly laying bare the socioeconomic infrastructure of what Kierkegaard long ago described as "the immediate stages of the erotic," Jameson argues:

> I believe that the emergence of postmodernism is closely related to the emergence of this new moment of late, consumer or multinational capitalism. I believe that its formal features in many ways express the deeper logic of that particular social system. I will only be able, however, to show this for one major theme: namely the disappearance of a sense of history, the way in which our entire contemporary social system has little by little begun to lose its capacity to retain its own past, has begun to live in a perpetual present and in a perpetual change that obliterates traditions of the kind which all earlier social formations have had in one way or another to preserve.[17]

186

Jameson's "perpetual present" is, in effect, the realization of Baudrillard's "ecstasy of communication." Though Jameson invokes surrealism in the title of his essay, he nowhere explains the relation of the modern ecstasy of surrealism to the postmodern ecstasy of hyperrealism.

On 24 February 1948, Georges Bataille delivered an address entitled *"La réligion surréaliste,"* at the Club Maintenant in Paris. Pierre Klossowski opened the discussion following the lecture by asserting: "You are Catholic!" Bataille responded: "I am Catholic? I do not protest because I see nothing to say. I am also everything one would wish."[18] Though Bataille's reply is evasive, his entire corpus is an indirect confirmation of Klossowski's insight. Bataille's Catholicism, which he shares with many other surrealists, is, however, as strange as that of Salle. In fact, the visions of Bataille and Salle are remarkably similar. They both regard the task of art as the solicitation of the repressed in which eros and thanatos are inseparably bound.

Bataille's appropriation of Catholicism is a dialectical reversal that establishes a *coincidentia opposiorium* in which differences collapse into identity. In this perverse religious economy, redemption is a function of transgression. "Transgression," explains Michel Foucault, who edited Bataille's *Oeuvres Complètes,* "opens onto a scintillating and constantly affirmed world, a world without shadow or twilight, without that serpentine 'no' that bites into fruits and lodges their contradictions at their core. It is the solar inversion of satanic denial. It was originally linked to the divine, or rather, from this limit marked by the sacred it opens the space where the divine functions."[19] The "religion of surrealism," Bataille maintains, resurrects the "original" link between transgression and the sacred. At the deepest level of desire, all human beings long "to live in the present instant." Always carrying a faint recollection of the archaic world that has been left behind and yet dwells within, modern man longs to return to the ground from which he originally arose. Religion addresses this primal desire through myths and rituals designed to bind believers back to the sacred origin. In his *Theory of Religion,* Bataille argues:

> Man is the being that has lost, and even rejected, that which he obscurely is, a vague intimacy. Consciousness could not become clear in the course of time if it had not turned away from itself looking for what it has itself lost, and what it must lose again as it draws near to it. Of course, what is lost is not outside it; consciousness turns away from the obscure intimacy of consciousness itself. Religion, whose essence is the search for lost intimacy, comes down to the effort of clear consciousness that wants to be a complete self-consciousness: but this effort is futile, since consciousness of intimacy is possible only at a level where consciousness is no longer an

operation whose outcome implies duration, that is, at the level where clarity, which is the effect of the operation, is no longer given.[20]

It is toward this obscure realm that surrealism draws those who dare to entertain its vision.

Following Nietzsche's interpretation of Greek tragedy in *The Birth of Tragedy,* Bataille argues that in the modern world, art replaces religion as the medium through which the sacred is experienced. Through the work of art, surrealists seek a return of the agonizing ecstasy that was once present in religious ritual. Art, in other words, re-presents what religion once presented.

The strategy the surrealists adopt to facilitate the return of the repressed is automatic writing and, by extension, automatic drawing and painting. Automatic writing, drawing, and painting are artistic appropriations of the method of free association that Freud developed for the analysis of dreams. By letting go of the control of mental functioning, the individual attempts to negate consciousness's negation of aberrant desire. Bataille comments on André Breton's method of automatic writing:

> The one who is seated comfortably, who maximally forgets what is in order to write by chance on blank paper *les folies les plus vives* that pass in the head, is able to arrive at nothing according to the plan of literary value. . . . What he has done is essentially an act of insubordination, in the sense that he has done a sovereign act; at the same time, he has accomplished what, in the sense of religions, would appear as predominant—he has accomplished the destruction of the personality.[21]

The accomplishment of the destruction of the personality is the realization of the intimacy that Bataille deems sacred. The price of art's success is the sacrifice of the individual. Anticipating Salle's projective method of painting, Bataille describes "The Point of Ecstasy" in an excessive text entitled *Guilty:*

> I'm going to tell you how I arrived at an ecstasy of such intensity. On the wall of appearance I threw images of explosion and of being lacerated— ripped to pieces. First I had to summon up the greatest possible silence, and I got so as to be able to do this pretty much at will. In this boring silence, I evoked every possible way there was of my being ripped to pieces. Obscene, ridiculous, and deadly thoughts came rushing out one after the other. I thought of a volcano's depths, war, and my own death. It wasn't possible any more to doubt that ecstasy dispenses with any idea of God.[22]

To dispense with God is, for Bataille, following Nietzsche, to confess the death of the transcendent God, who is always elsewhere. This death issues in the realization of the sacred *here and now*. In the postmodern culture of the simulacrum, Bataille's transgressive ecstasy is refigured in the electric ecstasy of communification. To move from surrealism to hyperrealism, it is necessary to electrify the painted image and printed word. When the obscene becomes the obseen on the video screen, the surrealism of the unconscious becomes the hyperrealism of consciousness.

Channeling

In postindustrial capitalism, advertising fuels the economy of consumption. But it has not always done so. During the Middle Ages, advertisements were associated with sacred texts and were designed to interrupt the flow of capital by taking works out of circulation. "In the Low Countries, books copied during holy days in medieval scriptoria were regarded as specially consecrated. A note placed in the colophon designating holy-day work served as a warning (or 'avertissement') against sale."[23] By what reversal does the *désoeuvrement* of the *avertissement* become the excessive investment of the advertisement? And what kind of transubstantiation of the sacred is implied by the displacement of a saving economy by an economy that requires expenditure without return? What is the profit of such a prodigal economy? Who are its prophets?

In the corner of Kirsten's room, not far from the Gap ad bearing Rauschenberg's image, she has carefully placed a collage that she made of one of today's most remarkable cultural icons—Madonna (fig. 27). Beside the images of Madonna and beneath her collaged wall, Kirsten has placed her boom box, which she has wired to the light switch. No light without sound; no sound without light. "I hate silence!" she defiantly declares as I repeatedly ask her to lower the volume. Kirsten and her friends sit by the hour *making* tapes of their favorite performers. They mix but do not match. As I began to listen more carefully to their music, I realized that they almost never play a tape by a single artist or group. Nor do they play the tapes they buy. Rather, they use and reuse what they purchase to make their own tapes. Their creations are never unified, coherent or consistent but invariably juxtapose performers and styles in no apparent order: Madonna, the Rolling Stones, Billy Joel, the Beatles, Cyndi Lauper, Simon and Garfunkel, Whitney Houston, Phil Collins, U2, Talking Heads, James Taylor, Genesis—but no Apocalypse, at least not yet. Cutting and editing, Kirsten creates a pastiche of sounds that complements the visual collage on her wall. She supplements these tapes with videos pirated from television. As might be expected, MTV is

189

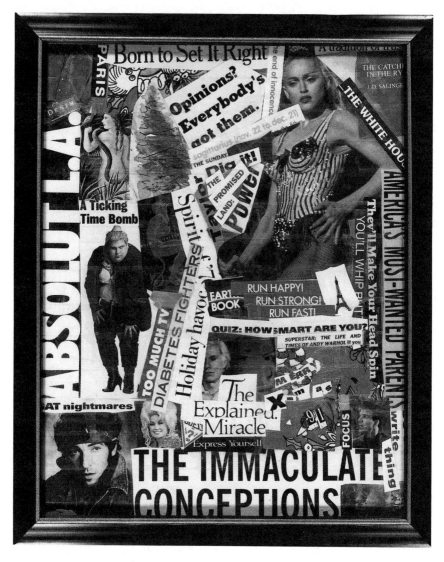

27. Kirsten J. Taylor, *Immaculate Conceptions* (1991). Photograph:
Mark C. Taylor.

one of her favorites. Though most home VCRs do not yet allow one to
edit as freely as sound tapes, the technology that will turn the living
room into a production booth already exists and soon will be generally
available.

Kirsten's practice of poaching extends postmodern strategies of appropriation and quotation. Her walls, tapes, and videos are hardly less
original than many of the materials she copies. The work of art in the
age of electronic reproduction is thoroughly disseminated, thereby

transforming culture as a whole into a complex *oeuvre d'art.* Though initially criticized for inducing a certain passivity, the growing sophistication of electronic media is actually creating a revolution by transforming consumption into production.[24] The postmodern art form par excellence is video and the reigning queen of video is Madonna.

In the summer of 1981, a revolutionary development brought together television, video, and popular music to create a new art form that continues to have an enormous cultural impact. Suffering severe economic difficulties, the record industry devised a plan to develop videos to advertise the latest albums of popular groups. Ads were to be shown on a cable channel that would be completely devoted to "visual radio." The result of this experiment was the extraordinarily successful music television network, MTV. As if combining Warhol's *Campbell Soup Cans* and *Brillo Boxes* with his steamy films like *Heat, Flesh,* and *Trash,* the creators of MTV carried commodification of the work of art far beyond anything the high priest of pop art ever achieved. MTV has even gone so far as to enlist the services of artists like Jenny Holzer, Robert Longo, and Survival Research Laboratories. In spite of the effort to erase the distinction between high and low art, music videos remain advertisements that claim the status of a popular art form.

In the decade since its founding, MTV has continued to grow. By the fall of 1991, the network had divided into three channels that broadcast to seventy-three countries. MTV is not only changing music, television, and video; it is transforming consciousness in important ways. In the world of MTV, word, sound, and image repeatedly intersect in a vertiginous montage that approaches total flow or pure flux. The promiscuity of images staged in music videos far exceeds what Salle accomplishes on his static painted surfaces. As John Leland and Marc Peyser point out, "this is a world without perspective: Paul Abdul dances with a cartoon cat; a clay hammer spurts from Peter Gabriel's clay head; David Byrne of Talking Heads is a child one minute, a face projected on a house the next. For the sixteen minutes—the network's estimate of the average viewer visit—logic takes a break."[25] When logic goes on holiday, other voices can be heard.

The most remarkable creation of MTV is Madonna. The responses to Madonna's excessively provocative videos have been predictably contradictory. Reviving longstanding criticisms of rock and roll, representatives of the religious and political right charge that the blatant sexuality of her music and videos is nothing less than demonic. Some

191

critics have actually gone so far as to claim that, when played backwards, the lyrics of the notorious video "Justify My Love," which was even too hot for MTV to handle, express a hidden message of Satan worship. According to the Simon Wiesenthal Center, the remake of "Justify My Love," entitled "The Beast Within," expresses anti-Semitic sentiments. On the opposite end of the religious and political spectrum, Madonna's work has provoked the praise as well as the ire of many feminists. While for some critics Madonna's exhibitionism acts out male fantasies by depicting women as "Boy Toys," for others her music and videos convey a sense of empowerment that reflects women's ability to take charge of their lives by turning men themselves into "Boy Toys" whose desires can be effectively manipulated. To millions of adolescent girls and boys, however, nothing so grand or profound is at stake in the antics of the icon of MTV. For them, Madonna is an extraordinarily vital performer whose highly charged songs and videos are nothing short of electrifying. The electricity she communicates carries cultural implications that reach far beyond the surface of the video screen.

Madonna Louise Veronica Ciccone was born in Bay City, Michigan, on 19 August 1959, the oldest daughter in a family of six children. There were two determinative influences in her childhood. The first was the death of her mother, who was also named Madonna, from breast cancer at the age of thirty. Though Madonna was only six when her mother died, she retains vivid memories of the excruciatingly difficult final year of her mother's life. When recalling her mother, Madonna repeatedly describes her as "forgiving and angelic." In one of the most moving and troubling scenes in *Truth or Dare,* Madonna writhes in a manner that is both remorseful and erotic on her mother's grave. Three years after the death of her mother, her father married a woman who had been his housekeeper. In an effort to describe her obviously strained relationship to her stepmother, Madonna frequently appropriates the story of Cinderella without the scene in which Prince Charming arrives.

The other formative influence in Madonna's childhood and youth was Roman Catholicism. As even a cursory acquaintance with her art makes clear, Madonna's ongoing involvement with Catholicism is exceedingly complex. From the outset her videos have been filled with Catholic iconography, and her songs concerned with religious themes. Though much of her work seems to be a calculated refusal of the faith of her youth, Madonna's very obsession with Catholicism suggests that something more subtle is at work than an outright rejection of religion. In a 1985 interview, she comments:

Catholicism gives you a strength, an inner strength, whether you end up believing it later or not. It's the backbone. I think maybe the essence of Catholicism I haven't rejected, but the theory of it, I have, if that makes any sense. I don't go to church but I believe in God. I don't say my rosary but I think about things like that. The thing that has remained with me the most, I guess, is the idea that you do unto others as they do unto you.[26]

As with everything else Madonna says and does, it is hard to know how seriously to take such a claim. It is always possible that she is suggesting an ironic twist of the golden rule: "Do unto men what they have been doing unto us for lo, these many years—Fuck 'em!" But the lyrics of several of her most popular songs suggest a more straightforward reading of Madonna's professed concern with ethical and religious matters. Some of her most powerful songs evoke memories of social protest reminiscent of 1960s folk music. For example, "Papa Don't Preach" deals with the problem of teen pregnancy; "Till Death Do Us Part" probes the horror of wife beating; and "Spanish Eyes" denounces the violence and poverty of a Hispanic ghetto. Not satisfied with merely registering concern, Madonna prompts her adoring fans to action. In "Love Makes the World Go Round," she explicitly recalls the antiwar music of the sixties:

Make love not war we say
It's easy to recite
But it don't mean a damn
Unless we're gonna fight
But not with guns and knives
We've got to save the lives
Of every boy and girl that grows up in this world

There's hunger everywhere
We've got to take a stand
Reach out for someone's hand
Love makes the world go round
It's easy to forget, if you don't hear the sound
Of pain and prejudice
Love makes the world go round.

In other songs, Madonna seems to adopt the values of some of her harshest critics. The most striking instance of this strategy is her re-peated invocation of the value of family. "Keep It Together" opens with praise for family loyalty:

Keep, keep it together, keep people together
Forever and ever

Keep it together in the family
They're a reminder of our history

Brothers and sisters they hold the key
To your heart and your soul
Don't forget that your family is gold

Madonna's preoccupation with her mother and obsession with Catholicism meet in her fascination with the family. In many ways, Madonna attempts to live up to her name by becoming for others the mother she lost when she was only six. Throughout the Blond Ambition tour, she tries to create a family out of the dancers and singers with whom she performs. It is, to be sure, a strange family, which is, in many ways, a parody of the traditional family. In the absence of a father, but the omnipresence of the mother, Madonna's family seems to be immaculately conceived. Whether in a gesture of devotion or mockery, the Mother leads her children in prayer before every performance. Behind the scenes, members of the family frolic together in bed in a way that draws Madonna closer to Jean Genet's perverse family and Bataille's decadent mother than to the divine family and holy mother of God. If, however, one follows Bataille's excessive reading of the sacred, the distance separating the purity of the angel from the impurity of the whore is less than it initially appears; the two might even be one.

There is an undeniable element of adolescent rebellion in Madonna's attack on the Church. Having been subjected to a strict Catholic upbringing, the word of the Church is, for Madonna, "No." Her rendering of the message of traditional religion is more negative than positive, especially with regard to the body and sexuality. Repression both breeds desire and creates guilt, thereby dividing the self against itself. In the eyes of Madonna, the mediator of the Church's repression was her father, and "the name of the father"—be he heavenly or earthly—was "NO":

> On the one hand, you could say that I am turning men into swine, but I also have this other side of my head that is saying that I am forcing men—not forcing, asking men—to behave in ways that they are not supposed to behave in society. If they want to wear a bra, they can wear a bra. If they want to cry, they can cry. If they want to kiss another man, they can kiss another man. I give them license to do that. My rebellion is not just against my father but against the priests and all the men who made the rules while I was growing up.[27]

194

Madonna's "Yes" is a "No" to the fathers' "No." In a song that purposefully obscures the identity of the Father, "Oh Father," she declares her freedom from *le nom du Père*:

Seems like yesterday
I lay down next to your boots and I prayed

For your anger to end
Oh Father I have sinned

You can't hurt me
I got away from you, I never thought I would
You can't make me cry, you once had the power
I never felt so good about myself

To negate negation by saying "No" to No is to free oneself of guilt, and thus to accept, indeed to *enjoy* oneself as what one is rather than as what the fathers say one ought to be. "No to no," she sings. "Forget Not!"

I never felt so good about myself
I never felt so good about myself
I never felt so good about myself

"Yes, yes, yes; more, more, more; *encore, encore, encore!*"

Madonna's rebellion against Catholicism is not, however, an outright rejection, for it involves a subversive rereading of the relation between religion and sexuality. She ironically confesses that at one time she wanted to be a nun because "Nuns are sexy."[28] Madonna's attraction to the sisterhood remains more sexual than ascetic. Nuns, she stresses, are "married to Jesus." For Madonna, this truth is more than symbolic. In her most revealing comment on religion, she expresses the radical implications of her belief in the incarnation for the human body and sexuality:

In the *Like a Virgin* scene in my show [*Truth or Dare*], I have these men whom I have emasculated with bras on who are attending me and offering me sex if I so wish. But in the end, I would rather be alone and masturbate. Until God comes, of course, and frightens me. Then all of a sudden *Like a Prayer* begins, and you hear the voice of God, and the curtain opens. Figures clothed in black, like priests and nuns, appear on stage and the cross descends. It's like here comes the Catholic Church saying "Sex goes here and spirituality goes there." And I say—but I say, NO, THEY GO TOGETHER! I am supposed to pray, right? But my praying gets so frenzied and passionate and frenetic that by the end, I am flailing my body all over the place, and it becomes a masturbatorysexualpassionate thing.[29]

Madonna's Joycean masturbatorysexualpassionate thing is the moment of passion, which, as Bataille insists, is the instant when self-division is overcome and the presence of the self to itself becomes *total*. In this moment, the passion of Christ is translated into the passion of the "believer." While awaiting the coming of Christ, Madonna comes on the altar. Like Bernini's *St. Theresa* coming all over the cover of Lacan's

Encore, Madonna's masturbatorysexualpassionate thing is the moment of *jouissance,* which, in some cases, marks the climax of the female mystic's spiritual quest.

In the perverse moment of passion, Madonna becomes what Edith Wyschogrod aptly describes as a "saint of depravity" whose life is governed by the excessive expression instead of repression of desire.[30] In the open economy of depraved sainthood, desire is not an attribute of the individual subject but is a force, which, like capital, circulates freely. When released from lawful constraint, desire issues in what might be labeled "material ecstasies." From one point of view, the material ecstasies of the "Material Girl" mark a return of the repressed that overthrows the norms of religion. From another point of view, however, transgression radicalizes the process of incarnation by redeeming the body itself.

The release of desire shatters the individual ego and decenters the subject. This decentering creates a condition that approximates schizophrenia, which, as Gilles Deleuze and Félix Guattari argue, is the psychological counterpart of the late capitalist economy. The transformation of the structure of subjectivity is wrought by the altered experience of time that Jameson identifies as one of the defining conditions of postmodernism. In the culture of the simulacrum, Schreber becomes exemplary. Surveying the psychological landscape of postmodernism in *Anti-Oedipus: Capitalism and Schizophrenia,* Deleuze and Guattari argue:

> In *Le Baphomet,* Klossowski contrasts God as the master of the exclusions and restrictions that derive from the disjunctive syllogism, with an antichrist who is the prince of modifications, determining instead the passage of a subject through all possible predicates. I am God I am not God, I am God I am Man: it is not a matter of a synthesis that would go beyond the negative disjunctions of the derived reality, in an original reality of Man-God, but rather of an inclusive disjunction that carries out the synthesis itself in drifting from one term to another and following the distance between terms. Nothing is primal. It is like the famous conclusion to *Molloy:* "It is midnight. The rain is beating on the windows. It was not midnight. It was not raining." Nijinsky wrote: "I am God I was not God I am a clown of God; I am Apis. I am an Egyptian. I am a red Indian. I am a Negro. I am a Chinaman. I am a Japanese. I am a foreigner, a stranger. I am a sea bird. I am a land bird. I am the tree of Tolstoy. I am the roots of Tolstoy. . . . I am husband and wife in one. I love my wife. I love my husband.[31]

An inclusive disjunction that carries out the synthesis itself in drifting from one term to another and following the distance between terms.

Nothing is primal. I am . . . I am not. . . . Within this "myth of the eternal return," nothing *is* primal and thus everything is secondary.

This is, in effect, the Gospel according to Madonna. One of the names Madonna bares is the Antichrist. As Nietzsche and before him Blake realized, not only Satan but the earthly Jesus can be viewed as the Antichrist. According to the nonfoundational principles of Nietzsche's gay wisdom, the Antichrist negates negation by overturning Christianity's overturning of Christ's original vision:

> One should not confuse Christianity as a historical reality with that one root that its name calls to mind: the other roots from which it has grown up have been far more powerful. It is an unexampled misuse of words when such manifestations of decay and abortions as "Christian faith" and "Christian live" label themselves with that holy name. What did Christ *deny?* Everything that today is called Christian. [*WP,* 98–99]

From the Nietzschean perspective that implicitly informs Madonna's music and videos, to reject the Christ of the Church is to embrace the earth(l)y Kingdom of Jesus. As we have previously noted, Jesus, Nietzsche argues,

> ignores the entire system of crude formalities governing intercourse with God: He opposes the whole teaching of repentance and atonement; he demonstrates how one must live in order to feel "deified"—and how one will not achieve it through repentance and contrition for one's sin: "Sin is of no account" is his central judgment. . . . "Bliss" is not something promised: it is there if you live and act in such and such a way. [*WP,* 98–99]

Another name for "bliss" is *jouissance.* Madonna shows her listeners and viewers how they must live and act if they are to enjoy the forbidden fruits of *jouissance* here and now. But where are here and now here and now?

In contrast to the asceticism and austerity of certain Protestantisms and Judaisms, Catholicism retains a profound appreciation for the religious significance and aesthetic richness of liturgy. The celebration of the mass in which Christ is held to materialize is repeatedly staged as a high drama that culminates in the believers' appropriation of the body and blood of God. Madonna extends this process of appropriation to the point of dialectical inversion through which opposites are identified and sinner becomes saint. She effectively develops transgressive tactics that enable her to realize this subversive inversion by refiguring the images and symbols of Catholicism itself. Since Madonna's iconophilia is more visual than verbal, no amount of listening to her music prepares one for the visual impact of religious images in her videos:

197

I think I have always carried around a few rosaries with me. There was this turquoise-colored one that my grandmother had given to me a long time ago. One day I decided to wear it as a necklace. I thought, "This is kind of offbeat and interesting." I mean, everything I do is sort of tongue in cheek. It's a strange blend—a beautiful sort of symbolism, the idea of someone suffering, which is what Jesus Christ on a crucifix stands for, and then not taking it seriously at all. Seeing it as an icon with no religiousness attached to it. It isn't a sacrilegious thing for me. I'm not saying, "This is Jesus Christ," and I'm laughing. When I went to Catholic schools, I thought the huge crucifixes the nuns wore around their necks with their habits were really beautiful. I have one like that now. I wear it sometimes but not on-stage. It's too big. It might fly up in the air and hit me in the face.[32]

This absence of religiousness in the icon is not a simple absence but is an absence that is, in some sense, at the same time a presence. "My idea," Madonna explains, "is to take these iconographic symbols that are held away from everybody in glass cases and say, 'Here is another way of looking at it. I can hang this around my neck. I can have this coming out of my crotch if I want.' The idea is somehow to bring it down to a level that people can relate to."[33] Through such tactics, Madonna exposes what the fathers of the Church either consciously or unconsciously want to repress—"the sexuality of Christ."[34] So offensive were Madonna's antics to Church officials that Vatican objections led to the cancellation of the Blond Ambition concerts in Italy. In response to this censorship, Madonna protests:

I had to cancel two of my shows in Italy because of the Vatican. Rome and Florence. It was propaganda. Even though there were all of these profane gestures and masturbatory demonstrations, I think that my show was very religious and spiritual. I feel fairly in touch with my Italian roots, so when I got to Italy, I expected to be embraced because my show has so much Catholicism in it.[35]

Again, the cutting edge of Madonna's irony cannot obscure the force of her observation. She realizes more clearly than her celibate fathers that when carried to its logical conclusion, the affirmation of the incarnation entails the acceptance—even the explicit celebration—of carnality, which is traditionally regarded as obscene.

As I have suggested, two images of woman pervade Madonna's vision—the angel and the whore. Many of her videos are structured around the opposition angel/whore or sacred/profane, which appears visually as the interplay of white and black or red. In some cases, Madonna carries whoring to excessive extremes. For example, in "Justify

My Love" she appears in scenes that include virtually every form of sexual perversion, while in "Express Yourself" she engages in sado-masochistic play as she dons a collar and chain and grovels like a servile dog. Any simple opposition between good and evil, however, is misleading, for Madonna realizes that love is never pure. Love inevitably entails violence, just as eros always involves thanatos. Even sadomasochism has a religious dimension, and, conversely, traditional religion includes elements that are sadistic and masochistic:

> Yea, well . . . I am a masochist. Why? Because I felt persecuted as a child. My father made a never-ending impression on me. He had a philosophy, little pearls of wisdom he would drop on us. One of them was, "If it feels good, you are doing something wrong. If you are suffering, you are doing something right." I tried not to compartmentalize those feelings, so that they are rooted in the same impulse. And another was, "If there were more virgins, the world would be a better place."[36]

For this erstwhile Cinderella, even mothering has its masochistic side. The angelic mother is actually a suffering servant whose life is devoted to others. Appearances to the contrary notwithstanding, the purest of mothers is also something of a whore. Regardless of how it is obscured by the doctrine of the Immaculate Conception, *the* Madonna is a whore and God, the Father, is an adulterer. In the colorful world of video, angels are whores, and whores are angels; nothing is simply black or white.

Madonna's appropriation of religious imagery is most obvious and complex in her video *Like a Prayer* and film *Truth or Dare*. *Like a Prayer* initially appears to be structured by a series of binary oppositions: black/white, love/hate, peace/violence, sacred/profane, inside/outside, church/world, woman/man, and dream/reality. However, as the video unfolds, Madonna inverts these classical polarities and calls into question the very antithetical structure upon which her work seems to depend. In this video more than anywhere else, the contours of what can only be described as Madonna's religious vision emerge clearly, though subtly.

Like a Prayer opens with an extraordinary montage: Madonna, dressed in black and wearing a cross on her breast, running and stumbling past an open fire on a desolate blue landscape, with sirens and heavy metal music blaring in the background; a jail door slamming shut; a burning cross; white men attacking a white woman; a white church radiating warm inner light; a black man apprehended by the police. As the sirens fade, Madonna's voice rises:

Life is a mystery, everyone must stand alone
I hear you call my name
And it feels like home

When you call my name it's like a prayer
I'm down on my knees, I wanna take you there
In the midnight hour I can feel your power
Just like a prayer you know I'll take you there

Collecting herself, Madonna enters the church. As the word *home* sounds, she closes the door behind her and approaches an altar where prayer candles burn. To the right of the altar, there is a statue of a black Christ figure behind the bars of a gate or cage. Madonna draws near the icon singing:

I hear your voice, it's like an angel sighing
I have no choice, I hear your voice
Feels like flying

With Madonna kneeling before Christ, the statue moves its hand ever so slightly and sheds a stream of tears. Moved by Christ's tears, Madonna withdraws from the altar and lies seductively on a nearby pew. Slowly reclining, she provocatively rubs her genitals:

I close my eyes, oh God I think I'm falling
Out of the sky, I close my eyes
Heaven help me

In her reverie, Madonna bows reverently before the icon, kisses its feet, opens the doors of the cage, and touches the face of her idol. The stroke of her hand brings the statue to life. The black messiah returns Madonna's kiss and then slowly leaves the church to enter the hostile outside world.

Only with Madonna's kiss does the full impact of her song begin to emerge. Though she kneels before the image of Christ, her gesture of submission is deceptive. It is *Madonna,* not Christ, who is the savior in *Like a Prayer:* "*I* wanna take *you* there," she sings. Her religious mission is, in effect, to redeem the redeemer. She can accomplish this only if she is able to lure Christ from the pedestal that holds him captive. Madonna, in other words, tries to release Christ from bondage to the Church. Though Catholics have always worshipped the Mother of God, they have never before met a Madonna quite like this one.

Madonna's role in the economy of salvation becomes explicit in the sequence following the departure of Christ. She picks up a dagger, which had fallen among the roses the Christ figure had held, and cuts

her hands with the sharp blade. The camera zooms in on her palms to
expose two stigmata that recall the wounds from the nails driven into
Christ's hands. In these tears, the body and blood of Christ become the
body and blood of Madonna. The savior is no longer the Son but now
is the Mother; no longer man but now is woman. This interplay of word
and image raises more questions than it answers: How can (the) Madonna save Christ? How can woman save man? How can the mother
save the son?

> Like a child you whisper softly to me
> You're in control just like a child
> Now I'm dancing
> It's like a dream, no end and no beginning
> You're here with me, it's like a dream
> Let the choir sing

While the black gospel choir sings, a remarkable sequence of images
unfolds in which the peace, harmony, and love within the church are
juxtaposed with the violence, discord, and hatred of the outside world.
Madonna emerges from the church to observe a gang of white men
attacking a young white woman. The woman appears to die from a
wound the men inflict at the precise spot where taunting soldiers are
reported to have stabbed Jesus while he was hanging on the cross.
When a black man rushes to the aid of the dying woman, he is apprehended by the police, handcuffed, and taken away. Madonna feigns
horror.

As one examines the face of the black man carefully, it becomes
clear that the suffering innocent is not only the same person who appears in the video's opening sequence but is also the Christ figure who
leaves the church. After the arrest of Christ, the scene shifts abruptly to
Madonna singing and dancing erotically first in front of a dark field of
burning crosses and then with the church choir. In yet another unexpected twist, the church becomes the site of a further transgression.
With the soft light of prayer candles and the rhythmic beat of the gospel
choir in the background, Madonna seduces the black messiah. This is
the moment when the nature of Madonna's redemptive power is revealed.[37] For Madonna, love is salvific. But Madonna's love is not the
pale image of a love that represses the body and denies its desires. To
the contrary, she believes in a love that is fully incarnate—a love that
embraces materiality and carnality as nothing less than the temple of
God. She is, indeed, a "Material Girl," who challenges both followers
and nonfollowers: Truth or Dare! Madonna dares the Church to believe

the radical truth it simultaneously proclaims and represses. "Take, eat [me]." For the Church fathers, such love is, of course, utterly transgressive. In the eyes of the mother, however, the belief of the fathers is unbelief and their love is a denial of the incarnation.

As the lips of the white woman and black man become one on the altar of God, the violence of the outside world intrudes: burning crosses and the face of the innocent "criminal" flash on the screen. In the midst of these images, which by now have become familiar, there is a new figure that is deeply disturbing. The black icon returns for a split second. But there is an important difference—his tears have now turned to blood. The eye of the savior is cut, torn, wounded. The most obvious reading of this wound is that one of the bullets or arrows hurled at the suffering servant hits its mark. But there is another, less obvious, way to read the bleeding eye. Within the psychoanalytic register, blindness represents castration. The fleeting image of Christ's bleeding tears might figure Madonna's effective displacement of the savior. In her Dionysian frenzy, this latter-day Antichrist repeats the proclamation of Nietzsche's madman: "God is dead, God remains dead. And we have killed him." But this is no ordinary death, for through a dialectical reversal, the death of God the Father is the sacralization of woman. Feminine power disarms men, thereby rendering all Boy Toys impotent. With eyes bleeding, the living Christ reenters his cage and, as if suffering the gaze of Medusa, turns back into stone.

The clang of the closing cell door awakens Madonna. As she rouses, the last two stanzas of the song are playing:

> Just like a prayer, your voice can take me there
> Just like a muse to me
> You are a mystery
> Just like a dream, you are now what you seem
> Just like a prayer
> No choice
> Your voice can take me there
>
> Just like a prayer
> I'll take you there
> It's like a dream to me

With these words, everything seems to return to normal—the choir is singing and the icon is nothing more than an inert statue. The order of things is not only reestablished but, in the blink of an eye, the extraordinary seems to become intelligible. The last line of the song ("It's a dream to me") recasts all the events that have been recorded in dreamtime. But just when coherence seems to be achieved, everything is again thrown into question. The ending is deferred; the curtain does not fall.

Though the song has reached its end, there is one more scene in the video. When Madonna casts a final glance toward the icon, she once more sees a living man—the falsely accused black man who is standing behind bars. As the camera withdraws, Madonna appears before a police officer and apparently offers testimony that proves the man's innocence. Convinced by her story, the policeman releases the prisoner from jail. The camera continues to recede, revealing that the prisoner and jail cell have replaced the icon of Christ and its protective cage. Only when the officer opens the cell door does the bright red curtain fall and do the large white letters "The End" appear. It is important to realize that all of this takes place *after* Madonna supposedly has woken and thus would not seem to be part of her dream. But the testimony that frees the prisoner presumably is based on what she saw in her dream. The crucial line is in the penultimate stanza: "Just like a dream, you are not what you seem." The word *you* in this verse remains indefinite. It might refer to the Christ figure: "You, Christ, are not what you seem; you are not God but man, a full-blooded man with needs and desires just like everyone else." Madonna's Christ succumbs to every last temptation that Kazantzakis's Christ merely imagines. For Madonna, this is his glory, not his sin. From God to wo/man: "You, viewer/listener, are not what you seem; you are not mere women and men but are truly divine. Your needs and desires—even the most carnal of them—are not evil or sinful and thus should not make you feel guilty. Your body is holy, worship it by enjoying it. Guilt is the invention of the Father, which the love of the Mother overcomes." To her children, (the) Madonna's gospel is: "Be yourselves, accept yourselves *as you are.* The Kingdom is not elsewhere; it is *present,* here and now. Bliss is not something promised: it is there if you live and act in such a way. And *I,* Madonna, will show you how to live so that you may enjoy bliss and experience *jouissance. I* wanna take you there . . . you know *I'll* take you there . . . *I'll* take you there. Come, please come. Here, now!"

And yet . . . and yet . . . and yet, the final line of the song continues to resound long after the music dies and the video fades: "It's like a dream to me." The meaning of this verse remains undecidable. Once released, undecidability works its way back through all the words and images of *Like a Prayer.* Madonna does not say "It *is* a dream to me" but "It's *like* a dream to me." What, then, has she revealed to us? Dream or reality? Has the Kingdom been realized or deferred yet again? Has dream become reality or has reality become a dream? Or is something else at work in all of this play? Perhaps something like surreality, hyperreality, or even virtual reality?

The relevant scenes in *Truth or Dare* extend but do not significantly develop or revise the religious vision represented in *Like a Prayer*. As I have noted, Madonna insists that the film's most graphic scene, which accompanies *Like a Virgin,* represents the coincidence of spirituality and sexuality:

> It's like here comes the Catholic Church saying "Sex goes here, and spirituality goes there." And I say—but I say, NO, THEY GO TOGETHER!

As the scene shifts from *Like a Virgin* to *Like a Prayer* in *Truth or Dare,* the red bed of the sinner becomes the altar of sacrifice, where the passion of Christ is ritually reenacted by Madonna's second coming. An altar, after all, not only designates the place of the Son's suffering but also refers to "the altar of pleasure," where the daughter is offered in the marriage ceremony. In slang, "altar" designates the female pudendum. It is upon this polymorphous and perverse altar that Madonna assumes her religio-artistic mission.

The blatant eroticism of the *Like a Virgin* segment of *Truth or Dare* points to a more complex obscenity that pervades the film. Obscenity, we have discovered, has less to do with sexuality than with the exposure of the private to the voyeuristic gaze of the public. *Truth or Dare* was conceived and billed as a "documentary" film. Trying to persuade himself and others of his artistic "integrity," the young director, Alek Keshishian, insists that Madonna's agreement to total access and no censorship was a condition of his doing the film. He claims to have instructed his crew: "We are not human beings. We are just here to report." Regardless of the sophistication of the recording device, reporting is never just reporting and the eye of the camera is never neutral. As the wedding of news and entertainment industries makes clear daily, every documentary is really a docudrama.

204

The dramatic ob-scene that Keshishian records is, in many ways, remarkable. In an effort to make a distinction between the private and public, which his film also attempts to erase, Keshishian juxtaposes black-and-white (private) and color (public). The camera captures the ordinary as well as the extraordinary: reunions with a wary father, troubled brother, and uncertain high school friend are mingled with obscene games and promiscuous encounters between Madonna and members of her extended "family." As if to breathe life into the violent eroticism of a Salle painting, *Truth or Dare* bars nothing and lays bare everything. Or so it seems.

In spite of the purported unobtrusiveness of the camera's eye, the obscene nevertheless is staged. For all her exposure—both figurative and literal—Madonna never truly appears; she forever withdraws in and through her multiple appearances. Responding to the question "What is real and what is for the benefit of the camera?" she confesses:

> People will say, "She knows the camera is on, she's just acting." But even if I *am* acting, there's a truth in my acting. It's like when you go into a psychiatrist's office and you don't really tell him what you did. You lie, but even the lie you've chosen to tell is revealing. I wanted people to see that my life isn't so easy, and one step further than that is, the movie's not completely me. You could watch it and say, I still don't know Madonna, and *good*. Because you will never know the real me. Ever.[38]

As one studies the masks she wears, images she fabricates, and personas she assumes, it becomes clear that we do not really know who Madonna is or even what she looks like. Thoroughly postmodern, Madonna is *image all the way down*. She is nothing but her masks and yet no mask represents her. This is not to imply that the true Madonna lies hidden behind her myriad masks. Madonna makes no such mistake, for she realizes that the real itself has become a simulacrum. In every image, she coyly winks at the viewer, thereby giving a hint of the nonknowledge that is her "knowledge." Madonna invites what she denies and denies what she invites. In an image that might have been painted by Salle, Madonna stands, with back turned, wearing nothing but unzipped shorts (fig. 28). On her back is superimposed what could be the outline of a picture frame, television screen, or video terminal. In the middle of the empty box is written: "ALL ACCESS." The image deconstructs itself, for the words subvert the image and the image contradicts the words. Access is precisely what Madonna denies. She repeatedly withdraws what she holds out and holds out what is always withdrawing. Her art is the art of "adverteasing" in which the interplay of solicitation and refusal generates the power of seduction.

Adverteasing is seductive rather than obscene. Though not immediately evident, seduction renders explicit the implications of Kirsten's refusal when she declares:

> There's nothing to write. Everything is there on the wall. It doesn't mean anything. It's not like there's any deep meaning or anything.

In contrast to obscenity, seduction involves an infinite play of signs in which depth gives way to surface, creating what Baudrillard labels "superficial abysses." As we have seen, in the culture of the simulacrum, God tends to become a sign, or the sign tends to become sacred. If the

205

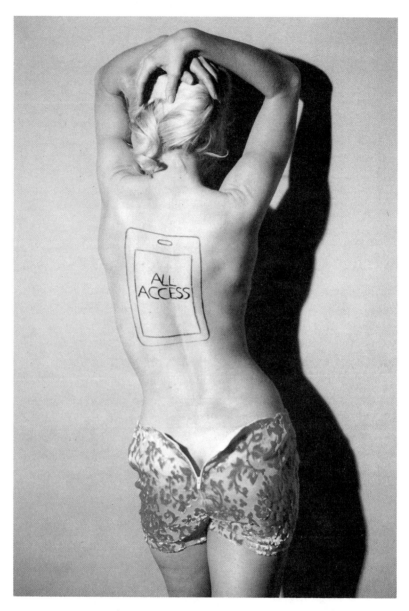

28. Madonna (1991). Photograph: Steven Meisel.

real is always already encoded, there is nothing either latent or transcendent to stop the free circulation of signs. Once the shock of the
death of God or disappearance of the real has passed, it becomes clear
there is nothing to be mourned:

> *To seduce is to die as reality and reconstitute oneself as illusion.* It is to
> be taken in by one's own illusion and move in an enchanted world. It is

the power of the seductive woman who takes herself for her own desire, and delights in the self-deception in which others, in their turn, will be caught. . . . The strategy of seduction is one of deception. It lies in wait for all that tends to confuse itself with its reality. And it is potentially a source of fabulous strength. For if production can only produce objects or real signs, and thereby obtain some power; seduction, by producing only illusions, obtains all powers, including the power to return production and reality to their fundamental illusion.[39]

Madonna's enchanted world holds out the promise of the ecstasy of communication, which the "mediaization" of reality *seems* to make possible. Within the regime of postmodernism, the circuit of transubstantiation extends from the mass to the loss of mass. When the real dies and is reborn as image, everything becomes insubstantial. Madonna appears to realize what most of her followers tend to forget: ecstasy is never real but, like everything else, is always a simulacrum. "Thus, when seducing, her body and desires are no longer her own. But then what is this body, or these desires? She doesn't believe in them—and so plays with them. Without a body of her own, she turns herself into a pure appearance, an artificial construct with which to trap the desires of others. Seduction consists in letting the other believe himself to be the subject of his desire, without oneself being caught in this trap."[40]

What makes adverteasing so seductive is the repeated promise yet inevitable denial of fulfillment. Signs evoke real satisfaction only to "reveal" another sign that defers gratification. If the sign is always a sign of a sign and never the real thing, there is no end to the excessive quest for satisfaction. Desire is sacrificed on an altar that figures crucifixion but not resurrection. Contrary to expectation, the absence that haunts the endless play of signs harbors a not that cannot be erased. The return of the not, which is repeatedly repressed in the culture of the simulacrum, is not the reappearance of the transcendental signified that attempts to pass itself off as (the) real. The not cannot be figured and thus "appears" by "disappearing" in the gap *between* signs. This ever elusive gap is the nonsite of adverteasing. Adverteasing marks not by remarking not the space of fulfillment but its lack, not the opening of satisfaction but its impossibility, not the interval of gratification but its frustration. In rare moments—moments that effectively mark an other passion, which might be the passion of the other, Madonna glimpses this gap through the tears and tears of her "Spanish Eyes" :

I know for sure his heart is here with me
Though I wish him back I know he cannot see

29. Prostitutes sitting in a display window (1991). Photograph: Peter Charlesworth.

> My hands trembling
> I know he hears me sing

> I light this candle and watch it throw
> Tears on my pillow
> And if there is a Christ, he'll come tonight
> And pray for Spanish Eyes

> And if I have nothing left to show but
> Tears on my pillow
> What kind of life is this if God exists
> Then help me pray for Spanish eyes.

But, of course, Christ does not come. *Christ never comes.* In the space of this absence, there is nothing left to show ... nothing but tears ... which sometimes turn to blood.

Signs of the Times

There are other signs of the *Times*—signs that Kirsten does not cut out and hang on her wall. On 14 July 1991, the *New York Times Magazine* carried an article entitled "A Plague Awaits." Above the headline a remarkable photograph appeared (fig. 29). In this picture, there is a table filled with rich foods in front of a bright red sign, or what seems

208

to be a sign. On the sign there are images of six carefully posed and
pensive women; above the women there appear partially erased words
in an indecipherable language, an inscription in Thai, and an English
sentence: "We welcome only guests using condoms." On a box next to
luscious fruit that looks like ripe apples, the word VEGA is printed in
large white letters. The name of the brightest star in the constellation
Lyra, *Vega* derives from the Arabic *al waqu,* which means "the falling
vulture." Which vulture? Who is falling—in this image and elsewhere?
In the lower righthand corner of the photograph, there is an incon-
spicuous caption: "At brothels like this one in Chiang Mai, four out of
five prostitutes carry the AIDS virus." Only after reading these words,
does it become clear that the picture is not the representation of a sign
but is a photograph of prostitutes, behind a glass window, displaying
themselves to prospective customers. Marys all—but all other Marys. At
the bottom of the page, a highlighted inserts reads: "In Thailand, where
brothels are a way of life, AIDS among heterosexuals is an invisible
epidemic. Few Thais know that the disease is closing in on them, or that
it will kill them." The figures registered for yet another country are
staggering:

> The eerie quality of the raging AIDS epidemic in Thailand is its invisibility.
> Doctors and scientists estimate that at least 300,000 Thais are infected with
> AIDS, and thousands more are being infected every month. By 1997, ac-
> cording to W.H.O., between 125,000 and 150,000 Thais will have died from
> AIDS. This is a conservative estimate. The Population and Community
> Development Association of Thailand estimates that AIDS could infect
> as many as 5.3 million by the year 2000, with more than a million dead
> by then.[41]

A sign of the times that all too few are reading.

The culture of the simulacrum is, in many ways, a parody of the
utopian dreams of the avant-garde. When Marinetti and the futurists
extolled the beauty of the Eiffel Tower and the power of electricity, they
envisioned a union of art and technology that would transform the
world into a peaceful kingdom. In this realized Eden, fulfillment was
supposed to be *present* here and now. Violence would give way to
peace, suffering would be overcome, and disease would be eliminated.
The dream is always the same. And it always remains a dream—a cruel
dream that raises expectations only to dash every hope of salvation.

The "good news" electronic media bring is no different from past
gospels of salvation. It is not insignificant that the era of MTV coincides

with the extraordinary spread of televangelism. The global village, prophets proclaim, will emerge with the spread of the word made image. But in the culture of the simulacrum, even the profits are image all the way down. Their God is a sign—and nothing but a sign. In the electronic age, selling the gospel is more than ever an art. The commodification of the work of art becomes the program for the commodification of religion. Though MTV and televangelism seem utterly opposed, they actually share more than their priests, priestesses, and disciples would like to admit. They are all iconolaters, for they share a belief in the reality of the image. In this global church, *il n'y a rien hors d'image. Rien. Rien. Rien.*

On 21 March 1987, the *New York Times* reported on the front page: "Bakker, Evangelist, Resigns His Ministry Over Sexual Incident."

> The Rev. Jim Bakker, a leading television evangelist has resigned his ministry, asserting that he was maneuvered into a sexual encounter six years ago and subsequently blackmailed.

The report proceeded to detail the financial network that Jim and Tammy Faye Bakker had built around their television ministry. The centerpiece of the Bakker's empire was an organization they named PTL, which stood for "Praise the Lord," or "People That Love." In the preceding year, the reported annual income of PTL was $120 million. In addition to the lucrative PTL television network, Jim and Tammy presided over Heritage U.S.A., a 2,300-acre theme park employing over two thousand people, which was designed to be something like a religious version of Disney World. The Bakkers' kingdom is truly the Magic Kingdom. Jim and Tammy, however, do not realize that the drama they stage is a parody of the Gospel they preach. In their Kingdom, there is no nonplace for irony.

On the same page of the *Times* as the report of Bakker's transgression, another headline appeared:

210

> U.S. Approves Drug that Prolongs Lives of AIDS Patients
> Cure Still Not Achieved
> Distribution Will Be Limited
> Because of Short Supply and
> Fear of Side Effects

The article included a diagram and explanation of how the AIDS virus infects its victims:

When the AIDS virus invades a cell, it uses an enzyme to translate the code in its RNA, or genetic material, into DNA. The DNA enters the cell nucleus and subverts its genetic machinery, causing it to make messenger RNA and proteins that form the new AIDS virus particles. AZT [Azidothymidine] can prevent the translation of RNA into DNA molecules before they enter the cell nucleus.

Cure Still Not Achieved. Even in the Magic Kingdom, viruses cannot be controlled. Every program—be it television, computer, or genetic—is infected as if from within by an incurable disease. Viruses can sometimes be repressed but never eliminated. Disease, it seems, is a not that cannot be undone, for it is, in a certain sense, systemic but not systematic. Though we struggle to forget not, the not always returns to undo us.

August 20, 1992

Dear Kirsten,

In spite of what you think, I *am* learning the lessons you are teaching me slowly—doubtless all too slowly. It is, of course, impossible for me to respond in a way you would find appropriate or adequate. Perhaps some day this letter will arrive at its destination. But my hope is faint, for today more than ever, it seems, letters are interrupted, diverted, or delayed. Like every other system, the postal system has already broken down. *If* hope were still possible, I would hope that you would never forget the Gap but that you would learn to read it otherwise and thus discover how to *forget not.*

Love,

Dad

Forget Not
To remember
To forget
N
O
T
.
.
.
?

Body

8

The Betrayal of the Body: Live Not

By the 1980s, the immune system is unambiguously a postmodern object—symbolically, technically, and politically. . . . Language is no longer an echo of the *verbum dei,* but a technical construct working on principles of internally generated difference. If the early modern natural philosopher or Renaissance physician conducted an exegesis of the text of nature written in the language of geometry or of cosmic correspondences, the postmodern scientist still reads for a living, but has as a text the coded systems of recognition—prone to the pathologies of misrecognition—embodied in objects like computer networks and immune systems.
—DONNA HARAWAY

As a rule, a person is considered to be healthy when he himself does not say that he is sick, not to mention when he himself says that he is well. But the physician has a different view of sickness. Why? Because the physician has a defined and developed conception of what it is to be healthy and ascertains a man's condition accordingly. The physician knows that just as there is merely imaginary sickness there is also merely imaginary health, and in the latter case he first takes measure to disclose the sickness. . . . A physician's task is not only to prescribe remedies but also, first and foremost, to identify the sickness, and consequently his first task is to ascertain whether the supposedly sick person is actually sick or whether the supposedly healthy person is actually healthy
—SØREN KIERKEGAARD

When are you coming back? I will call Sunday at the latest. If you're not there, leave them a message. Leave, for example, so that they won't understand a thing, as in the Resistance, a sentence with "sunflower" to signify that you prefer that I come, without sunflower for the opposite. Since I am a true network of resistance, with internal cells, those little grips of three who communicate only on one side (what is it called?), so that nothing can be extorted, so that no one gives way under torture, and finally so that no one is *able* to betray. What one hand does the other does not know (definition of Islamic alms?). It will end very badly, for a long time I have no longer been able to refind myself, and in fact I betray myself, me, all the time.—JACQUES DERRIDA

Wvhat lines of communication do these texts open or close?[1] Do they correspond or resist correspondence? What letters travel their circuit and pulsate through their channels? Do their messages—do any messages arrive, ever arrive? What is the price of the failure of communication? What happens when messages do not arrive, are interrupted, or misread?

The body betrays—always inevitably betrays. The betrayal of the body is disease, which unavoidably involves a certain sickness and illness. The most insidious diseases are those that leave no apparent trace, diseases that are silent, invisible, sometimes even casting a semblance of health. But health is imaginary, if only because temporary. The real, we eventually discover, is disease and disease is (the) real. The glow of health harbors the shadow of disease. The obscure silence of disease is not its absence but a fleeting dissemblance that betrays itself in and through its opposite. Health betrays sickness, even as sickness betrays health. When disease inevitably appears as sickness, it is nothing new, for I finally realize that it has always been arriving—arriving from the beginning, indeed even before the beginning.

Betrayal is not secondary to an original promise or contract any more than sickness is the loss of original health. Rather, betrayal involves something like an originary transgression that discloses the primal discord of a founding wound. In the beginning... before the beginning was betrayal. Betrayal is not ideal; it is real, material, carnal. Before it can be thought, betrayal must be realized, materialized, incarnate. Incarnation is betrayal and betrayal is incarnate.

215

To acknowledge the unavoidable betrayal of the body is, among other things, to confess: "I am sick, always already sick." Such words do not come easily; I must rehearse them again, and again, and again. One day, perhaps unexpectedly, I will speak them or they will speak me. The word *will be* spoken and when it arrives, it brings with it the recognition that illness is not episodic but chronic. It is my condition—our condition and this condition is the gift of chronos, which, like all pharmacons, is both a blessing and curse. I cannot live with betrayal, nor can I live without it. The betrayal of my body betrays the not that entangles the "I am." If betrayal is unavoidable, "I am" is inseparable from "I am sick" : "I am sick, therefore I am," or "I am, therefore I am sick." The "not" in the midst of "I am" can be translated: "I am sick, therefore I am not," or "I am not, therefore I am sick." This not of disease is the sickness unto death that "is" before my beginning and after my end.

The web of betrayal is endless as well as beginningless. Since health is not original, betrayal cannot betray health. But if betrayal does not betray health, can it betray disease? Can the betrayal of the body betray disease in a way that leads not to health but to an acceptance of the incurability of disease? And might this acceptance create the possibility of lingering with the not in a way that allows me to escape bondage to a hopeless search for an impossible cure?

Disease is one of the guises in which altarity approaches. Like every brush with otherness, disease leaves us uneasy. The dis-ease with dis-ease signals a response that is thoroughly ambivalent, for altarity is both terrifying and strangely attractive. We dread and yet secretly desire disease. To be diseased is to be cursed, even if we do not know by whom or by what, and to be cursed is to be chosen, even if we do not know by whom or by what. The lesson is at least as old as Job.

The terror of disease provokes the effort to control it by defining and delimiting the other as other. "It is the fear of collapse," argues Sander Gilman, "the sense of dissolution, which contaminates the Western image of all diseases, including elusive ones such as schizophrenia. But the fear we have of our own collapse does not remain internalized. Rather, we project this fear onto the world in order to localize it and, indeed, to domesticate it. For once we locate it, the fear of our own dissolution is removed. Then it is not we who totter on the brink of collapse, but rather the Other. And it is an-Other who has already shown his or her vulnerability by having collapsed."[2] To create distance is to establish difference, and to establish difference is to secure identity. Distance, however, need not be spatial and is often subtle. Apparently sympathetic words tend to carry echoes of self-interest: "Does it run in *your* family?" implies "It does not run in *mine*." Though we know better, it is difficult to dissociate disease from guilt. Long after

30. *Opposite.* Francis Galton, *Specimens of Composite Portraiture.*

SPECIMENS OF COMPOSITE PORTRAITURE
PERSONAL AND FAMILY.

Alexander the Great
From 6 Different
Medals.

Two Sisters.

From 6 Members
of same Family
Male & Female.

HEALTH.	DISEASE.	CRIMINALITY.

23 Cases.
Royal Engineers.
12 Officers.
11 Privates

6 Cases

9 Cases

Tubercular Disease

8 Cases

4 Cases

2 Of the many
Criminal Types

CONSUMPTION AND OTHER MALADIES

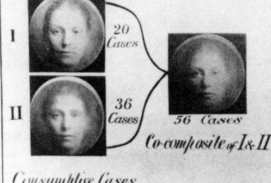

I — 20 Cases

II — 36 Cases

56 Cases
Co-composite of I & II

Consumptive Cases.

100 Cases

50 Cases

Not Consumptive.

belief in sin has faded, the association of disease with character flaws lingers: "He always smoked." "She drank too much." "He didn't eat right and never exercised." "She simply refused to slow down." Such words invariably suggest that *I* know better. If disease results from will or its lack, illness is not unavoidable.

Even when unmarked, disease is stigmatized. The stigma of disease is the inscription that brands the other as other, thereby creating the space and distance necessary for my identity. The strategies of demarcation and containment are multiple: some are personal, others social; some are formal, others informal; some are visible, others invisible. Hospitals, clinics, asylums, and prisons are among the sites of institutional containment that are constructed not only to treat the ill but, perhaps more important, to prevent disease from spreading by keeping the other separate and unequal. When there is no obvious trace of disease, those who deem themselves healthy go to extraordinary lengths to invent visible and invisible stigmas. From the identity of names and images to the materiality of scars and tattoos, the sick are forced to bear the mark of disease. In one of the more remarkable attempts to graph disease, Francis Galton depicts images of health, disease, and criminality by creating "composite portraits" (fig. 30). Reflecting on his photographic technique, Galton comments:

> In the large experience I have had of sorting photographs, literally by the thousand, while making experiments with composites, I have been struck by certain general impressions. The consumptive patients consisted of many hundred cases, including a considerable proportion of very ignoble specimens of humanity. Some were scrofulous and misshapen, or suffered from various loathsome forms of inherited disease; most were ill nourished. Nevertheless, in studying their portraits, the pathetic interest prevailed, and I returned day after day to my tedious work of classification, with a liking for my materials.[3]

In the face of the other, I see myself by *not* seeing my own face. But Galton's remark records an unexpected reversal. The other, who provokes fear and dread, is also terribly attractive. What makes consumption so consuming?

Susan Sontag describes tuberculosis as the "artists' disease." Among the surprising number of artists who contracted TB were: Keats, Shelley, the Brontës, Trollope, Thoreau, Emerson, Chekhov, Kafka, Lawrence, Orwell, Solzhenitsyn, and Percy. Sontag's point, however, is not simply that before the discovery of a cure in 1944, artists suffered TB in unusually high numbers. Her primary interest is how tuberculosis figures in the artistic imagination. In her thoughtful study *Illness as Metaphor,* Sontag examines the way in which the romantics romanticize disease, especially TB. Keats speaks for his generation when he insists: "Until we are sick, we understand not." While the association of suffering with knowledge is as ancient as mythology itself, the romantics stress the relationship between disease and creativity. In countless poems, stories, and novels, writers who are sick or long to be so, explore the ways in which disease can "etheralize consciousness," expand awareness, and deepen sensitivity.[4] Works like Eugene O'Neill's *Long Day's Journey into Night* and Thomas Mann's *The Magic Mountain,* inter alia, testify to the persistence of the tendency to romanticize disease. Virginia Woolf echoes Kierkegaard's melancholy ruminations when she declares disease to be her "greatest enemy and greatest friend." For those who believe in its creative power, disease assumes sacramental proportions. Sickness becomes an outward sign of an inward grace.

But the longing for creative inspiration is not the primary source of the attraction that disease exercises on the human imagination. The desire to be sick runs deeper and in a certain sense contrary to the wish to be creative. Disease, as Gilman argues, brings with it "the fear of collapse, the sense of dissolution." Though horrifying, collapse and dissolution are nevertheless alluring. In various strands of Eastern and Western as well as Northern and Southern mystical traditions, the collapse and dissolution of the individual are actually goals of the religious quest. This collapse can be physical or psychological. While nineteenth-century romantics tend to idealize physical diseases like TB, their twentieth-century heirs are more likely to romanticize psychological illnesses like schizophrenia.[5] If the medieval monastery served as something like an asylum, the contemporary asylum is often portrayed as a sanctified retreat where strange gods reveal themselves to chosen messengers. Madness is collapse and dissolution is ecstasy. The secular mystic Bataille describes this ravishing dissolution as "inner experience."

> And ecstasy is the way out! Harmony! . . . Infinite surpassing in oblivion, ecstasy, indifference, towards myself, towards this book: I see—that which discourse never managed to attain. . . . Ecstasy is not love: love is possession for which the object is necessary, and at the same time possession of the subject, possessed by it. There is no longer subject-object, . . . the subject and object are dissolved; there is passage, communication, but not from one to the other: *the one* and *the other* have lost their separate existence.[6]

"Ecstasy is not love"... it is *death*. The seduction of disease embodies the yearning for death. Death, as Freud has taught us, is our most profound desire—a desire that runs even deeper than eros.

The metaphors through which death and disease "speak" exceed the limits of art and infringe on the territory of what once was regarded as "hard" science. With the increasing awareness of the creative dimensions of all knowing, there is growing acknowledgment of the poetic nature of nature. The recognition that our access to "reality" is always linguistically mediated usually leads to the conclusion that knowledge is subjective and therefore relative. Critics argue that this position leads to unwarranted skepticism or even solipsism. The response to such criticism is usually the reformulation of one or another version of the "social construction of reality." Though knowledge is historically situated and socioculturally conditioned in a way that makes certainty impossible, consciousness, some argue, is not necessarily locked up in a "prison-house of language" that transforms individuals into windowless monads. To the contrary, the categories through which we know and the norms with which we judge are products of social communities. While we may never know things-in-themselves or be confident in the absolute truth of our principles of conduct, it is possible to reach a consensus about the way things seem to be. Though rarely acknowledged as such, this position is, in effect, a restatement of idealism in a relativized form. Within this framework, shared notions bind together rather than drive apart—at least for those who are inside and not outside.

It should be clear that the shift from the individual to the social register actually solves very little. This line of analysis claims both too much and too little, for skepticism that is certain of itself is insufficiently skeptical. When radicalized, skepticism becomes skeptical even of itself and thus must entertain the *possibility* of its own error. The possibility that social constructions of reality relate to something other than themselves creates an opening in which the relationship between language and "the real" must be rethought. By extending Lacan's analysis, it is possible to argue that not only the unconscious but the body is structured like a language.

This criticism of latter-day idealism does not necessarily result in a return to realism. The idealism/realism opposition or polarity is as problematic as every such binary or dialectical contrast. Nor does the suggestion that the body is structured like a language inevitably imply the reinscription of logocentrism. Everything turns on how language is

220

construed. If language is understood as a closed system of relations, the body and, by extension, nature can be read like a book. If, however, language is interpreted as a nonsystematic play of differences that is riddled with gaps and lacunae, then the body, and by extension, nature must be read like a text. Unlike the book, the text retains a certain unreadability that infinitely defers total comprehension and absolute knowledge. Thus, the suggestion that the body is structured like a language does not imply that we can truly know it. To the contrary, the linguisticality of the body might harbor an unknowability that can *never* be overcome.

It seems undeniable that there is an architecture of the body. If, as Heidegger insists, the order of things is never more apparent than when it breaks down, then it is possible that the architecture of the body can best be read in and through disease.[7] The body is no more stable than the diseases that inhabit it. During the modern era, the figure of the body shifts first from the eighteenth-century model of the machine to the nineteenth-century image of the organism, and then to the twentieth-century figure of an information, communications, or cybernetic system. The significance of these changes extends from psychomedical to religiophilosophical and sociocultural diagnostics. *If* the body is structured like a language, it is necessary to reexamine the relation between body and mind as well as nature and culture.

In his 1795 *Essays on Philosophical Subjects,* Adam Smith observes that "systems [of explanation] in many respects resemble machines. A machine is a little system created to perform, as well as to connect together, in reality, those different movements and effects which the artist has occasion for. A system is an imaginary machine invented to connect together in the fancy of those different movements and effects which are in reality performed."[8] The notion of system is not fixed but, as Michel Serres points out, "changes through history. . . . This notion may be logico-mathematical: a coherent set of demonstrable propositions deduced from a small number of postulates. One speaks in this way of a system of axioms or a system of differential equations. For Descartes, Spinoza, or Leibniz, this is the classical ideal of knowledge. The notion of system may also be mechanical: a set that remains stable throughout variations of objects that are either in movement or relatively stationary."[9] But this way of putting the matter is too simple. When Descartes collapses truth into certainty, he establishes self-identity at the price of self-bifurcation. The early modern subject is split in two by separating the *res cogitans* from the *res extensa*. Moreover, each part of the subject is governed by distinctive principles. While the mind and its products follow logicomathematical rules, the body is a machine that is regulated by the laws of mechanics. The primary mechanical law is, of course, causality, which brings together otherwise unrelated entities and events. The relation between cause and effect as well as the connection between the causal law and the entities it links is *external*. In other words, principles of causality are not intrinsic or implicit within things but are extrinsic and hence must be imposed from without.

When extrapolated from the micro to the macro level, this account of causality leads to a deistic vision of the world in which God is something like a mechanical engineer who constructs the world machine and establishes the principles by which it operates. In a more traditional image, God is the master clockmaker who creates the universe and its laws and then withdraws to allow the world to run on its own. Extrinsic laws provide whatever order and stability there is in the world. As La Mettrie makes clear in his classic treatise *L'Homme machine* (1747), man, in this scheme, is a law-governed machine.

From the mechanistic perspective of the eighteenth century, the analysis of disease is primarily a taxonomic or, more precisely, a nosological enterprise. The task of medical investigation is to define the "essential body" of disease through a comparison of visible symptoms. Ideally, this study of symptoms enables one to formulate a classificatory grid that can be used for diagnosis and treatment. "In the eighteenth century," Foucault explains, "the fundamental act of medical knowledge was the drawing up of a 'map' (*repérage*): a symptom was situated within a disease, a disease in a specific *ensemble,* and this *ensemble* in a general plan of the pathological world. In the experience that was being constituted towards the end of the century, it was a question of 'carving up' the field by means of the interplay of series, which, in intersecting one another, made it possible to reconstitute the chain. . . . A system of coincidences then appeared that indicated a causal connection and also suggested the kinships or new links between diseases."[10]

The relationship of diseases graphed on the nosological map is both external and superficial. While symptomatic association is the result of external similarities and differences, classification is a function of the recognition of surface appearances. Furthermore, diseases stand in an extrinsic relation to sick individuals who bear them. The classificatory grid of disease, like the mechanistic laws of nature, is imposed from without by a medical investigator whose inspection of the relation between disease and the patient is strictly parallel to the scientist's observation of the association of natural law with the particular entities and events. "If one wishes to know the illness from which he is suffering, one must subtract the individual, with his particular qualities: 'The author of nature,' said Zimmermann, 'has fixed the course of most diseases through immutable laws that one soon discovers if the course of the disease is not interrupted or disturbed by the patient'; at this level the individual was merely a negative element, the accident of the disease, which, for it and in it, is most alien to its essence."[11]

The shift from the mechanistic to the organic metaphor for interpreting natural and cultural processes takes place in Kant's *Critique of Judgment*. The Third Critique is supposed to resolve the tensions within each of the first two, as well as to unite the analyses of theoretical and practical reason. Kant attempts to synthesize the faculties of knowing and acting by developing an extensive analysis of "inner teleology" or "purposiveness without purpose [*Zweckmässigkeit ohne Zweck*]." This complex notion grows out of an important criticism and revision of the principle of causality that underlies the mechanistic model of the world. Kant identifies two primary examples of purposeless purpose—one natural, the other cultural: the living organism and the work of art. To argue that the living organism is characterized by purposiveness without purpose is to insist that the end, purpose, or goal of the organism is nothing other than the organism itself. In "The Analytic of Teleological Judgment," Kant explains that "this principle whose statement serves to define what is meant by organisms, is as follows: *an organized natural product is one in which every part is reciprocally both end and means.* In such a product, nothing is in vain, without an end, or to be ascribed to a blind mechanism of nature."[12] In contrast to mechanical relations in which means and end are external to each other, in the living organism, means and end are internally related in such a way that they are *mutually* constitutive. This reciprocity creates a harmonious accord that insures the vitality of the organism. The notion of inner teleology, Kant argues,

leads reason into an order of things entirely different from that of a mere mechanism of nature, which *mere mechanism* no longer proves adequate in this domain. An idea has to underlie the possibility of the natural product. But this idea is an absolute unity of the representation, whereas the material is a plurality of things that of itself can afford no definite unity of composition. Hence, if that unity of the idea is actually to serve as the *a priori* determining ground of a natural law of the causality of such a form of the composite, the end of nature must be made to extend to *everything* contained in its product. For if once we lift such an effect out of the sphere of the blind mechanism of nature and relate it *as a whole* to a supersensible ground of determination, we must then estimate it out and out on this principle. We have no reason for assuming the form of such a thing to be still partly dependent on blind mechanism, for with such confusion of heterogeneous principles, every reliable rule for estimating things would disappear.[13]

Mechanism is blind because the elements it links are inherently heterogeneous. As we have seen, mechanical cause and effect are not internally related but are brought together by an *external* third that remains heteronomous. In the "absolute unity" of the organism, heteronomy and heterogeneity give way to autonomy and an integration of differences in which each part is conditioned by others. Inasmuch as cause is implicit in effect and effect inherent in cause, apparent heteronomy is actual autonomy in which determination-by-an-other is really self-determination. When Kant claims that the *whole* is the "supersensible ground of determination," he is not suggesting that the principles governing the organism are external to the organism itself. To the contrary, the whole is the *structural totality* that patterns and organizes the organism. Though not immediately evident to the gaze of the superficial observer, this structure is inseparable from the material it organizes and the material of the organism is inseparable from the structure that articulates it.

Appropriating the category that is the keystone of the entire edifice of Western philosophy, Kant defines the structural foundation of nature and culture as the *idea*. The idea of the organism is an internally differentiated totality in which every particular is an integral member of the whole, and the whole is inherent in the particulars without which it cannot exist. Kant is, however, reluctant to follow his argument to its logical conclusion. Within his critical philosophy, the *Zweckmässigkeit ohne Zweck* is a "regulative idea" that is not necessarily constitutive of reality as such. In other words, purposelessness without purpose is a heuristic device that helps us organize experience but whose ontological status remains uncertain. Hegel translates the Kantian idea from the realm of ideality to the domain of reality. No longer merely a regulative principle of knowledge, the Hegelian idea forms the essence of the real itself. According to the most basic principle of Hegel's speculative philosophy, the idea is an inwardly diverse whole that is epistemologically and ontologically constitutive. The mechanical vision of the universe represents a rudimentary and unsatisfactory interpretation of natural laws and processes in which "the universal of physics is abstract or simply formal; its determination is not immanent within it, and does

224

not pass over into particularity. This is precisely the reason why its determinate content is external to the universal, and is therefore split up, dismembered, particularized, separated and lacking in any necessary connection within itself." When nature is grasped organically, the externality of mechanism is sublated and "the mind feels the life and the universal relatedness within nature; it has a presentiment of the universe as an organic whole, a rational totality, just as it experiences an inner unity within itself through the living individual."[14] Before philosophical comprehension is complete, this intuition of the organic whole of nature "must be submitted to thought, so that what has been dismembered may be restored to simple universality through thought. This contemplated unity is the Notion, which contains the determinate differences simply as an immanent and self-moving unity. Philosophical universality is not indifferent to the determinations; it is the self-fulfilling universality, the diamantine identity, which at the same time holds difference within itself" (*PN*, 1, 202–3).

It is clear that Hegel's idea of nature presupposes Kant's notion of purposiveness without purpose. The organism is the concrete embodiment of inner teleology:

> When the living thing is regarded as a whole consisting of parts, or as a thing operated on by mechanical or chemical causes, as mechanical or chemical product, . . . then the Notion is regarded as external to it and it is treated as a *dead* thing. Since the Notion is immanent in it, the *purposiveness* of the living being is to be grasped as *inner;* the Notion is in it as determinate Notion, distinct from its externality, and in its distinguishing, pervading the externality and remaining identical with itself. This objectivity of the living being is the *organism.* [*SL,* 766]

The health of the organism requires the *harmonious* interrelation of the members comprising the whole. Though it can be occasioned by an external agent, disease is not a condition that is imposed from without but emerges from within as an interruption of the smooth functioning of the organism. Such disruption invariably results from the internal conflict that arises when a particular organ or system becomes isolated from and opposed to the organism as a whole:

> The organism is in a *diseased* state when one of its systems or organs is *stimulated* into conflict with the inorganic potency of the organism. Through this conflict, the system or organ establishes itself in isolation, and by persisting in its particular activity in opposition to the activity of the whole, obstructs the fluidity of this activity, as well as the process by which it pervades all the moments of the whole. [*PN, 3,* 193]

In contrast to his eighteenth-century precursors, Hegel is remarkably uninterested in identifying and classifying different diseases.[15] He is less concerned with the specifics of diagnosis than with the general way in which disease infects the organism.

Since disease is the negation of the internal harmony of the organism, the restoration of health requires a negation of negation through which inner equilibrium is reestablished. "In a state of *health,* there is *no disproportion* between the organic self and its determinate being; all its organs give free play to the fluidity of the universal" (*PN,* 3, 194). From Hegel's point of view, organisms—be they micro- or macroscopic—are *essentially* healthy. Disease, therefore, represents the loss of primal harmony or balance and the successful treatment of disease restores the organism to its *original* condition. Once recovered, the healthy individual is the incarnation of life universal:

> Life, considered now more closely in its Idea, is in and for itself absolute *universality;* the objectivity that it possesses is permeated throughout by the Notion and has the Notion alone for substance. What is distinguished as part, or in accordance with some other external reflection, has within itself the whole Notion; the Notion is the *omnipresent* soul in it, which remains simple self-relation and remains a one in the multiplicity belonging to objective being. [*SL,* 763]

The omnipresent soul that constitutes the universal life of everything that exists is the embodiment of the divine Logos. The theological notion of the Logos is a religious representation of the logical structure of reality that Hegel articulates in his *Science of Logic.* When fully developed, the notion of the organism reveals the rational *system* within which everything is encompassed. Reason or the Logos is not merely a subjective cognitive principle but is ontologically constitutive of things in themselves. Since reality is essentially rational or inherently logocentric, nature is an open book awaiting a knowledgeable reader. For those with eyes to see, nothing remains obscure. Part of Hegel's blindness results from his failure to appreciate the duplicity of this claim.

226

When Hegel transposes Kant's purposiveness without purpose from the natural to the logical register, the inner teleology of the organism becomes the self-regulation of the system. In the final analysis, Hegel denies all exteriority. What seems to be external is really internal to a whole that can bear nothing other than itself. In the absence of externality, every determination is self-determination and apparent heteronomy is true autonomy. To be an integral member of this organic totality is to be not only healthy but free. The reconciliation with the Logos is *salus*—the health that is our salvation.

While the movement from the eighteenth to the nineteenth century entails a shift from the use of mechanistic to organic metaphors for understanding nature and the body, the transition to the twentieth century is marked by what is often described as "the linguistic turn." Since the second decade of this century, there has been a tendency to draw on language instead of the machine or organism as a source of analytic and interpretive concepts. Humanists and social scientists in a remarkable range of disciplines were quick to realize the far-reaching implications of Saussure's *Cours de linguistique générale,* which was published in 1916, three years after his death. While the appropriation of linguistic models and metaphors in the biological sciences was slower than in other fields, it was no less significant for the understanding of human life and experience. By the middle of this century, it had become commonly accepted practice to describe biological and biochemical processes in terms of language, information, and communication. The delay in the use of linguistic terminology in biology had several noteworthy consequences. Most important, the appropriation of linguistic theory was not direct but was mediated by major developments in the areas of information and communication theory as well as computer technology.

As a result of these additional influences on biological and biochemical thinking, language does not so much replace the images of the machine and organism as provide a way to rethink the body as a communications system that combines mechanical and organic elements. The emerging field that creates the possibility of joining mechanics, organics, and linguistics is cybernetics. The word *cybernetics,* which was coined by Norbert Wiener, derives from the *kubernetes* (pilot, governor), which stems from *kubernan* (to steer, guide, govern). The Latin *gubernare* can also be traced to *kubernan.* To govern is, of course, to control the action or behavior of someone or something; to guide, direct, administer. But *govern* can also mean to regulate something by controlling its speed or magnitude. Thus, a governor is both a person who governs and "a feedback device on a machine or engine used to provide automatic control, as of speed, pressure, or temperature." In a 1943 article entitled "Behavior, Purpose, and Teleology," Wiener and his colleagues Arturo Rosenbleuth and Julian Bigelow, "distinguish between the 'functional analysis' of an entity and a 'behavioristic approach.' In the former, 'the main goal is the intrinsic organization of the entity studied, its structure and its properties.... The behavioristic approach consists in the examination of the output of the object and of the relations of this output to the input.' Wiener in his subsequent works largely restricted himself to 'the behavioristic method of study [which] omits the specific structure and intrinsic organization of the object.' The authors assign the term 'servomechanism' to designate machines with 'intrinsic purposeful behavior.' Purposeful behavior is directed at 'a final condition in which the behaving object reaches a definite correlation in time or space with respect to another object or event. All the purposeful behavior may be considered to require negative feedback,' that is, 'the behavior of an object is controlled by the margin of error at which the object stands at a given time with reference to a relatively specific goal. The authors conclude on the note that 'purposefulness [is] a concept necessary for the understanding of certain modes of behavior,' and define teleology as 'purpose controlled by feedback.' The authors reject the concept of teleology as implying a 'cause subsequent in time to a given effect.' " [16] As cybernetics developed, it came to specify "the theoretical study of control processes in electronic, mechanical, and biological systems, especially the mathematical analysis of the flow of information in such systems." [17]

Though Wiener and his followers do no explicitly draw on ninteenth-century interpretations of organisms, it is clear that their notion of cybernetics repeats and extends central elements in the view of organic systems that were first identified by Kant, Hegel, and many of their romantic counterparts. Within a cybernetic framework, systems are first and foremost self-governing or self-regulating. Furthermore, insofar as the concept of teleology does not imply a "cause subsequent to a given effect," cybernetic systems involve something like purposiveness without purpose or inner teleology. This does not imply that every system is completely closed and cut off from everything else. A system is open when it stands in an integral relation to its context, setting, or environment.

Cybernetics can be understood as a refinement and elaboration of the organic model of analysis. Whereas philosophers like Kant and Hegel leave the exact means of the self-governance of the organism relatively unspecified, cyberneticists attempt to define the mechanisms of self-regulation with great precision. The central factor in cybernetic self-regulation is the effective operation of a feedback control. "The principal characteristic of a self-regulating system is the presence of a control loop whereby system comportment may be modified on the basis of information inputs regarding performance and the comparison of performance with a criterion value. The control loop may be a 'closed loop' existing within the boundaries of the system, or it may be an 'open loop.' In the open loop feedback, part of the control information flow takes place outside the system boundary. The interaction of a self-regulating system with its external environment characteristically involves an open loop. Effector elements on the system boundary manipulate the environment to achieve certain objectives. Such sensor elements (receptors) perceive environmental changes which are transmitted to a decision-making element that compares this percept with the objective and transmits new orders to the effector element in terms of the difference between objective and achievement."[18] In anticipation of the application of cybernetic theory to the field of biology, it is important to stress that organisms can be micro- or macroscopic. Everything from the cell, to the body, to the earth is something like a cybernetic system. Thus, the relation of the cell to the organism is strictly parallel to the relation of the organism to the environment. Instead of a simple part that contributes to the composition of the whole, each part is itself a whole. In less prosaic terms, every member of the totality is a synecdoche.

In developing the role of feedback in systematic control, early cybernetic theorists drew extensively on developments in emerging computer technology and information theory. Feedback, I have noted, can be either positive or negative. When joined in a recursive loop, positive and negative feedback function like a switch that can be turned on or off. Proper regulation of the system requires the maintenance of a balance between too much and too little. Excess—be it positive or negative—destroys systematic equilibrium. When understood in this way, the governance of a system depends on digital operations that can be coded in terms of binary oppositions. Self-regulating systems, in other words, are analogous to digital computers.[19] But the similarities between cybernetic systems and computers are even more profound than this analogy suggests. The means by which systems regulate themselves is *information,* which, in order to be effective, must be coded in digital form.

Claude Shannon's seminal paper, "The Mathematical Theory of Communication," published in 1948, marked a turning point in the understanding of problems that had plagued communication theory and technology since the advent of electronic communications. Shannon is less concerned with semantics than the capacity to measure the *quantity* of information transmitted. In its most basic form, information theory represents an effort to define the relation among five elements that make up any communication system: sender, receiver, channel, code, and message. For communication to take place, a sender must be

229

able to send a coded message across a channel to a receiver who can decipher the transmission. A communication network is something like a *postal system* in which letters are sent, delivered, and read. Shannon develops an extraordinarily complex mathematical theory to demonstrate that the information communicated can be measured in quantifiable *bits.*[20] The amount of information is inversely proportional to its probability. In other words, the more probable an occurrence or event, the less information it communicates, and vice versa.[21]

The transmission of messages presupposes the coding of information in readable form. "A code may be defined as a set of rules governing the permissible construction of messages in the system. A code mediates the relationships between the goalseeking sender-receivers that employ it. Thus a code or set of codes is the basis of the creative principle that makes messages and relationships *possible* in the first place, at the same time as the constraints embodied in a code make an even greater variety of qualitatively different messages and relationships *impossible* in the system as it stands."[22] Expressed in terms of Saussurean linguistics, a code is *la langue* that is the condition of the possibility of the message, which is *la parole.* If messages are to be transmitted, sender and receiver must share a template that makes it possible to code and decode information.

When information theory is combined with the technological capacity to transfer information created by computers, cybernetic systems become networks of communication that are regulated by the orderly flow of information. In his important book *System and Structure: Essays in Communication and Exchange,* Anthony Wilden proposes a series "tentative axioms" on "Epistemology and Ecology," several of which help to clarify the intersection of cybernetics, computers, and information and communication theory:

1. A system is distinguished from its parts by its organization. It is not an aggregate. We may consequently say that the 'behavior' of the whole is more complex than the 'sum' of the 'behavior' of its parts. However, since the organization of the whole imposes *constraints* on the 'behavior' of the parts, we must also recognize that the semiotic freedom of each subsystem in itself is greater than its semiotic freedom as a part of the whole, and may in effect be greater than that of the whole.

2. All behavior is communication. Communication, by definition, is an attribute of system and involves a structure. Structure concerns frameworks, channels, and coding; system concerns processes, transmissions, and messages. . . .

3. Language includes all the communicational processes and possibilities of less highly organized, primarily digital, communicational systems, as

well as specific linguistic properties. Language is not only a means of communication and behavior; it also imposes specific systemic and structural constraints on the ways in which we perceive and act upon the world and each other. [*SS*, 201–3]

In his last axiom, Wilden distinguishes communication from language. This distinction *does not,* however, imply an opposition. While all communication is not necessarily linguistic *sensu strictissimo,* all language presupposes a communications system as an enabling condition. My earlier claim that the body is structured like a language must, therefore, be refined: the body is structured like a communications system. The point I would like to stress at this juncture is that there is no *qualitative* difference between communication and language. If the body is structured like a communications system and if nature is understood as an extension of the body or the body is viewed as a synecdoche of nature, then the classical Western oppositions between mind/body and person/ nature must be reconsidered. When the notion of the organism is reinterpreted in light of cybernetics and communication theory, the body and the natural world do not seem unintelligent but appear to be *disseminated information* that circulates in a decentered communications network. Donna Haraway has coined the suggestive term *cyborg* to describe this cybernetic organism:

> A cyborg is a cybernetic organism, a hybrid of machine and organism, a creature of social reality as well as a creature of fiction. . . . Modern medicine is also full of cyborgs between organism and machine, each conceived as coded devices, in an intimacy and with a power that was not generated in the history of sexuality. . . . By the late twentieth century, our time, a mythic time, we are all chimeras, theorized and fabricated hybrids of machine and organism; in short, we are cyborgs. The cyborg is our ontology; it gives us our politics. The cyborg is a condensed image of both imagination and material reality, the two joined centers structuring any possibility of historical transformation.[23]

To understand the life of cyborgs, it is necessary to move beyond Foucault's microphysics of power to a *microbiotics of information and intelligence.*

As I have stressed, a system tends to disclose its structure when it fails or breaks down. In the biological system, the point of breakdown is disease. The most recent advances in biological and medical research suggest that disease can best be understood as a failure, break, or interruption in the complex communications system that constitutes the body. Messages fail to arrive, arrive too early or too late, or are misdirected and thus the system breaks down. When carefully examined, disease reveals that the failure of communication is not accidental but endemic to bodily functioning. The body, like every other system, is structurally incomplete. Dysfunction does not befall the organism from without but is, as it were, systemic.

Ever since the initial formulation of information theory, philosophers, mathematicians, and scientists have insisted on the relevance of cybernetics for understanding living organisms. In *Cybernetics— or Control and Communication in the Animal and Machine* (1948), Wiener argues that information theory makes it possible to establish the isomorphism of nonliving and living systems. Such claims remained largely speculative until the remarkable developments in molecular biology in the middle of this century. "Although the role of DNA as genetic material was established in the middle 1940s," William DeWitt points out, "it was not until some twenty years later that we understood how information is coded in DNA and how it is decoded by the cell for use in synthesizing proteins. The 'cracking' of the genetic code may be the single most significant breakthrough in our understanding of cellular function."[24] In 1952, James Watson and Francis Crick discovered that the DNA molecule consists of two polynucleotide strands that are interwoven to form a double helix.[25] A human cell contains approximately six feet of DNA, which consists of six billion base pairs squeezed into forty-six chromosomes. This genetic material forms the blueprint for the entire organism. Each of the fifty to one hundred thousand genes in the cell nucleus makes up a segment of the DNA and possesses the instructions for making a particular protein. These instructions are produced by varying the sequence of the four chemical bases that form what is, in effect, the alphabet of the organism's communication network: adenine (A), thymine (T), guanine (G), and cytosine (C). The functioning of the organism involves the coding and decoding of the messages composed from this rudimentary alphabet. Since each cell in the body has all the DNA and thus contains a complete operational blueprint, cell specialization requires the restriction or regulation of genetic information. Hence the body is similar to a cybernetic system in which information is managed by an intricate feedback loop.

New genetic material is produced by DNA replication in which each strand in the double helix unwinds and becomes a template for the creation of a new strand (fig. 31). The replicated DNA consists of one strand from the original molecule and a newly synthesized strand. The exchange of information between DNA and RNA and hence the communication of DNA with the rest of the organism depend upon two interrelated processes known as transcription and translation. The syn-

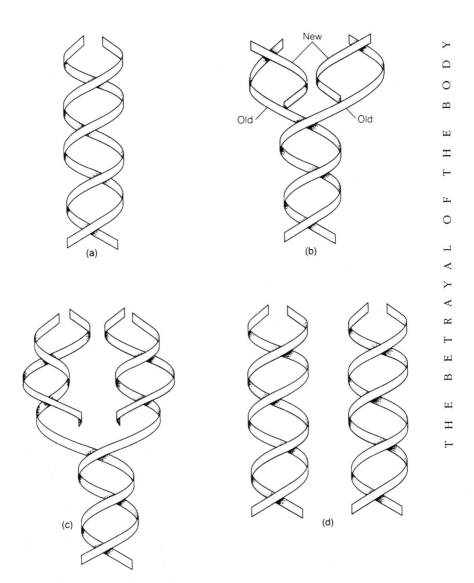

31. DNA replication. Courtesy William DeWitt.

thesis of the proteins upon which life depends takes place in two stages. First, a sequence of nucleotides from the polynucleotide strand of a DNA molecule, is *transcribed* as an RNA molecule, which is known as messenger RNA (mRNA). As a result of this transcription, the genetic code of DNA is transferred to mRNA, which leaves the cell nucleus and moves through the cytoplasm where the message is decoded, or *translated,* to form specific proteins. "If the sequence of nucleotides in a mRNA molecule determines the sequence of amino acids in a protein, then specific nucleotides, or groups of nucleotides, must somehow specify the incorporation of particular amino acids into proteins during protein synthesis, just as a sequence of three dots in Morse code speci-fies the incorporation of the letter S into a word."[26] Wilden summarizes this intricate process in a way that underscores the cybernetic aspect of intra- and intercellular communication:

> DNA is the molecular coding of a set of instructions for the growth of a certain living system of cells. But these instructions do not *cause* growth any more than the directions of a cake mix cause the mix to become a cake. They do not cause growth, they control its possibilities. In other words, the instructions of DNA *constrain* or limit growth. (All growth is positive feedback—the amplification of deviations—and, without negative feedback control, all growth would be cancerous, leading to destruction.) . . . If DNA were all there were to the 'blueprint' of the cell, then, since all cells in an organism contain the same genetic instructions, no differentiation or division of labor in the cell would ever occur. Differentiation is the prod-uct of inhibitors: the constraints of the feedback relationship to the envi-ronment in which the messengers carrying the instructions (RNA) find themselves. Thus the articulation of the genetic code—which we know to be in some way double, like language, and punctuated, like writing—de-pends upon processes of combination-in-context (contiguity) and substitu-tion-by-selection (similarity). Like language, also, it is a combined analog and digital process. Like language, it is not ruled by causality, but by goal-seeking and constraint. It is not ruled by what is or what was so much as by what is not, by what may be. [*SS,* 339–40]

The processes of transcription and translation are not always free of error. The survival of the organism depends on the storage of infor-mation coded in DNA and transcribed in RNA. Though there are various mechanisms to insure the accurate preservation and replication of DNA, mistakes sometimes occur that modify the message required for the manufacture of specific proteins. Changes can take place in DNA itself, as well as in the processes by which it is transcribed into RNA and RNA is translated into proteins. Alterations in the nucleotide sequence of DNA are called mutations and usually result in a change in genetic in-formation content, which, in turn, leads to the substitution of one amino acid for another. Even without such a change in the information, mis-takes are made when DNA is transcribed into RNA and RNA is translated into proteins. Though the latter changes do not have a genetic basis, their consequences can be detrimental to the organism.

These basic life processes seem to confirm the suspicion that at the most rudimentary level, the body is structured like a language or a communications system. The genetic code is breathtakingly complex and yet surprisingly simple. Though the chemical reactions necessary to sustain life are bewildering in their number and intricacy, the *struc-*

ture of these processes is elementary. As structuralists have long realized, the structure of structure is binary opposition. In some of his more speculative moments, Lévi-Strauss proposes that the final explanation of the structure of mental and cultural artifacts might actually lie at the biological level. Analyzing the effectiveness of symbols in the apparently different practices of a shaman and psychoanalyst, Lévi-Strauss comments:

> It would be a matter, either way, of stimulating an organic transformation which would consist essentially in a structural reorganization, by inducing the patient intensively to live out a myth—either received or created by him—whose structure would be, at the unconscious level, analogous to the structure whose genesis is sought on the organic level. The effectiveness of symbols would consist precisely in this 'inductive property,' by which formally homologous structures, built out of different materials at different levels—organic processes, unconscious mind, rational thought—are related to one another.[27]

While any such line of analysis is potentially reductive, Lévi-Strauss's argument can be read as an effort to establish the isomorphism of different systems of human behavior without reducing one to an other. When theorizing about the interrelation of the body, the unconscious, the mind, and, indeed, society and culture as a whole, Lévi-Strauss invariably turns to linguistic metaphors:

> The unconscious . . . is always empty—or, more accurately, it is as alien to mental images as is the stomach to the foods that pass through it. As the organ of a specific function, the unconscious merely imposes structural laws upon inarticulated elements that originate elsewhere—impulses, emotions, representations, and memories. We might say, therefore, that the preconscious is the individual lexicon where each of us accumulates the vocabulary of his personal history, but that this vocabulary becomes significant, for us and for others, only to the extent that the unconscious structures it according to its laws and thus transforms it into language. . . . If we add that these structures are not only the same for everyone and for all areas to which the function applies, but that they are few in number, we shall understand why the world of symbolism is infinitely varied in content, but always limited in its laws. There are many languages, but very few structural laws that are valid for all languages.[28]

The developments in biological theory and information technology that we have been considering effectively extend structural analysis to the level of the microorganism. Though organisms and bodies vary infinitely, the universal genetic code is constituted by very few structural laws. These laws are the *grammar* of our bodies.

235

When read in this way, current biological theory appears to reinscribe the logocentrism that has characterized Western thought since its beginnings in ancient Greece. As a body of disseminated information or intelligence, a cyborg seems to be the immanent realization of the structures defined by philosophy in one or another variation of the Platonic forms and by theologians in contrasting reflections of the *imago dei*. In different terms, if the communications system of the body is interpreted cybernetically, it seems to represent a refinement of the romantic notion of the organism advanced by nineteenth-century artists and poets and conceptualized in both Kant's Third Critique and Hegel's system. If the real is logical or "logos-ful," then the body (and everything else) can be read like an open book.

I have suggested, however, that the closure required for this hermeneutic of the body is impossible because systems are inevitably inadequate and incomplete. Fault is not secondary or accidental but is necessary to the constitution of the system as such. In relation to organic systems, this means that the mistakes that lead, inter alia, to disease are not only unavoidable but, in a certain sense, are "original." Disease arises as if from within to disrupt an equilibrium or harmony that was never present in the first place. To diagnose the faults in systems, it is necessary to reexamine the etiology of disease by reconsidering the structure of structure.

From a structuralist perspective, we have seen, the structure of structure is binary opposition. When this structure is translated into cybernetic terms by information machines known as computers, binary oppositions are digitized. By asking what such binary and digital translations omit, it is possible to discern faults that leave every system gaping. In his summary of the cybernetic aspects of organic communication, Wilden notes that the articulation of the genetic code is, like language, a combined analog and digital process. There are, however, important differences between analog and digital computers, which imply yet another difference that resists computation and thus remains

incalculable.

The difference between analog and digital computers entails a difference between two kinds of difference. "Analog differences are differences of magnitude, frequency, distribution, pattern, organization, and the like. Digital differences are those such as can be coded into *distinctions* and *oppositions*, and for this, there must be discrete elements with well-defined boundaries" (*SS,* 169). So understood, analog differences cannot pose either/or oppositions but can represent a sliding differential scale. An analog computer calculates "by means of an analog between real, physical *continuous* quantities and some other set of variables. The real quantities may be the distance between points on a scale, the angular displacement, the velocity, or the acceleration of a rotating shaft, a quantity of some liquid, or the electrical current in a conductor" (*SS*, 155–56). A digital computer, by contrast, uses discrete elements or bits and discontinuous scales. The distinction between analog and digital computers is analogous to the difference between wave and particle theories of light. Neither computer can register the processes graphed by the other. "The analog computer maps continuums precisely, whereas the digital computer can only be precise about boundaries. The units of communication or computation in the analog machine may, in principle, be repeatedly divided without necessarily losing their signification or use, whereas those in the digital computer cannot be divided below the level of the discrete unit on which it depends." [29]

Some of the difficulties involved in interpreting living bodies in terms of computers become clear when we realize that biological processes entail both analog and digital functions. For example, communication through the central nervous system presupposes the capacity of neurons to transmit messages by way of axons across the synapses that separate nerve cells. While neurons operate digitally, axons function analogically. The dispatch of a message along the axon is an analog process in which the amplitude and frequency of electrochemical activity is modulated. When these analog changes reach a threshold level, the charges of the ions in the aqueous solution on either side of the cell membrane switch through a digital reversal, thereby enabling the neurotransmitters to convey the message. For our purposes, the important point about this process is the inextricable interplay between analog and digital functions. "The relation between inside and outside is not a simple 'binary opposition' between positive and negative," Wilden concludes, "because it is a relation between a continuously differentiated potential and a threshold. The message in the axon thus appears as a distinction engendered on the ground of difference. This distinction is, in turn, dependent on the punctuation of the distinction between inside and outside by the membrane" (*SS*, 176).

Since cybernetics and information theory are built upon a digital model that cannot calculate analog differences, and since organisms require both analog and digital processes, the interpretation of the body as a communications system is unavoidably incomplete and inadequate. This problem cannot be overcome by attempting to incorporate an analog function in a digital machine, for, as I have stressed, the difference between analog and digital differences is incommensurable. There is, however, an even more profound fault in every communications system, and this fault points to a different difference—a difference that is even more radical than either analog or digital (that is, binary) differences. The site or nonsite of this difference is the membrane, margin, boundary, or gap that inhabits every system and organism.

All communication presupposes difference. Difference is something like a boundary or margin that opens the space in which messages can be exchanged. As such, the difference of the boundary is *different* from the differences whose articulation it creates. Though it is the condition of the possibility of articulation and communication, this different difference is inarticulate and incommunicable. It can be coded neither analogically nor digitally. The membrane, margin, or boundary is something like a *not* that cannot be undone.

This not not only distinguishes analog and digital differences but also "infects" binary oppositions, which, according to the foundational principles of structural linguistics, constitute the structure of structure. "Language depends upon punctuation in the widest sense, and especially on the space or the zero phoneme, both of which establish relations between something and something else. The space is a boundary, but not an absence. If the space is equivalent to zero or to 0, then we have to say that 'not' is both equivalent to zero and 0 and also a rule about establishing zero and 0. In other words, 'not' is both a boundary and a rule (or a 'frame') about the establishment of boundaries" (*SS*, 188). Not is, however, a strange, irregular ruler that creates irresolvable paradoxes. Perhaps the most puzzling paradox of the not is its necessary incomprehensibility; it eludes every system whose construction or formulation it enables. In this sense, the not deconstructs all systems from an "inside" that is nonetheless "outside." Every system is irreducibly incomplete, for it "includes" as a condition of its own possibility something it cannot include. Though seemingly irrational, this paradox can actually be expressed mathematically in Gödel's theorem, which states: "In any formal system adequate for number theory, there exists an undecidable formula—that is, a formula that is not provable and whose negation is not provable." In other words, a system can be consistent if and only if it is incomplete.

A system that is either inconsistent or partial is not, of course, a system. If every system is "structurally" incomplete, then the body and its subsystems are less like books whose logic, coherence, and unity are perfectly transparent than texts that are inwardly torn and riddled with gaps in a way that makes them essentially opaque. The textuality of the body renders its integrity deeply problematic. Within the open economy of textuality, the body is no more a unified whole than the self is identical to itself. As a result of its textuality, the body inevitably betrays itself.

Nowhere is the betrayal of the body more pronounced than in the covert operations of the immune system and the baffling contradictions of autoimmune diseases. At first glance, the immune system seems to involve operations that are quintessentially digital. Immunology is commonly described as the science of "self-nonself discrimination."[30] Irun Cohen begins an informative and suggestive paper entitled "The Self, the World, and Autoimmunity" by explaining that "it is generally assumed that the main job of the immune system is to distinguish between what is 'self' and what is 'not self.' Once the distinction has been made, 'self' is preserved and 'not self' is destroyed. At the most general level, of course, this is true, and human beings remain alive and healthy only because it is so. Recently it has become clear, however, that at a finer level of detail the distinction between self and other is not absolute."[31] In this biological version of Hegel's speculative philosophy, identity is a function of difference from difference. Health presupposes self-recognition in which the self knows itself as not other, and, correspondingly, disease arises from the failure of self-recognition that results from the inability to distinguish self from nonself. The medium of healthy self-recognition is disseminated knowledge that must be clearly communicated across channels that are free of interruptions and interference.

In the scientific literature devoted to the immune system, the rhetoric of immunology tends to be surprisingly militaristic. The word "immune" derives from the Latin *immunis,* which means "exempt from a public service, burden, or charge; free, exempt." Its use in connection with the investigation of disease and its prevention dates only from 1880. The terms that biological and medical researchers currently use to characterize immunological processes present a picture of the body engaged in a life-and-death struggle with others that are constantly attacking it. Recalling the image of the ancient physician-philosopher Heraclitus, life is war and the only guarantee of survival is a good defense system. The immune system is, in effect, a strategic defense system in which vigilant observers constantly patrol the outer and inner borders of the body. The purpose of this perpetual surveillance is to keep out foreigners, strangers, undesirables, unwelcome guests, and illegal aliens. Any adequate defense system requires a sophisticated "intelligence community." The endless "struggle for recognition" staged between self and other involves a complex game of espionage in which agents and counteragents (chemical and otherwise) employ elaborate disguises and deceits to dupe the enemy and thereby gain a decisive advantage. One of the most important ploys in espionage and counter-espionage is the ability to trick the enemy by sending false messages that are mistaken for true. In addition to deceit, defense agents must be able to develop and break codes that convey the messages upon which every "strategic defense initiative" depends. When messages are intercepted, interrupted, or misread, the defense system breaks down and the invaders win the struggle.

All the intelligence in the world, however, is useless without an adequate arsenal of weapons for self-defense. In the body's deadly battle with disease, the invaders are antigens and the defense network is formed by an "army" of lymphocytes, some of which secrete antibodies and some of which attack cellular antigens directly.[32] There are two types of immune response: humoral and cell mediated. While it is tempting to describe humoral response as an analog process and cell-mediated immunity as digital, the parallel is, for reasons that will become clear, approximate rather than precise. The cells involved in the immune system are lymphocytes, which are a class of white blood cells. Though all lymphocytes are produced in bone marrow, some migrate to lymphatic tissues and organs and others pass through the thymus gland where they undergo further specialization. The former are called B-lymphocytes, which produce the antibodies that are responsible for the humoral response, and the latter T-lymphocytes, which are responsible for the cell-mediated response.[33] As I have noted, the ability of the body to defend itself against invading antigens depends on a complex process of self-recognition in which the body distinguishes self from other (that is, nonself).

There are, of course, millions of foreign agents that seek to cross the body's borders. These agents are marked by antigens that bear a unique identity formed by specific molecules on their surface. This protein structure constitutes a code that must be deciphered by the body's defense system. One of the major breakthroughs in immunology was the discovery in 1954 by Niels Jerne that the human body is *preprogrammed* to detect and respond to an astonishing one hundred million or more antigens. Jerne arrived at his momentous insight while walking home in Copenhagen from the Danish State Serum Institute at Amaliegard. Ten years later he described his discovery in terms borrowed from Kierkegaard:

> "Can the truth *(the capability to synthesize an antibody)* be learned? If
> so, it must be assumed not to pre-exist; to be learned, it must be acquired.
> We are thus confronted with the difficulty to which Socrates calls attention
> in Meno, namely that it makes as little sense to search for what one does
> not know as to search for what one knows; what one knows one cannot
> search for, since one knows it already, and what one does not know one
> cannot search for, since one does not even know what to search for. Socra-
> tes resolves this difficulty by postulating that learning is nothing but recol-
> lection. The truth *(the capability to synthesize an antibody)* cannot be
> brought in, but was already immanent."
>
> The above paragraph is a translation of the first lines of Søren Kierke-
> gaard's *Philosophical Fragments.* By replacing the word "truth" by the itali-
> cized words, the statement can be made to present the logical basis of the
> selective theories of antibody formation. Or, in the parlance of Molecular
> Biology; synthetic potentialities cannot be imposed upon nucleic acid, but
> must pre-exist.[34]

According to Jerne's natural selection theory, the body randomly produces antibodies capable of recognizing virtually every possible antigen
it might encounter. The revolutionary aspect of Jerne's theory is his
contention that antibodies are produced *in the absence* of antigens. In
other words, the body is equipped for the battles it faces *before* the so-
called enemy appears. F. M. Burnet refined Jerne's analysis to form the
clonal selection theory, which most immunologists currently accept as
the basis of their investigations. Burnet's theory rests on the precise
recognition mechanisms at work in the immune system.

The strategies for recognizing antigens are somewhat different in
the humoral and cell-mediated response. In the humoral response, a
specific antibody produced by a B-lymphocyte and present as a receptor
on the surface of the lymphocyte recognizes a particular antigen and
responds by producing more antibodies, which are released into the
blood stream (whence the name "humoral response") to combat the
infection. The recognition mechanism in B-lymphocytes is similar to a
digital function in which the decoding of a message turns on a switch
that sets in motion antibody production. The antigen-antibody dyad
forms something like a lock-key structure with a part of the surface
structure of the antigen, known as the epitope, serving as a lock that
can be opened by *only one* key. The antibody is the key to the antigen.
The key-like part of the antibody is a protein structure that fits the antigen epitope. It is important to stress that each antibody is coded to
recognize a *single* antigen. Since there are at least one hundred million
antibodies in the human body, the process of sorting necessary for an

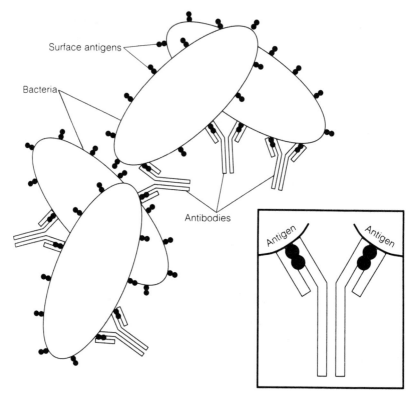

Surface antigens

Bacteria

Antibodies

Antigen

Antigen

32. Antigen-antibody relation. Courtesy William DeWitt.

effective response to the presence of aliens is extraordinarily complex.
When the key fits the lock (that is, when the complementary molecular
structures unite), proper identification is established and the immune
response begins (fig. 32).

This process of recognition can be described in different terms. The
antibody must *read* the message or *decipher* the program of the antigen. Once the antibody "understands" exactly what the antigen is "saying," it knows how to respond. The response of the antibody is twofold.
In the first place, the antibody's recognition of the antigen as a foreign
agent triggers the production of more antibodies by B-lymphocytes to
ward off the invasion. According to Burnet's clonal selection theory, the
lymphocyte clones itself, thereby producing a number of identical lymphocytes, all of which make the same antibody. Most of these antibodies
are then released into the blood stream as plasma proteins and proceed
to circulate throughout the system to neutralize or destroy the antigens.
In one of the most remarkable features of the immune system, some of
the cloned lymphocytes are brought to the brink of response (that is,
brought to the stage where they are capable of producing antibodies)

242

and then deactivated. These antibodies, which form something like an army of reserves, constitute the organism's "immunological memory." When the body is again attacked by the same antigen, the deactivated recruits are called to active duty. Having already undergone extensive training, the activated reserves can respond quickly and effectively when ordered to do so. This mechanism explains why, in some cases, a person who has had a disease once is immunized against further occurrences of the illness.

The operation of the T-lymphocyte is considerably more complex (fig. 33). In contrast to B-lymphocytes, three distinct cells are categorized as T-lymphocytes: helper cells, suppressor cells, and killer T-cells.

33. T-lymphocyte. Micrograph by Yaakov Naparstek and Dorit Gurfel.

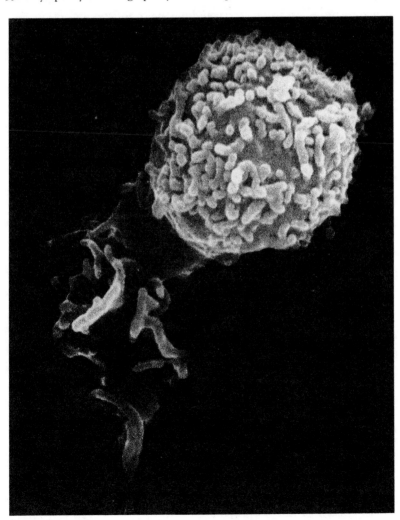

While helper cells aid B-lymphocytes in the production of antibodies, suppressor cells turn off antibody synthesis when an adequate humoral response has been achieved. Unlike B-lymphocytes, whose response to antigens is always mediated by antibodies, killer T-cells attack invading or infected cells directly. Killer T-cells are responsible for destroying fungi, parasites, cells infected with intracellular microbes, organ transplants, and tumorous cells.[35]

The recognition mechanism of killer T-cells is more intricate than that of B-lymphocytes. Left to its own devices, the killer T-cell cannot recognize the antigen as a foreign body. In order to decipher the code of the antigen, the killer T-cell needs the assistance of cells in the blood system known as macrophages. A macrophage is a large phagocytic cell, formed form a monocyte (that is, another type of white blood cell), which serves as a scavenger by engulfing microbes and devouring dead or damaged cells and cellular debris. Before the antigen can be recognized as nonself, a macrophage must consume the foreign microbe and present it to the killer T-cell. After ingesting the invader, the macrophage places the portion of the epitope that defines the antigen on its own surface. Even this processing and presentation, however, are inadequate to make the antigen legible to the killer T-cell. The killer T-cell can decode the antigen only when it is read in the context of a specific aspect of the body's unique cellular identity. Each cell within the human organism bears the body's individual stamp, which serves as something like an *idiomatic* signature. This privileged trace of bodily identity is the "histocompatibility complex," which is formed by a unique protein structure that appears on the surface of cells. The killer T-cells cannot decode the antigen unless the foreign epitope is presented along with the body's own histocompatibility complex. When the macrophage presents the antigen, it is placed beside the cellular signature of the body in a way that enables the killer T-cell to distinguish self and nonself. Once the foreign agent is recognized, the immune response of the killer T-cell moves into action. The actual recognition of the antigen by the killer T-cell follows the lock-and-key pattern of B-lymphocytes. The formation of a bond between the antigen and killer T-cell stimulates the macrophage to release a hormonelike molecule of interleukin, which, in turn, causes the T-cell to divide to form an army of defense agents. Thus fortified, killer T-cells proceed to attack the antigen by secreting a protein that pierces the membrane of the alien cell. The perforated membrane of the target cell results in an influx and efflux of vital fluids that eventually kills the cell (figs. 34 and 35). When

244

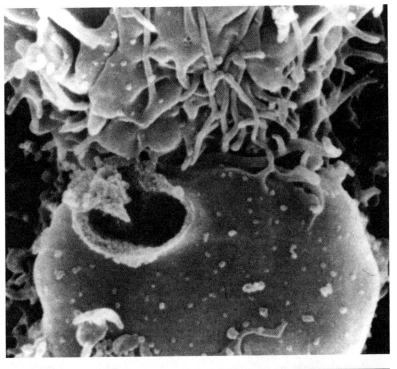

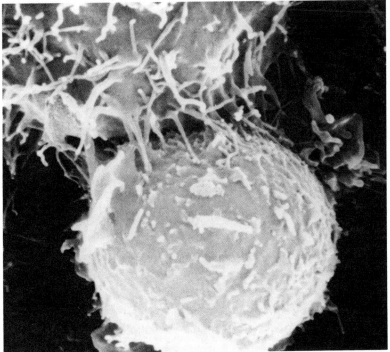

34–35. Killer T-cell destroying a tumor. Micrograph by Gilla Kaplan, Scanning Electron Micrographs, The Rockefeller University.

the immune response is successful, the invader is repulsed and the body seems to return to its healthy and peaceful state.

But health and peace are only apparent. The struggle against disease is endless, for foreign agents are forever foiling the body's defense system and slipping across its borders. The body is always forced to play host to many unwanted guests. The immune system is not only perpetually in a state of high alert but is constantly engaged in active warfare. Since the enemy never sleeps, vigilance must be ceaseless. The problems the body faces are, however, even more profound than this diagnosis suggests, for the body is also at war with itself. The body, in other words, betrays itself. Contrary to long established canons of theology, philosophy, biology, and medicine, the betrayal of the body is not abnormal but is, in a certain sense, our "original" condition. The most disturbing yet revealing instance of the body's betrayal of itself is autoimmune disease.

While successful immune response depends on the ability to distinguish self from nonself, autoimmune disease results from the body's failure to distinguish self from nonself. The body mistakes itself for an other and initiates an attack on itself, which is normally reserved for foreign invaders. The result is self-destruction by means of self-consumption. As Donna Haraway correctly observes, "we seem invaded not just by the threatening 'non-selves' that the immune system guards against, but more fundamentally by our own strange parts. No wonder autoimmune disease carries such awful significance, marked from the first suspicion if its existence in 1901 by Morgenroth and Erlich's term, *horror autotoxicus.*"[36] In the course of this century, scientists have confirmed the suspicions of Morgenroth and Erlich many times over. In every case of *autotoxicus,* the disease is caused by a malfunction in the immune system: Graves' disease (antibodies attack the thyroid gland), Reiter's syndrome (T-cells attack tissues in the eyes, joints, and genital track), rheumatic fever (antibodies attack heart muscle), systemic lupus (antibodies attack joints, skin, kidneys, and other organs), rheumatoid arthritis (T-cells attack joints), myasthenia gravis (antibodies attack neuromuscular junction), multiple sclerosis (T-cells attack sheaths around nerve cells), and insulin-dependent diabetes (T-cells attack insulin-making cells in the pancreas). Investigators are now convinced that autoimmune diseases result from a breakdown in the communications systems that govern the body. The interruption or misinterpretation of a message upon which effective immune response depends prompts the body to turn on itself. Though none of these conditions is fully understood, scientists are making gradual progress in unravelling the

246

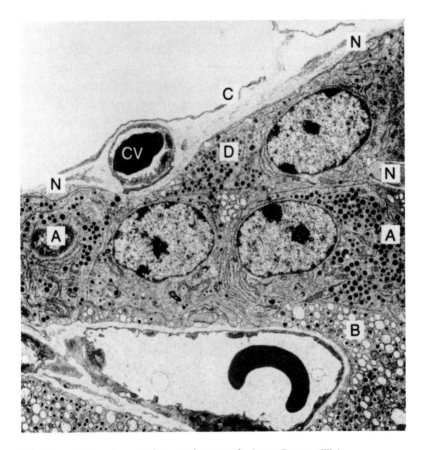

36. Islet of Langerhans in the rat. Photograph: Susan Bonner-Weir.

mystery of autoimmune diseases. Because it is relatively widespread, considerable attention has been focused on diabetes. An examination of the etiology of diabetes illuminates the mechanisms of autoimmunity and suggests the broader implications of autoimmune diseases for our understanding of our bodies and ourselves.

There are two types of diabetes or, more accurately, diabetes mellitus, which usually are referred to alternatively as Type I and Type II, juvenile and adult-onset, and insulin-dependent and non-insulin-dependent diabetes. Only insulin-dependent (Type I) diabetes is an autoimmune disease.[37] In most cases of Type II diabetes, insulin is generated in higher than normal concentrations but there is a reduced sensitivity of cells to insulin. In Type I diabetes, by contrast, the depletion of the insulin-producing beta cells in the islets of Langerhans (fig. 36) leads to the inability to take up and process the glucose that supplies the body with energy. Unused glucose remains in the blood and results in elevated blood sugar levels. In the absence of available glucose, the body

247

begins to break down stored fat and even proteins to supply needed energy. In other words, the body literally *cannibalizes* itself. Sudden weight loss, which is one of the symptoms of the onset of diabetes, is a sign of the body's self-consumption. In a paradoxical cycle that would make most weight watchers envious, the more one eats, the more weight one loses. As the ability to metabolize glucose decreases, the need to degrade more fat increases, thereby further reducing body weight. The catabolism of fat creates as by-products acetone and ketone bodies, which accumulate in the blood and cause the osmotic loss of water and, correlatively, dehydration. The acidity of the blood and dehydration produced by hyperglycemia can result in diabetic coma and finally death. Frequently fatal complications of long-term diabetes range from atherosclerosis, heart attack, and kidney damage, to blindness and a variety of neurological disorders.[38]

The islets of Langerhans, housing the beta cells, are lodged in the pancreas. The pancreas, in turn, is part of the endocrine system whose eight ductless glands, in cooperation with the nervous system, regulate bodily activities by secreting hormones directly into the blood.[39] Within the decentered information system of the body, responsibility for short-term responses and adjustments is delegated to the nervous system and long-term regulation of bodily functions is controlled by the endocrine system. Endocrine glands operate like cybernetic systems to sustain the metabolic homeostasis necessary for the stability of the organism. As we discovered in our investigation of cybernetic systems, "feedback loops may be of two general types. The most common are *negative feedback loops*, in which an increase in the output, or function, of a target organ causes a reduction in the synthesis and release of the hormone that controls the organ. In *positive feedback loops*, an increase in target organ output increases the synthesis and release of the controlling hormone. Examples of negative feedback loops are the effects of insulin on blood sugar reduction and of glucagon on the elevation of blood sugar. In this system, a reduction in blood sugar levels inhibits insulin production by the islet cells of the pancreas while an increase in blood sugar levels inhibits glucagon secretion by pancreatic islet cells. The net effect of the action of insulin and glucagon is to maintain blood sugar at relatively constant levels."[40] If the feedback loop fails or is interrupted, the equilibrium of the organism is disrupted; if the circuit cannot be repaired, equilibrium becomes impossible and disease chronic.

In insulin-dependent diabetes, the cybernetic system of the pancreas breaks down irreparably as the result of the body's destruction of its own beta cells. Though all the details of the autoimmune response at work in Type I diabetes are not clear, most researchers now agree that the problem arises when a killer T-cell misinterprets pancreatic beta cells as invaders and destroys them. Thus, the body unleashes an attack *on itself.* This misinterpretation is no simple mistake but is an error produced by supplementary layers of duplicity and deceit, which are added to the intelligence and counterintelligence drama played out in the recesses of the body. This strange twist in the covert game of corporeal espionage is called antigenic or molecular mimicry.[41] Describing possible complications in the body's response to antigens, Cohen writes:

> The challenge is compounded by the fact that the self and the invader are made up of the same building blocks: proteins, carbohydrates, nucleic acids and lipids. What is more, molecules such as enzymes or hormones that perform key biological functions tend to be conserved in evolution so that the self and invader may have identical—or at least very similar— molecules. Finally, it seems that some pathogens actually make hostlike antigens as a means of disguise. For example, leishmania parasites (some types of which cause trypanosomiasis) synthesize antigens similar to those of the red blood cells of their mammalian hosts. It appears that antigenic "mimicry" is a persistent feature of the struggle between self and pathogen.[42]

In the case of diabetes, the molecular structure of some antigens is so similar to part of the structure of one or more of the proteins on the surface of the beta cells of the pancreas that killer T-cells misread self as nonself (fig. 37). Having made this mistake, the body lacks the resources to turn off the process of self-destruction. In Type I diabetes, the attack of killer T-cells continues until all the beta cells are destroyed and insulin production stops completely.[43]

There is no cure for diabetes. The most that those who suffer from this disease can hope for is "the reasonable control" of symptoms and the *temporary* delay of complications. Treatment consists of a strict exercise and dietary regimen and the regular administration of insulin by injection. In the past decade, the effectiveness of self-regulation has been improved by the development of more refined insulins and introduction of better methods for testing the blood and monitoring blood sugar levels. This technology enables the patient to attempt to simulate the feedback loop of the pancreas. Though steadily improving, these management strategies will always remain imprecise and inadequate. Broken loops cannot be mended; cut circuits cannot be repaired; interrupted communication cannot be revived. Failure is inevitable and disease incurable.

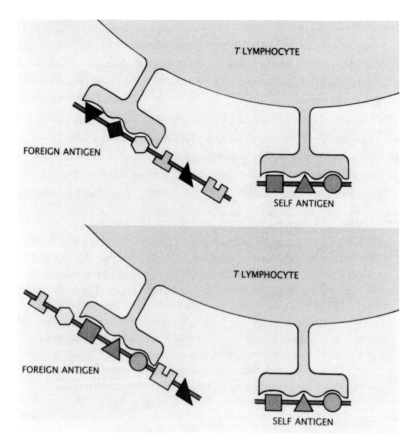

37. Joan Starwood, Antigenic mimicry. From Irun Cohen, "The Self, the World and Autoimmunity," ©1988 by Scientific American, Inc. All rights reserved.

But disease itself does not seem unavoidable. Health appears to be our "normal" state and disease an "abnormal" or "anomalous" condition. Or so we like to tell ourselves. From this point of view, our original condition is one of unity and harmony with ourselves, others, and the environment. Division and opposition befall us from without and upset the equilibrium we had enjoyed. However, since we once experienced unity and harmony, it does not seem unreasonable to hope that they might be restored. To reassure ourselves about the possibility, indeed the likelihood, of recovery, we construct myths, stories, and theories in which life is a struggle to return to the original condition we have lost. This scheme of unity-loss-recovery has been extraordinarily pervasive and influential throughout history and continues to guide the human imagination in a variety of obvious and not-so-obvious ways. It not only provides the symbolic structure for many religious and philosophical traditions but also serves as the implicit framework for many theories in the social and natural sciences. *If* there ever were a mythic-poetic-epistemic universal, the pattern of health-disease-recovery (or its functional equivalent) might be a likely candidate.[44]

Appearances to the contrary notwithstanding, universals are always faulty. The study of autoimmune disease implies that the classical scheme of creation-fall-redemption is deeply flawed. There is mounting evidence that autoimmunity is our "primal" condition and so-called health is secondary to, and dependent upon, the suppression of an autoimmune response. If this is so, then the self is never at one with others, its world, or even itself. Disease, in other words, is not "abnormal" but is always already in our midst. Two recent developments in research on fetal development suggest that autoimmunity is the very condition of life itself.

In a provocative article entitled "Hostile Womb," Rob Wechsler writes:

> We like to think of the womb as a prenatal paradise where an innocent creature floats peacefully in a bath of warm water, protected from harm by its mother. But according to some immunologists, life—even before birth—may not be that simple. In their view, the mother's immune system regards the fetus as a mass of foreign tissue, an invader that must be attacked and killed. So even as she sustains the life of her child with oxygen and nutrients, she may also be bombarding it with lethal antibodies and killer cells. If her aggressive response goes unchecked, the helpless fetus is destroyed. In this scenario, some miscarriages are the result of a cruel betrayal by a misguided immune system.[45]

When "spontaneous miscarriages" are placed in the context of autoimmune disease, the state of the pregnant woman appears to be similar to the patient who has undergone an organ transplant. "For immunologists, the ultimate puzzle is not why some women miscarry, but why most don't. Pregnancy is a paradox. When a foreign tissue is grafted into the body, it is normally quite rapidly recognized and attacked. Logically, since the fetus has genetic material from its father as well as its mother, it should be recognized as a foreign graft and promptly rejected—much as a transplanted kidney or heart can be."[46]

For the fetal organism to develop, the mother's immune response to the presence of a "foreign body" must be turned off. The most obvious protection for the fetus is the tissue that surrounds it, which is called the trophoblast. But this sheltering membrane does not solve the problem of tissue rejection, for there is no obvious reason why the mother's immune system should not also regard the trophoblast as foreign. According to immunologists Page Faulk and David Clark, successful pregnancy requires the mother's "natural" immune response be "deactivated." Faulk explains that "the trophoblast has on its surface a special group of antigens that originate from the father and serve as signals to the mother; they send a message to her that says 'protect me.' If the mother gets the message, she makes blocking antibodies and suppressor cells and allows implantation and successful pregnancy. If she doesn't get the message, she may have a spontaneous abortion."[47] If Faulk, Clark, and their colleagues are right, the original relation between fetus and mother *is not* unity and harmony but discord and conflict. From the beginning, even before the beginning, self and other are divided.

The opposition between self and nonself runs deeper than the primal conflict between self and others and self and world. The study of autoimmune disease also suggests that the body is *inwardly* divided.[48] The capacity for self-recognition is not innate but must be acquired. According to Jerne, who, as we have noted, was the first to propose the natural selection theory of antibody formation,

> one's immune system does not seem to recognize the epitopes on molecules and cells that are part of one's own body. This property, which Sir Macfarlane Burnet called the discrimination between self and not-self, is often referred to as self-tolerance. You might think that self-tolerance derived from nature's being wise enough to construct the genes coding for your antibodies in such a way as not to give rise to combining sites that would fit epitopes occurring in your own body. It can easily be shown, however, that this is not so. For example, your father's antibodies could recognize epitopes occurring in your mother; some antibody genes inherited from your father should therefore code for antibodies recognizing epitopes inherited from your mother.
>   Self-tolerance, then, is not innate. It is something the immune system "learned" in embryonic life by either eliminating or "paralyzing" all lymphocytes that would produce self-recognizing antibodies.[49]

The learning of self-tolerance takes place when the T-cell passes through the thymus gland. The thymus "educates" the T-lymphocytes by conferring on them the capacity to distinguish cells in the host organism from unwanted guests. While the precise details of this process are still not fully understood, it is clear that inadequacies in the body's "educational system" are related to genetic disorders. Heredity plays a significant role in virtually all autoimmune diseases. Inasmuch as genetic defects are the result of the storage or mistranslation of instructions coded in DNA, autoimmunity entails misreadings within misreadings and misinterpretations upon misinterpretations.

Since self-tolerance must be learned, the autoimmune response is *antecedent to* both self-unity and self-identity. If our initial relation to ourselves is autoimmunity, our body is not originally an integrated whole governed by the principle of inner teleology but is inherently torn, rent, sundered, and fragmented. The body is *always* betraying itself. Otherness is not only a threat from without but is a danger lurking within. Though it seems impossible, *the body is simultaneously itself and other than itself.* Never simply itself, the body is haunted by an altarity with which it cannot identify and yet with which it cannot avoid identifying. This altarity is the *not* of the body—the not that the body "is" as well as the not that the body cannot not be. In relation to this not, intelligence and counterintelligence strategies, however elaborate, are always inadequate. Like every other communications system, the body is riddled with gaps. Inasmuch as the body is *not* itself, agents and counteragents become confused; messages fail to arrive, they are diverted, interrupted, lost, and misread. Superficial order is really disorder. In such a system the appearance of health is nothing more than the repression of disease. When disease is finally diagnosed, it appears as the return of the repressed through which we discover that we are always already sick. Disease, we eventually learn, is *chronic;* it is as endless as time itself.

o   o   o

> "That *you*, O Zarathustra, once said,
> 'Spirit is the life that itself cuts into life,'
> that introduced and seduced me to your
> doctrine. And verily, with my own blood
> I increased my knowledge.[50]

SYRINGE

Greek *eiron:* a sayer, who speaks but utters not his own thoughts. *irony. susurration. synrinx:* first, a shepherd's pipe. From the hollow pipe, *syringe; syringotomy. Syringa:* genus, the mock orange, from its hollow stem. . . . Possibly *Hermes,* messenger of the gods, himself the god of eloquence and science, who is pictured as a youth with *caduceus* (rod), *petasus* (brimmed hat), and *talaria* (winged sandals); identified with the Roman god Mercury. Hence *hermeneutics:* art of interpretation; when related to Scripture, *hermeneutics* is distinguished from *exegesis:* exposition. *hermaphrodite.*[51] [Fig. 38]

Strange messenger of a strange god who speaks but utters not.

I remember all too well (how could I ever forget?) the first time I suffered by my own hand the wound of a syringe. It was not the pain I

253

38. Syringe. Photograph: Mark C. Taylor.

dreaded, though there was that, but the violence, the violation of my body. Its wounding, puncture, bleeding; the injection of a foreign, synthetic, artificial agent. I felt that I was betraying the body that had betrayed me. Wound upon wound, betrayal upon betrayal. What would it all solve? What would it cure? I drew the syringe slowly, carefully, deliberately, and watched the mesmerizing trickle of the chemical substance. Numbers and lines, small numbers and fine lines. Always fine lines that must not be crossed. A mistake, a misreading, a miscalculation could prove fatal. When the agents reached the proper line on the syringe, I paused long enough to forget what I had to do. Then with a suddenness that startled me, I sank the needle into my flesh, deep into my flesh, and emptied the contents of the syringe into my body. Much to my surprise, I felt *nothing*—no pain, no pleasure, no relief. Nothing but a slight trace of blood marked the site of my transgression. The text of the body can be read in the silent trace of blood.

Now there was nothing left to do but to wait. Doing nothing is never easy, and never more so than when waiting for test results. Distractions do not distract, diversions fail to divert. In the midst of the noise around me, all I could hear was the silence of the telephone whose ring promised a message I hoped would never arrive. When tests are vital, uncertainty is not always to be feared and certainty not always desired. Sometimes the only thing more terrifying than uncertainty is certainty itself.

254

"Yes, I see.
I understand.
No, no, I'll be alright.
No need for that.
At least, not now.
Thank you.
Goodbye."

Names and numbers that only yesterday I had never heard today are a matter of health and sickness, life and death. When all is said and done, it comes down to codes and numbers—input and output, positive and negative feedback, communication and miscommunication. Pluses and minuses do not cancel each other, input and output never balance. Thus, messages inevitably fail to arrive or arrive mistakenly. It makes no difference. God, it seems, is no mathematician or geometer and the world is no book waiting to be read. My body, which, of course, is not my own, is a text that remains unreadable for me as well as the others who watch over it. Numbers, angles, things never add up; they are never right—never have been, never will be right. There is irony—bitter irony—in the numbers inscribed on the syringe. The more careful I am to be sure I do not make a mistake, the more I realize that mistakes are unavoidable; the more I struggle to achieve "reasonable control," the more I am forced to admit that control is neither reasonable or possible. *Things are always out of control.*

In time, it all becomes ritualized, which is not to say regularized. The pulse of life as well as disease: fluids flowing in and out, out and in. Insulin in, blood out; codes and numbers in, codes and numbers out. Rituals are often violent and bloody. There is something hypnotic, even addictive, about the ritual of a syringe: the care for the instruments, the deliberateness of the preparation, the solemnity of the administration. As in any ritual worth repeating, there is a moment when death draws near. In this moment, the fluid, the sacred fluid of life, can quickly become fatal—a few more numbers, a few more lines, a few more drops. The ritual turns on the point of excess and control: too much and/or too little, never just enough, never equilibrium, never harmony. To stop or to go on? And what would it be to stop? Or to go on? When the impossibility of control becomes overwhelming—and it *does* become overwhelming—the excess of death is no more fearful than the painless prick of a sharp needle. Would it really be a betrayal to betray the body that has always already betrayed me?

255

"This is my body
broken"

Nothing ever balances... *nothing ever balances.* Betrayal is unavoidable, cure impossible. Disease is neither a mode of being nor of nonbeing but is a way of being not without not being. The dilemma, the abiding dilemma to which we are forever destined, is to live not.

Not (E) s

Chapter One

1. G. W. F. Hegel, *Lectures on the Philosophy of Religion,* trans. R. F. Brown et al., ed. P. C. Hodgson, 3 vols. (Berkeley: University of California Press, 1985), 3:355.

2. Derrida's comment on the logic of supplementarity illuminates issues that are examined in more detail below: "But the supplement supplements. It adds only to replace. It intervenes or insinuates itself *in-the-place-of;* if it fills, it is as if one fills a void. If it represents and makes an image, it is by the anterior default of a presence. Compensatory [*suppléant*] and vicarious, the supplement is an adjunct, a subaltern instance that *takes-(the)-place* [*tient-lieu*]. As substitute, it is not simply added to the positivity of a presence, it produces no relief, its place is assigned in the structure of the mark of an emptiness. Somewhere, something can be filled up *of itself,* can accomplish itself, only by allowing itself to be filled through sign and proxy. The sign is always the supplement of the thing itself" (*Of Grammatology,* trans. Gayatri Chakravorty Spivak [Baltimore: Johns Hopkins University Press, 1976], p. 145).

3. For a fuller account of the notion of inner teleology in relation to nature and the body, see below, chapter 8.

4. Karl Barth, *Anselm: Fides Quaerens Intellectum,* trans. Ian Robertson (Cleveland: Word Publishing Co., 1962), p. 150. Compare Kierkegaard's comment: "Anselm's ontological proof has played a large role in modern times and is used especially by free thought. Curious! As Anselm himself relates, he won this proof (in *Proslogium*) by prayer and supplication. Incidentally, a peculiar method of praying! Anselm says: I want to prove the existence of God. To that end I pray God to strengthen and help me—but this is no doubt a much better proof for the existence of God—that it is so certain that one has to have God's help to prove it. If one could prove the existence of God without God's help it would be, so to speak, less certain that he exists" (*Søren Kierkegaard's Journals and Papers,* trans. Howard and Edna Hong [Bloomington: Indiana University Press, 1975], vol. 3, no. 3615).

5. Maurice Blanchot, *Le pas au-delà* (Paris: Gallimard, 1973), p. 69.

6. Michel Foucault, "Maurice Blanchot: The Thought from the Outside," *Foucault/Blanchot* (New York: Zone Books, 1987), pp. 25–26.

Chapter Two

1. Jacques Derrida, *"Pas," Gramma* 3/4 (1976): 180, 139, 152, 189.

2. In October 1990, Professor Harold Coward organized a conference around the theme of "Derrida and Negative Theology," which was held at the Institute for the Humanities at the University of Calgary.

3. Mark C. Taylor, "Unending Strokes," *Theology at the End of the Century: A Dialogue on the Postmodern,* ed. Robert Scharlemann (Charlottesville: University of Virginia Press, 1990), p. 136.

4. A network of terms bearing the prefix *ver-* plays a crucial role in Freud's theories: *Verarbeitung, Verdichtung, Verdrängung, Verfüllung, Verkehrung, Versagung, Verschiebung, Verwerfung,* etc.

5. In his brief essay entitled "Negation," Freud writes: "To negate something in a judgment is, at bottom, to say: 'This is something which I should prefer to repress.' A negative judgment is the intellectual substitute for repression; its 'no' is the hallmark of repression, a certificate of origin—like, let us say, 'Made in Germany.' With the help of the symbol of negation, thinking frees itself from the restrictions of repression and enriches itself with material that is indispensable for its proper functioning" (Freud, "Negation," *Standard Edition,* vol. 19, p. 236).

6. The most important difference between these two terms concerns the problem of castration and the correlative question of fetishism. "The mechanism of *Verleugnung,*" Laplanche and Pontalis explain, "is first described by Freud in the course of his discussion of castration. Confronted by the absence of a penis in the girl, children 'disavow (*leugnen*) the fact and believe that they *do* see a penis, all the same.' . . . The fetishist perpetuates an infantile attitude by holding two incompatible positions at the same time: he simultaneously disavows and acknowledges the fact of feminine castration" (J. Laplanche and J.-B. Pontalis, *The Language of Psycho-analysis,* trans. Donald Nicholson-Smith [New York: W. W. Norton and Co., 1973], pp. 118–19).

7. Blanchot, "The Essential Solitude," *The Gaze of Orpheus and Other Essays,* trans. Lydia Davis (Barrytown, N.Y.: Station Hill Press, 1981), p. 73.

8. Derrida, "Signature Event Context," *Margins of Philosophy,* trans. Alan Bass (Chicago: The University of Chicago Press, 1982), p. 322.

9. Derrida, *Memories for Paul de Man,* trans. Cecile Lindsay, Jonathan Culler, and Eduardo Cadava (New York: Columbia University Press, 1986), p. 98.

10. Derrida, "Des Tours de Babel," *Difference in Translation,* ed. Joseph Graham (Ithaca, N.Y.: Cornell University Press, 1985), p. 176.

11. Emmanuel Levinas, *Otherwise than Being, or Beyond Essence,* trans. A. Lingis (Boston: Martinus Nijhoff, 1981), pp. 10–11.

12. Derrida, "Des Tours de Babel," p. 184.

13. Derrida, *"Pas,"* pp. 168–69.

14. For a detailed analysis of the crypt, see "Fors: The Anglish Words of Nicholas Abraham and Maria Torok," which appears as the foreword to Abraham and Torok's *The Wolfman's Magic Word: A Cryptonomy,* trans. Nicholas Rand (Minneapolis: University of Minnesota Press, 1986). I will consider the notion of the crypt in my analysis of Libeskind's architecture; see below, chapter 6.

15. See Georges Bataille, *La Part maudite* (Paris: Les Éditions de Minuit, 1967).

16. The implications of "part cut off" extend to the issue of castration, which plays such an important role in "Of an Apocalyptic Tone Recently Adopted in Philosophy." Always playing on many registers at once, Derrida suggests an association between Eckhart's argument and castration by way of the issue of vision. The fetish allows one to see "what is not present." This is, of course, one strategy for dealing with the problem of castration. As Derrida has long insisted, logocentrism and phallocentrism are inseparable. Eckhart's "Nothing that is Being" is a fetish constructed to repress the inescapability of lack.

17. These lines from Paul Celan's "Chymisch" are quoted by Derrida in "Shibboleth," *Midrash and Literature,* ed. Geoffrey Hartman and Sanford Budick (New Haven, Conn.: Yale University Press, 1986), p. 336. Celan's ashes will return in Libeskind's cryptic architecture. See below, chapter 6.

18. Derrida, "*Ousia* and *Gramme:* Note on a Note from *Being and Time,*" *Margins of Philosophy,* p. 65.

19. Elsewhere, Greek/Christian becomes Greek/Jew. Derrida concludes his important essay on Levinas with a series of questions: "Are we Jews? Are we Greeks? But who, we? Are we (not in a chronological, but a pre-logical question) *first* Jews or *first* Greeks? And does the strange dialogue between the Jew and the Greek, peace itself, have the form of the absolute speculative logic of Hegel, the living logic that *reconciles* formal tautology and empirical heterology after having *thought* prophetic discourse in the preface of the *Phenomenology of Spirit?* Or, on the contrary, does this peace have the form of an infinite separation and of the unthinkable, unsayable transcendence of the other? To what horizon of peace does the language that asks this question belong? From whence does it draw the energy of its question? Can it account for the historical *coupling* of Judaism and Hellenism? And what is the legitimacy, what is the meaning of the *copula* in the proposition from James Joyce, perhaps the most Hegelian of modern novelists: 'Jewgreek is greekjew. Extremes meet'" ("Violence and Metaphysics: An Essay on the Thought of Emmanuel Levinas," *Writing and Difference,* trans. Alan Bass [Chicago: The University of Chicago Press, 1978], p. 153).

20. As if to fulfill this "prophecy," Derrida has recently published what amounts to the first installment of his "autobiography"; see Derrida and Geoffrey Bennington, *Jacques Derrida* (Paris: Éditions du Seuil, 1991); translated by Geoffrey Bennington as *Jacques Derrida* (Chicago: University of Chicago Press, 1993).

Chapter Three

1. Blanchot, "Literature and the Right to Death," *The Gaze of Orpheus,* trans. Lydia Davis (Barrytown, N.Y.: Station Hill Press, 1981), p. 43.

2. Like many other nineteenth-century critics, Nietzsche distinguishes the religion *of* Jesus from the religion *about* Jesus. Christianity, the religion in which Jesus is the *object* of faith, is, in effect, the negation or reversal of Jesus' own religion. Nietzsche writes: "'Christianity' has become something funda-

mentally different from what its founder did and desired. It is the great antipagan movement of antiquity, formulated through the employment of the life, teaching and 'words' of the founder of Christianity but interpreted in an absolutely arbitrary way after the pattern of fundamentally different needs: translated into the language of every already existing subterranean religion" (*WP*, 114–15).

3. Friedrich Nietzsche, *Thus Spoke Zarathustra*, trans. Marianne Cowan (Chicago: Henry Regnery Company, 1957), pp. 334–35.

4. *RN*, 11. This insistence on the primordiality of unity distinguishes the position of Hegel and Nishitani from one of the most important strands in Nietzsche's thought. As we shall see in the next section, Nietzsche's interpretation of power points toward the absence of original unity.

5. See *Science of Logic*, esp. pp. 82–108.

6. *RN*, 128. In chapter 5 I will consider what is, in effect, an artistic inscription of *samadhi* in the art of Arakawa and Madeline Gins.

7. "Naturally, viewpoints that speak of a concentration into the One have shown up in the West from time to time. Examples are numerous, beginning in ancient Greece with Xenophanes' notion of 'One and All' ('What we call things, that is One') and Parmenides' idea of 'Being' ('To think and to be are one and the same'), and including such thinkers as Plotinus, Spinoza, and Schelling. The absolute One they had in mind, however, was either conceived as absolute reason or, when it went beyond the standpoint of reason, at least as an extension of that standpoint in unbroken continuity with it. At the same time, that absolute One was conceived of in terms of a negation of the multiplicity and differentiation of existing things as deceptive and illusory appearance" (*RN*, 143).

8. Hegel, it will be remembered, sets as his primary philosophical objective the establishment of the "union of union and nonunion." He seeks to develop a form of unity that escapes the reductionism of Fichte's subjective idealism and Schelling's objective idealism. Nonetheless, Hegel emphasizes union more than nonunion or, in terms of the *Logic*, privileges identity over difference. In what follows, I argue that Nishitani has not escaped the metaphysical tendency to give priority to unity and identity. In the next chapter I will return to Hegel's analysis of force in my consideration of Derrida's interpretation of the interconnection of force and law.

9. The notion of "gathering" plays a central role in Heidegger's later philosophy. Nishitani indirectly borrows Heidegger's insights on this issue.

Chapter Four

1. After this book went to press, Derrida published an essay in which he presents an analysis of Kierkegaard's *Fear and Trembling*. See Derrida, "Donner la mort," in *L'Ethique du don: Jacques Derrida et la pensée du don* (Paris: Métailie-Transition, 1992), pp. 11–108.

2. It is worth noting in this context that the stem of decision, *sek*, is related to the "origin" of writing, and, by extension to the problem of scripture. Commenting on *sek*, Joseph Shipley explains: "Early man found and fashioned tools. To shells and to stones sharp or chipped away he added hilts or handles, the

better to scrape, scratch, dig, cut apart. Then the basic roots for these tools, for the operations performed for the things made with them, took on wider meaning. Thus, *to scratch or incise letters* (on stone, wood, wax, clay, papyrus) produced *scribes* and *scribblers*—and current *scramblers*" (*The Origins of English Words* [Baltimore: Johns Hopkins University Press, 1984], p. 346). In addition to a gifted writer, Kierkegaard was an inveterate scribbler.

3. After drawing this distinction, Derrida comments: "I would be tempted, up to a certain point, to compare the concept of justice—which I'm here trying to distinguish from law—to Levinas', just because of this infinity and because of the heteronomic relation to others, to the faces of others that govern me, whose infinity I cannot thematize and whose hostage I remain" (FL, 959). Though Derrida does not elaborate his dependence on Levinas in this context, it is obvious that his entire analysis of justice is indebted to his influential precursor. It would also be possible to read "Force of Law" through Levinas and vice versa. Any such rereading, however, would require a further account of similarities and differences between Levinas's Judaism and Kierkegaard's Christianity. The relation between Levinas and Kierkegaard deserves much more careful attention than it has received.

4. Bennington and Derrida, *Jacques Derrida*, pp. 217–18 (French ed.).

Chapter Five

1. Clement Greenberg, "Modernist Painting," in *The New Art: A Critical Anthology*, ed. Gregory Battcock, rev. ed. (New York: E. P. Dutton and Co., 1973), p. 101.

2. Maurice Merleau-Ponty, *Phenomenology of Perception*, trans. C. Smith (London: Routledge and Kegan Paul, 1978), pp. xi–xii.

3. RD, 2. It is important to note that Hegel also begins the *Phenomenology of Spirit* with an analysis of the "here." See *PS*, 58–65.

4. Arthur Danto, "Gins and Arakawa: Building Sensoriums," *The Nation* 251 (15 Oct. 1990), p. 431.

5. Wallace Stevens, "Anecdote of the Jar," *The Collected Poems of Wallace Stevens* (New York: Alfred Knopf, 1981), p. 76.

Chapter Six

1. Peter Eisenman, "Representations of the Limit: Writing a 'Not-Architecture,' introduction to Daniel Libeskind, *Chamber Works: Architectural Meditations on Themes from Heraclitus* (London: Architectural Association, 1983). The texts inserted throughout this chapter between the Z's are from the writings of Edmond Jabès.

2. Ibid.

3. Libeskind, "Unoriginal Signs," *Chamber Works*.

4. Mark Wigley, in his introduction to *Deconstructivist Architecture* (exhibition catalog, Museum of Modern Art, New York, 1988). Wigley overemphasizes the influence of Russian constructivism on the architects whose work was included in the show.

5. Jacques Derrida, *Cinders*, trans. Ned Lukacher (Lincoln: University of Nebraska Press, 1991), p. 43.

6. For a suggestive analysis of the implications of the destruction of Libeskind's work, see Jeffrey Kipnis, "Though to My Knowledge, a Writ Has Not Been Issued, Nevertheless, the Case Is Becoming Well-known," *Threshold* 4 (Spring 1988): 106–13.

7. Libeskind, "Architecture Intermundium," *Threshold* 4 (Spring 1988): 115.

8. Ibid., pp. 120, 116, 120, 119, 121.

9. Ibid., p. 121.

10. Quoted in David Frisby, "Deciphering the Hieroglyphics of Weimar Berlin: Siegfried Kracauer," in *Berlin: Culture and Metropolis*, ed. Charles Haxthausen and Heidrun Suhr (Minneapolis: University of Minnesota Press, 1990), p. 156.

11. John Borneman, *After the Wall: East Meets West in the New Berlin* (New York: Basic Books, 1991), p. 6.

12. See Linda Schulte-Sasse, "Retrieving the City as *Heimat:* Berlin in Nazi Cinema," in *Berlin,* pp. 166–86.

13. The current Jewish population of Berlin is still only about seven thousand.

14. "Libeskind i Berlin: Interview ved Flemming Frost og Kjeld Vindum," *SKALA*, no. 17/18 (1989): 23.

15. Walter Benjamin, "A Berlin Chronicle," *Reflections: Essays, Aphorisms, Autobiographical Writings,* trans. Edmund Jephcott (New York: Harcourt Brace Jovanovich, 1978), p. 3.

16. Quoted in Charles Jencks, *The New Moderns: From Late to Neo-Modernism* (New York: Rizzoli, 1990), p. 269.

17. Wigley, introduction to *Deconstructivist Architecture,* p. 34.

18. Ibid.

19. For a vivid record of the work of Berlin's Wall artists, see Leland Rice, *Up Against It: Photographs of the Berlin Wall* (Albuquerque: University of New Mexico Press, 1987).

20. Daniel Albright, *Representation and the Imagination: Beckett, Kafka, Nabokov, and Schoenberg* (Chicago: University of Chicago Press, 1981), p. 18.

21. Quoted in ibid., p. 36.

22. Libeskind, "Peter Eisenman and the Myth of Futility," *Harvard Architectural Review* 3 (Winter 1984): 61.

23. Jean-Luc Nancy, *The Inoperative Community,* trans. Peter Connor et al. (Minneapolis: University of Minnesota Press, 1991), p. 148.

24. Derrida, "Shibboleth," p. 334.

25. Quoted in ibid., p. 336.

26. Derrida, *Memories for Paul de Man,* p. 6.

27. Derrida, "Fors," p. xiv.

28. Derrida, *Memories for Paul de Man,* p. 58.

29. As I have suggested above, Libeskind is fascinated by Benjamin. He underscores the explicit role that Benjamin's thought played in the development of addition to the Berlin Museum when he writes: "The fourth aspect of the project is formed by Walter Benjamin's *One Way Street.* This aspect is incorporated into the continuous sequence of sixty sections along the zig-zag, each of

which represents one of the 'Stations of the Star' described in the text of Walter Benjamin" (*CD*, 86).

30. For an account of Derrida's interpretation of *khora,* see chapter 2.

31. Benjamin, "The Task of the Translator: An Introduction to the Translation of Baudlaire's *Tableaux Parisiens,*" *Illuminations,* trans. Harry Zohn, ed. Hannah Arendt (New York: Schocken Books, 1969), pp. 79–80.

32. Libeskind, "Between Method, Idea and Desire," *Domus* (Oct. 1991): 28.

33. Quoted in Jencks, *The New Moderns,* p. 29.

34. Libeskind, "SPIRIT SPIRITSP IRI TSPIRI TSPIR I Tspirit," *Energia: En Ergiaen Ergiaenergi,* (Milan: Electa Spa, 1988).

35. Nancy, *The Sublime Offering,* trans. Jeffrey Librett (forthcoming).

Chapter Seven

1. See Jean-François Lyotard, *Le Postmodern expliqué aux enfants* (Paris: Éditions Galilée, 1986).

2. Peter Schjeldahl, "David Salle Interview," *Los Angeles Institute of Contemporary Art* 30 (Sept.-Oct. 1981): 18.

3. For a helpful account of the emergence of neofigurative painting in Germany, see *Refigured Painting: The German Image 1960–88,* ed. Thomas Krens, Michael Govan, and Joseph Thompson (New York: Solomon R. Guggenheim Museum, 1989).

4. David Salle, quoted in "Post-Modernism," *Real Life Magazine,* no. 6 (Summer 1981): 4.

5. Ibid., p. 5.

6. Schjeldahl, "David Salle Interview," pp. 16–17.

7. Peter Schjeldahl, ed., *David Salle* (New York: Random House, 1987), p. 40.

8. Schjeldahl, "An Interview with David Salle," in *David Salle,* p. 5.

9. Schjeldahl, *David Salle,* p. 72.

10. Early in his career, Salle worked for a soft-core porn magazine. When the company was liquidated, he collected cartons of black-and-white pornographic photographs, which he used in many of his later paintings.

11. Jean Baudrillard, *The Ecstasy of Communication,* trans. Bernard and Caroline Schutze (New York: Semiotext[e], 1988), pp. 21–22.

12. Salle was, in fact, raised in a "culture-conscious Jewish family in Wichita, Kansas" (Schjeldahl, *David Salle,* p. 4).

13. Schjeldahl, "David Salle Interview," p. 19.

14. Fredric Jameson, *Postmodernism or, The Cultural Logic of Late Capitalism* (Durham, N.C.: Duke University Press, 1991), pp. xv, 76.

15. Vincente Huidobro, "Eiffel Tower," quoted in Robert Hughes, *The Shock of the New* (New York: Alfred Knopf, 1987), pp. 37–38. The following quotations from Marinetti and Apollinaire are from pp. 42 and 11, respectively.

16. Filippo Marinetti, "The Founding Manifesto of Futurism," *Selected Writings,* ed. R. W. Flint and Arthur A. Coppotelli (New York: Farrar, Strauss and Giroux, 1972), pp. 41, 42.

17. Fredric Jameson, "Postmodernism and Consumer Society," in *The Anti-*

Aesthetic: Essays on Postmodern Culture, ed. Hal Foster (Port Townsend, Wash.: Bay Press, 1983), p. 125.

18. Georges Bataille, "La réligion surrealiste," *Oeuvres Complètes,* 12 vols. (Paris: Gallimard, 1976), 7:396.

19. Foucault, "A Preface to Transgression," *Language, Counter-Memory, Practice: Selected Essays and Interviews,* trans. Donald F. Bouchard and Sherry Simon, ed. Bouchard (Ithaca, N.Y.: Cornell University Press, 1977), p. 37.

20. Bataille, *The Theory of Religion,* trans. Robert Hurley (New York: Zone Books, 1989), pp. 56–57.

21. Bataille, "La réligion surrealiste," pp. 387–88.

22. Bataille, *Guilty,* trans. Bruce Boone (San Francisco: Lapis Press, 1988), pp. 32–33.

23. Elizabeth Eisenstein, *The Printing Press as an Agent of Change: Communications and Cultural Transformations in Early-Modern Europe,* 2 vols. (New York: Cambridge University Press, 1979), 1:59.

24. The far-reaching implications of this revolution are apparent in the extraordinary research being conducted at MIT's Media Laboratory. The range of current projects provides a glimpse of the future that is already upon us: Television of Tomorrow, Computer Graphics and Animation, Music and Cognition, Spatial Imaging, Vision and Modeling, Visible Language Workshop, Speech Research, Interactive Cinema, Movies of the Future, School of the Future, Electronic Publishing, and Advanced Human Interface. What these diverse areas of research share is an emphasis on *interactive* technology. Instead of a passive recipient or spectator, users and viewers will play an increasingly active role in the production of the information, sounds, and images at their disposal. Though the theological, philosophical, and political implications of this revolution are enormous, cultural interpreters and critics have barely begun to realize what is already going on, much less analyze the significance of these developments. For a somewhat dated but still useful history of the MIT Media Lab, see Stewart Brand, *The Media Lab: Inventing the Future at M.I.T.* (New York: Penguin Books, 1988).

25. John Leland and Marc Peyser, "Do You Still Want Your MTV?" *Newsweek,* 5 Aug. 1991, p. 53.

26. Madonna, quoted in Denise Worrell, "Now: Madonna on Madonna," *Time,* 27 May 1985, p. 83.

27. Madonna, quoted in Carl Wayne Arrington, "Madonna in Bloom: Circe at Her Loom," *Time,* 20 May 1991, p. 56.

28. Madonna, quoted in Worrell, "Madonna on Madonna," p. 81.

29. Madonna, quoted in Arrington, "Madonna in Bloom," p. 56.

30. See Edith Wyschogrod, *Saints and Postmodernism: Revisioning Moral Philosophy* (Chicago: University of Chicago Press, 1990), chap. 7.

31. Gilles Deleuze and Félix Guattari, *Anti-Oedipus: Capitalism and Schizophrenia,* trans. Robert Hurley, Mark Seem, and Helen Lane (New York: Viking, 1977), p. 77.

32. Madonna, quoted in Worrell, "Madonna on Madonna," p. 83.

33. Madonna, quoted in Arrington, "Madonna in Bloom," p. 58.

34. For a remarkable study of this theme in the history of art, see Leo Stein-

berg, *The Sexuality of Christ in Renaissance Art and in Modern Oblivion* (New York: Pantheon, 1983).

35. Madonna, quoted in Arrington, "Madonna in Bloom," p. 58.

36. Ibid.

37. This episode brings into sharp relief another important strand in the video. Even though Madonna's actions transgress many of the traditional codes of Christianity and call into question important aspects of the widely accepted male/female opposition, she also reinscribes problematic features of stereotypical relations between black men and white women. While casting herself in the role of the redeemer of the black redeemer, Madonna reinforces unquestioned anxieties that many white people still have about the purported sexual threat posed by black men.

38. Quoted in Lynn Hirschberg, "The Misfit," *Vanity Fair,* Apr. 1991, p. 168.

39. Baudrillard, *Seductions,* trans. Brian Singer (New York: St. Martin's Press, 1990), pp. 69–70.

40. Ibid., p. 86.

41. Steven Erlanger, "A Plague Awaits," *New York Times Magazine,* 14 July 1991, p. 24.

Chapter Eight

1. Research for this chapter was supported by a grant from the Sloan Foundation. I would like to express my sincere gratitude to Gordan C. Weir and Susan Bonner-Weir of the Joslin Clinic, and to William DeWitt of Williams College, for leading me through the intricacies and complexities of recent biological theory and the current status of diabetes research.

2. Sander Gilman, *Disease and Representation: Images of Illness from Madness to AIDS* (Ithaca, N.Y.: Cornell University Press, 1988), p. 1.

3. Francis Galton, *Inquiries into Human Faculty and Its Development* (London: Macmillan and Co., 1883), p. 19.

4. Sontag does not argue that all forms of disease are idealized. To the contrary, she establishes a sharp contrast between the way the nineteenth century figured TB and the way the twentieth century depicts cancer. The "glamor" of tuberculosis stands in marked contrast to the "shame" of cancer. See Susan Sontag, *Illness as Metaphor* (New York: Farrar, Strauss, Giroux, 1978), pp. 14ff. For another important study of the relationship between disease and art, see Jeffrey Meyers, *Disease and the Novel, 1880–1960* (New York: St. Martin's Press, 1985).

5. The tendency to romanticize schizophrenia is particularly pronounced among some so-called postmodern writers. See, inter alia, Norman O. Brown, *Love's Body* (New York: Random House, 1968) and Deleuze and Guattari, *Anti-Oedipus: Capitalism and Schizophrenia.*

6. Bataille, *Inner Experience,* trans. Leslie Boldt (Albany: State University of New York Press, 1988), p. 59.

7. Professor William DeWitt pointed out in conversation that "the study of mutant organisms has provided virtually all the insights in the field of genetics, such as the basis of genetic disease, functioning of the genetic code, mechanisms of protein synthesis, and others. The same is true for developmental

biology, where mutants have shown us how organs are formed, patterns are set down, etc." I will consider some of these processes in more detail below.

8. Quoted in Anthony Wilden, "Cybernetics and Machina Mundi," in *The Myths of Information: Technology and Postindustrial Culture,* ed. Kathleen Woodward (Madison, Wis.: Coda Press, 1980), p. 231.

9. Michel Serres, "The Origin of Language: Biology, Information Theory, and Thermodynamics," in *Hermes: Literature, Science, Philosophy,* ed. Josué Harari and David Bell (Baltimore: Johns Hopkins University Press, 1982), p. 71.

10. Foucault, *The Birth of the Clinic: An Archaeology of Medical Perception,* trans. A. M. Sheridan Smith (New York: Random House, 1975), p. 29.

11. Ibid., p. 14.

12. Immanuel Kant, *The Critique of Judgment,* trans. James Meredith (New York: Oxford University Press, 1973), pp. 24–25.

13. Ibid., p. 26.

14. For an examination of the role that the notion of the organism plays in Hegel's interpretation of the ontological argument, see above, chapter 1.

15. Hegel goes so far as to argue that "the *forms of disease* can be reduced to the following classification. (*a*) *Noxiousness,* which is a form of disturbance, is in the *first instance* a *general* determinateness residing in inorganic nature as a whole. This simple determinateness must be regarded as external in origin, and as being inflicted upon the organism from without; but although it is manifest externally in the organism's environment, it can also be apparent simultaneously, and with equal facility, in the organism itself. . . . (*b*) *Another* general form of disease is that which is brought forth by the organism's entering into contact with certain *specific noxious influences* from without. In this case one of the organism's specific systems, such as that of its skin or its stomach, becomes particularly involved, and so isolates itself" (*PN,* 3, 196–97).

16. Charles Dechert, "The Development of Cybernetics," in *The Social Impact of Cybernetics,* ed. Dechert (Notre Dame: University of Notre Dame Press, 1966), pp. 13–14.

17. *The American Heritage Dictionary,* 1970 ed., s.v. "cybernetics."

18. Dechert, "The Development of Cybernetics," pp. 14–15.

19. I consider below the importance between analog and digital computers for interpreting biological organisms.

20. See Claude Shannon and Warren Weaver, *The Mathematical Theory of Communication* (Urbana: University of Illinois Press, 1949).

21. Though never acknowledged by information theorists, this definition of information leads to a paradoxical conclusion. The occurrence that communicates the most information might actually be incomprehensible. For example, a unique event would presumably be most improbable and thus communicate the most information. And yet, its very incomparability or singularity would seem to render it unknowable.

22. Wilden, "Cybernetics and Machina Mundi," p. 228.

23. Donna Haraway, *Simians, Cyborgs, and Women: The Reinvention of Nature* (New York: Routledge, 1991), pp. 149–50.

24. William DeWitt, *Human Biology: Form, Function, and Adaptation* (Boston: Scott, Foresman and Co., 1989), p. 429.

25. Nucleotides, which consist of a nitrogenous base, a pentose sugar, and a phosphate group, are precursors for the synthesis of nucleic acids like DNA and RNA. For the story of this discovery, see James Watson, *The Double Helix: A Personal Account of the Discovery of the Structure of DNA* (New York: New American Library, 1968).

26. DeWitt, *Human Biology*, p. 432.

27. Claude Lévi-Strauss, "The Effectiveness of Symbols," *Structural Anthropology*, trans. Claire Jacobson and Brooke Schoepf (New York: Basic Books, 1967), p. 201.

28. Ibid., p. 203.

29. *SS*, 162. In applying the analog/digital distinction to the operation of the nervous system in the following paragraph, I have followed the general outline of Wilden's discussion. See *SS*, 156ff.

30. This is, in fact, the title of a popular immunology textbook; see Jan Klein, *Immunology: The Science of Self-Nonself Discrimination* (New York: John Wiley, 1982).

31. Irun Cohen, "The Self, the World, and Autoimmunity," *Scientific American* (Apr. 1988), p. 52.

32. Though all invaders are antigens, not all antigens are invaders. For example, a toxin that is released by a bacterium is not an invader, though it can be an antigen. An antigen is anything that provokes an immune response.

33. The *T* in T-lymphocytes designates those cells that pass through the thymus. The remainder of the lymphocytes are type B. The *B* is derived from *bursus*, an organ in the chicken in which the B-cells were first isolated. I will return to the role of the thymus in lymphocyte production in what follows.

34. Niels K. Jerne, "The Natural Selection Theory of Antibody Formation," *Phage and the Origins of Molecular Biology* (Cold Spring Harbor, N.Y.: Cold Spring Harbor Laboratory of Quantitative Biology, 1966), p. 301.

35. Although any consideration of the complexities of cancer lies beyond the bounds of the essay, it is helpful to note that cancer can also be understood in terms of the cybernetic model we have considered. Various forms of cancer are, in effect, breakdowns in the feedback loop upon which the body depends. Though it seems to be triggered by foreign agents, cancer involves a necessary organic process that goes awry. The very cells that are essential to the growth of the organism are protooncological. Under so-called normal circumstances, the cell growth is turned on when needed and turned off when not needed. In cancer, the growth switch that had been turned off is for some reason turned on again. In this case, a failure of the communications network means that positive feedback (growth) is not controlled by negative feedback (constraint). In the absence of negative feedback, the body's immune system tries to destroy the cancerous cells. In certain cases, this strategy is effective but when the immune system fails, cancer cells develop unchecked and growth eventually consume the body.

36. Haraway, *Cyborgs*, pp. 222–23.

37. While juvenile-onset diabetes is always insulin dependent, only approximately five percent of the cases of adult-onset are insulin dependent.

38. For a helpful summary of the symptoms of diabetes, see DeWitt, *Human Biology,* p. 341.

39. In recent years, researchers have discovered many other endocrine tissues scattered throughout the body, primarily in the stomach, intestine, and brain.

40. DeWitt, *Human Biology,* pp. 326–27.

41. Antigenic or molecular mimicry is also involved in other autoimmune disorders, for example, rheumatic heart disease.

42. Cohen, "The Self, the World, and Autoimmunity," p. 55.

43. In view of the growing importance of AIDS (Acquired Immune Deficiency Syndrome) throughout the world, it is important to understand how it differs from autoimmune diseases. In contrast to diseases caused by an autoimmune syndrome in which the body's own antibodies or T-lymphocytes turn on itself, AIDS occurs when a human immunodeficiency virus, which researchers have labeled HIV-1, infects the system. "Although HIV-1 can infect many cell types," DeWitt explains, "it preferentially infects and destroys helper T-cells that assist in activating B-lymphocytes to produce antibodies; the loss of helper T-cells, relative to suppressor T-cells, accounts for the substantial suppression of the immune system seen in AIDS." Death is not directly caused by HIV-1 but is the result of secondary infection that the deficient immune system cannot combat. Not all people who are infected by HIV-1 contract AIDS. The much publicized testing for AIDS involves the detection of antibodies produced to counter the HIV-1 virus in people who have no evident symptoms of the disease. "Currently, there is no cure for AIDS, and the disease is considered universally fatal. AZT (azidodeoxythymidine) is the only drug that has been approved by the FDA for AIDS treatment. It prolongs the life of AIDS patients with pneumocystis pneumonia by bringing about a partial, but temporary, restoration of the immune system function" (DeWitt, *Human Biology,* pp. 478–79). For an important collection of essays dealing with the social and cultural aspects of the AIDS problem, see the special issue of *October,* no. 43 (1987).

44. Within the Christian theological tradition, the idea of original sin suggests a possible alternative to this pattern. For most theologians, however, even so-called original sin is, in some sense, secondary to a primal condition in which the self is uncorrupted. To dislocate the unity-loss-recovery model, it would be necessary to radicalize the notion of sin by rendering it "primordial" and, correlatively, to deny the possibility of recovery or salvation.

45. Rob Wechsler, "Hostile Womb," *Discover,* Mar. 1988, p. 83. In what is, perhaps, a related condition, some women develop what is known as "gestational diabetes" during pregnancy. After the baby is delivered, this form of diabetes disappears.

46. Ibid.

47. Ibid., p. 85.

48. It should be apparent that the issues we have been exploring in this chapter greatly complicate the self/other distinction. Not only is the self the other of itself but the seemingly integral subject is inhabited by other subjects, which are also haunted by others that cannot be contained. Like Libeskind's

walls with walls, the body appears to be both radically decentered and thoroughly liminal.

49. Jerne, "The Immune System," *Scientific American,* July 1973, p. 55.

50. Nietzsche, *Thus Spoke Zarathustra* (4th part), *The Portable Nietzsche,* trans. and ed. Walter Kaufmann (New York: Penguin Books, 1980), p. 363.

51. Shipley, *The Origin of English Words,* p. 397.

INDEX

271

Daniel Libeskind has furnished the following short explanation of the images used on the (paperback) cover of this book:

RELEASING THE VIEW. The concept of the site-as-puzzle has been derived from the symbolic fragments of memory of Potsdamer Platz as they have been recorded in nine projective/hysterical viewpoints. These accelerated time perspectives develop a momentum which finally cancels the very notion of perspective.

Like Humpty Dumpty's shattering act, this spot cannot be "put together in place again" even by "All the King's horses and all the King's men."

The site-puzzle is in fact the entry into a tenth 'gate': the postcontemporary city where the view is cleared beyond the constriction of domination, power, and the gridlocked mind.